C000260137

The
Admiralty Regrets...
The Disaster in Liverpool Bay
by
C.Warren & J.Benson

Foreword by Derek Arnold - a survivor's son

Postscript by David Roberts - maritime historian

Avid Publications

HMS Thetis - Secrets and Scandal - aftermath of a disaster.
by David Roberts

The truth behind the cover-up of this terrible submarine disaster and the shameful treatment of those left behind. Contains interviews with relatives of victims and survivors; Son's, daughters, brothers, sisters and those very rare ladies, living *'Thetis'* widows. Why did the Official Inquiry blame nobody, explaining it away as 'an unfortunate sequence of events'? Why did the civil action on behalf of the widows fail? Did the Admiralty cover it up? How much did Churchill know?

A huge publicly subscribed disaster fund was collected for the relatives of those lost. How was this managed and distributed? Who got what and why? What ever happened to the money that was left? Why do a handful of living widows still today get just £9.62 per month from the fund, in one case LESS TAX?

'The Hillsborough of its day' .....- BBC Radio Merseyside

'Exposes how 'The Establishment' closed ranks...' Liverpool Daily Post

'A book that shocks'- Sea Breezes

ISBN 0 9521020 0 5 £8.99

'Lusitania'
by Colin Simpson
*'The Truth at last..a book that clamours to be read'...*The Times
ISBN 0 9521020 6 4 £9.50

'Life at Lairds - memories of working shipyard men'
by David Roberts
ISBN 0 9521020 1 3 £6.99

'Cammell Laird - the golden years'
by David Roberts.
With a Foreword by Frank Field MP.
ISBN 0 9521020 2 1 £5.99

Iron Clipper - *Tayleur* - the White Star Lines 'First Titanic'
by H.F.Starkey
ISBN 1 902964 00 4 £7.50

Schooner Port - Two Centuries of Upper Mersey Sail
by H.F.Starkey
ISBN 0 9521020 5 6 £8.95

Faster Than the Wind - The Liverpool to Holyhead Telegraph
by Frank Large
ISBN 0 9521020 9 9 £8.95

Just Nuisance AB
by Terence Sisson
The story of the only dog ever to be officially enlisted into the
British Royal Navy.   £7.99

'Off The Cuff' by Swasie Turner
A look at real life police work in and around the city of
Liverpool.
ISBN 0 9521020 4 8 £8.99

If The Cap Fits' by Swasie Turner
ISBN 0 9521020 7 2 £8.99

Foreword

by Derek Arnold- son of Leading Stoker Walter Arnold, who survived the loss of HM Submarine Thetis.

On the day of my father's birth on 28th October 1909, he came into the world with a membrane covering his face. The midwife who delivered him removed it, placed it in a wrap and commented that "anyone born with such a veil will never drown." How prophetic her words were to be. My father carried this little wrap with him wherever he went.

I was just twenty one days short of my first Birthday when the events involving the loss of the newly built submarine Thetis were taking place, but at that time I was naturally oblivious of both the dramatic circumstances in which the occupants of the vessel found themselves and the indelible mark the tragedy would make upon my own life.

As I grew up I became aware of a certain air of notoriety bestowed upon my father by all that knew, or claimed to know him. "Arnold of the Thetis" as he was frequently called, seemed to have the same connotation to it as 'Scott of the Antarctic', 'Clive of India' and so forth. As a naval family it was not unusual for us to move from place to place as and when father was posted, his popularity appeared to have preceded us wherever and whenever we arrived.

Of course the realisation that all of this camaraderie emanated from his part in the loss of 'Thetis', and the subsequent escape of four people from it, one of whom was 'Stoker Arnold of the 'Thetis', came over a long period of time, culminating on the day I started an apprenticeship at Cammell Lairds, the same shipyard that had built 'Thetis' fifteen years previously.

I was somewhat bemused at the oft heard comment, "that's Stoker Arnold's son". Even one of the yards top foremen came to have a curious look at 'how the lad was shaping up', a chap by the name of Frank Shaw as I recall .... now where had I heard that name before?

As it turned out, one of my co-apprentices of the same year was Frank Shaw's son, Tony, and when comparing notes with him, the awful events of June 1st 1939 seemed to adopt a more personal element. I began to realise that this event was regarded with enormous gravity, especially in the Merseyside area, and was recorded as the worst naval peacetime disaster.

It was at this point that I became determined to find out as much as I could about what was generally held to be a catalogue of errors culminating in the loss of the Thetis and the ninety-nine men who perished with her. The most obvious point of reference had to be my own father who, because of his quiet and undemonstrative nature, was quite reluctant to portray his part in the sinking and escape as anything more than both self preservation and a strong sense of duty to King and Country. It was, therefore, with a degree of recalcitrance that he unfolded not only his side of the story but the exploits of all his brothers and brothers-in-law who either met their maker via Davy Jones' locker or spent the major part of the second World War incarcerated in Prisoner of War camps. This was surely the stuff of which stories from the "Boys Own Adventure" comics were made.

It became apparent immediately that the thread which ran through the whole sorry episode was closely aligned to the 'them and us' attitude which pervaded society at that time and probably still does today to some degree. To Joseph H Public it was seen as a total break with tradition that the Captain was first and not the last to leave the sinking ship although in reality Captain Oram was really not the ships captain, far from it. The vessel was actually captained by Lt. Commander Guy Bolus who was in overall command. Oram's role was more to do with the submarine reconstruction programme which was proceeding at a rate of urgency in time for the conflict which all but the most optimistic knew was imminent. He had been invited, in this role, on the Thetis trials more as an interested observer than as an active participant and, in this capacity, was not even required to wear his uniform.

In short, Oram was an expendable item to be used as a messenger to the rescuers, his brief journey from sub to surface was truly an excursion into the unknown, and the chances of him perishing were far greater than his survival. He was not an engineer and therefore did not really understand what was required, so, in case he either drowned or forgot, the necessary instructions for rescue to the salvage crews, who were hopefully waiting, were written out and pinned to his suit lapels. Far from being the rat that deserted the sinking ship, Captain Oram displayed extraordinary courage by attempting the first escape.

The fact that Captain Oram escaped with a fellow officer, Lieutenant Woods, was additionally viewed with some scepticism by the public who, not unnaturally, thought that the officer class were "looking after their own". It was true that Woods was instrumental in starting the chain of events that plunged Thetis to the bottom of Liverpool Bay by opening the torpedo tube to the sea but, realistically, what experienced submarine officer would attempt such a foolhardy act?

Rather than lay the blame for the catastrophe at Wood's feet, Captain Bolus judged, correctly, that there had to be a fault either with the design or with the procedures that Woods had unwittingly uncovered. It was absolutely imperative therefore, that this man should be saved in order to explain to any enquiry, the processes that he had followed, or not, as the case may be. It must be remembered that Thetis was the first of a new class of submarine containing every modern gadget - if there was a fundamental fault which had the potential to sink the ship, surely this needed to be urgently researched. The only man who could explain what had really happened, step-by-step, was Woods, and therefore he was ordered to go.

It has always been my belief that the public more readily identified with the escape and rescue of my father and Frank Shaw than they did for Oram and Woods perceiving them as the very epitome of 'Jolly Jack Tar' and 'the bloke next door'. Certainly the people of the Merseyside area regarded them both as local heroes., This was a popular misconception as my father was not a scouser but a Hampshire man born and bred, who never lost or diluted his 'be oi 'ampshoire' accent. Obviously by living in Tranmere and being married to a Birkenhead girl, the assumption was made by locals that he was one of them, sadly, not true. Even so, some years ago, he was actually portrayed as a broad scouser in a radio dramatisation of the Thetis disaster.

He confided to me that the selection of the escapees was in no way conducted in the manner in which a film director would have delighted; no drawing of lots or men running around shouting "let me out". Nothing could have been more orderly and matter-of-fact. By the time the escapes began, Bolus knew that many on board would not be in anywhere near the physical condition to make the attempt as by this time Carbon Dioxide poisoning was becoming quite advanced, making thinking slow, and just moving around incredibly arduous due to the steep angle of the boats hull. Apart from that, probably only a third of those on board had any experience of Davis Escape Apparatus as a large proportion of the men on board were civilians, shipyard workers, caterers etc. so, on a reasoned estimate, few were suitable.

My father had been working the escape chamber mechanism for Oram and Woods and had witnessed the setback of the failed second escape attempt when four men had perished. This really was a dilemma. The boat had sunk because of a mechanical failure and it seemed that the escape equipment apparently also had a mechanical failure. Many of the men had initially thought, that morning, that it would be an adventure to escape from a submarine by floating to the surface to be picked up by the waiting rescuers, and be regaling their mates in the pub that night, probably without having to put their hands in their pockets. The realisation that the well organised naval escape routine was, after all, fallible brought home the reality of the situation to those who by this time still had the capacity for reasoning.

Bolus must have sensed this blow to morale because he said to father "would you have a try Arnold?" Weighing up the options of "do I wait for certain death here, or do I possibly die in an attempt to escape?" It took but a second to choose the latter. "For God's sake Arnold, do it right and give these chaps some hope" Bolus remarked.

It was just prior to this that Frank Shaw became involved. He happened, by chance, to be in the same compartment as the escape chamber. Overhearing Captain Bolus say to Arnold "take someone with you who looks as though he may make it", he volunteered himself and was readily accepted.

Now here was a man who had no idea at all of the process of escape. Of course father realised this and advised Shaw to do absolutely nothing until told, he would have to process them both. So saying, they climbed into the escape chamber and slammed the hatch shut.

It must have been a daunting experience for Frank Shaw, to have the cold seawater cascading into the chamber, rapidly filling it up. Several times he was tempted to don the facemask as the water lapped around his chin but was told sharply by his much-experienced companion, to wait until the very last minute.

I would not pretend to understand the intricacies of the Davis Escape Apparatus so therefore would merely relate to the reader that in order to function correctly during ascent, a valve had to be opened to equalise pressure and prevent a build up of pressure in the lungs which would have had the same effect as blowing up a balloon. In his haste, Shaw had omitted to complete this vital task, which did not go unnoticed by my father who grabbed his ankle as he commenced his ascent. Opening the valve, he released Shaw's leg to allow him to shoot to the surface and safety.

In expending this extra effort whilst breathing pure Oxygen, father vomited into his face mask, therefore, during his ascent he was actually drowning in his own juices. However, happily, as he broke the surface, he was immediately pulled into a waiting whaler from HMS Brazen. In Brazen's sick bay his protestations to be allowed up on deck to view further escapes fell on deaf ears and he was administered a heavy sedative against his will. He woke up some hours later to find himself well on the way to Plymouth, his involvement with Thetis temporarily over.

In contrast, however, Joe Oram was allowed to remain on the scene, which begs the question 'why' when he was not able to influence the rescue through lack of knowledge? Arnold, on the other hand, had worked on Thetis during her construction and was fully conversant with all the pipeline systems, valves and machinery. By the time father came round in Brazen's sick bay, it would not have mattered if the Naval Architect who had designed the ship had been present because by then the battle for survival was over and the sea had won.

The treatment meted to Shaw and Arnold after the tragedy could not have been more different. The trauma suffered by Frank Shaw was recognised by his employers, Cammell Laird, who immediately elevated him to 'staff' status. His own house ownership was not long in coming, at a time when house ownership was the preserve of the 'upper class' and his story was eagerly snapped up by the press in return for a significant consideration. Arnold, however, was incarcerated in hospital at Plymouth under strict orders not to say anything to anybody, especially the media, about the tragedy. The Royal Naval beurocratic system refused him his wages because he could not produce his pay-book, which now lay on the seabed. To refuse to obey orders in protest would be classed as mutiny, still a hanging offence in 1939, and certainly not an option that would have been considered by him.

It was during the next six months, the time it took to replace his pay-book, that father found out who his friends were. In those days, wages were poor for everyone and few people had money to spare for others. It was a struggle to feed my mother and myself and more poignantly so, it was demeaning to his character to be forced to accept charity. This seemed shoddy treatment indeed for someone the rest of the country regarded as a hero. At this point due deference must be paid to a man by the name of Fred Burdiss, a boilermaker from Newcastle who, in the years of the depression, was forced to seek work further afield and who settled eventually in Birkenhead to practice his skill at Lairds. It was Fred Burdiss who took it upon himself to ensure that the Arnold family had bread on the table and father a pint of best in his hand, almost certainly to the detriment of his own family's needs This Christian gesture would never receive any other accolade than the undying gratitude of the Arnolds at Birkenhead and therefore, to my mind, demands inclusion here as one of the many side stories which make up the complete tapestry.

Perhaps the person who showed the greatest fortitude in the whole Thetis affair was the wife of the captain, Mrs Bolus. Temporarily domiciled in Birkenhead while her husband oversaw the construction of his command, she must have been only too aware that her husband would not leave his ship until all the remainder of the people on board had gone. She was perceptive enough to know that by that time, the Captains chances would, to say the least, not be good. Despite this unspoken knowledge, Mrs Bolus spent her days during the crisis outside Cammell Lairds' Main Gatehouse offering comfort and counselling to other wives and relatives who were anxiously awaiting news. She transported to and from their homes other relatives who were distraught or needed to perhaps put children to bed. Perhaps by so doing, she did not dwell on the inevitable and dreaded the moment of truth. No story of the 'Thetis' could be complete without a reference to this brave and selfless lady.

On a personal note, I could never really understand why, when having stood side-by-side together, looking death squarely in the face, a more permanent friendship did not exist between Frank Shaw and my father. I cannot recall any occasion when one invited the other to an evening out, neither did one call socially upon the other although over the years they both attended the same functions, usually the anniversaries of the sinking, until they both died. To my knowledge there was no enmity either, they just never seemed to have generated any rapport, even though they both lived within a mile of each other. Perhaps the intervening war years gave them little chance to become better acquainted

Before concluding my catalogue of personalities, I must refer to a person that I came to know as a good friend some years later and whom I smilingly referred to as the man with the longest name in the telephone book, Johnny McGillicuddy. I was fortunate to know John, as he had served a similar apprenticeship to myself only at the time when a battered and sorry looking Thetis was re-docked at Lairds yard after being raised from the sea, beached at Anglesey for repairs and finally towed back to Lairds' yard. He could recall how the damage to the conning tower and periscope standards was repaired and the bow was extensively modified to eliminate the two external torpedo tubes.

John had certainly missed his vocation because he was the most entertaining raconteur I have even known. No matter how many times one heard his stories, they always held ones full attention. Arguably, his most interesting recollection was of the new Captain, Lt. C.B.Crouch, a man it seemed, who had been given a simple brief

- to make Thetis, now renamed Thunderbolt, seaworthy and battle ready with little tolerance of superstition by the crew. Crouch was of moderate build but of immense character. He was a no-nonsense type of man, perfect for the job in hand. His treatment of his officers and men could best be described as rigid. Thunderbolts' ultimate departure from Lairds wet basin was somewhat less sentimental than could be expected. Crouch was bellowing orders to his deck parties down a megaphone in terms guaranteed to bring more than a blush, not only to the cheeks of the wives and sweethearts gathered on the quayside, but similarly to the dockyard mateys tending the ropes.

That the end justifies the means could not have been in doubt as Thunderbolt, under Crouch's command served with distinction in the Mediterranean Theatre until, like so many other submarines at that time, she made her final patrol. In her case, she was depth charged in an attack by the Italian Destroyer Cicogna, and for the second time in her life, lifted her stern for all to see before taking the final plunge.

The ten year period following the Second World War brought a plethora of really good stories of exploits during the conflict. Best seller followed best seller and their authors became household names; Russell Braddon, Airey Neave, Douglas Bader and so on. In the mid fifties, the co-authors of this book contacted my father with a view to requesting his involvement with the production of the Thetis story, to be called 'The Admiralty Regrets', the opening statement of the dreaded telegram from the Navy informing the next of kin of their sailors loss. Consent was readily given and the research began. Some time later the completed version was submitted for publication and proved to be the definitive version of the tale of both heroism intertwined with a colossal lack of organisation in the rescue operation.

I was quite surprised when I was contacted by David Roberts who expressed a wish to produce a book recounting the Thetis disaster. My first impulse was to say "it's been done before", however David explained to me that it had been his experience to notice several books which were long gone out of print and in essence, lost to all but a few interested collectors. Books which told priceless stories, tales in essence which reflected both our maritime heritage and local interest in the Merseyside area.

Enthusiastic about the concept but sceptical about the outcome, I was very pleasantly impressed by a similar venture undertaken by David in recounting the story of the Lusitania. I could not help but think that the Thetis story would also be worthy of re-telling. As such, I was more than happy to allow David full access to all the material on the subject that was in my possession, so much so that his quick visits usually ended up as marathon sessions.

I am constantly amazed at the way that the 'Thetis' story keeps recurring. Only recently it featured as a question in a pub quiz on one of the current soap operas. Possibly every book written on the subject of the submarine service includes a reference to the tragedy.

As regards Stoker Arnold of the 'Thetis', he was subsequently involved in fighting during the War in practically every theatre of conflict. Following the Thetis inquiries in London he was posted to the submarine HMS Spearfish but found that the memories of his drowned comrades constantly haunted him, therefore the Navy transferred him back to general service on compassionate grounds. He joined the newly built cruiser HMS Fiji at Glasgow and sailed as a convoy escort heading towards Dakar. My mother was somewhat perturbed to hear Lord Haw Haw announce that the German Navy knew the Fiji had sailed and that 'U' Boats would ensure that she never returned. He was almost right for she was torpedoed and crippled. Thankfully she was able to make it back for repairs which were completed in time for her to proceed with all haste to join the Battle for Crete. This was indeed a sad time for the Navy. Operating with almost no air cover, ships were sunk with depressing frequency.

Fiji and Gloucester were sailing to rescue survivors from the destroyer HMS Greyhound when they were attacked by enemy aircraft and the Gloucester was hit. Unable to stop and render assistance, Fiji cast off her rafts for the swimming survivors as she steamed past at full speed. Later that day the lone cruiser was herself hit by a single bomb dropping down the funnel and bursting in the boiler room. As she lay stopped in the water she began to slowly roll over and the crew who were still on the hulk 'walked the hull', Stoker Arnold among them.

The Fiji took with her my Fathers two most valued possessions both quite unique items; his Thetis cap ribbon and the wrap containing the skin membrane which had covered his face when he was born.

Stoker Arnold returned home to join the Battleship HMS King George V which was engaged in protecting the convoys in the perilous waters to Russia, a far cry from the warm Mediterranean that he had previously sailed, any chance of 'getting ones feet wet' in these icy oceans would mean death within minutes, a harsh lesson found out to their cost by the crew of HMS Punjabi which was sliced in two by the Battleship. As she sank her own depth charges exploded in an enormous detonation which further damaged the KGV's hull plating. The only consolation was an extended repair stay in Gladstone dock at Liverpool, a heaven sent opportunity for anyone with family in

Birkenhead.

Repairs completed, 'King George V' sailed to head up the British Pacific Fleet. Their first encounter with Japanese aircraft was a puzzling affair as it appeared as though the planes were actually trying to crash onto the ships. They did not suspect at that time that they had experienced the first of the Kamikaze raids. Later, as the allies gained the upper hand, Kamikaze dangers were replaced by American pilots who returned to their Carriers in a hyped-up state, or 'bomb-happy' as the Matelots preferred to call it, blasting their cannons at anything that moved. My father told me that it was then that the Ostrich syndrome came into play. On the premise that "if I can't see you, you can't see me". Any object placed between you and the returning Grumman Wildcats, such as a bin lid, would render the amour piercing shells harmless and ineffective.

As the struggle petered out, 'KGV' returned from a month of bombarding the Japanese mainland only for the crew to wonder why the sky had suddenly taken a deep red tinge. It would be some time before they realised that they had witnessed the dawn of the Atomic age with the dropping of the first atom bomb.

Following the end of the war, joyous returns were commonplace but for the King George V much work was still to do in the Far East and by the time she returned, the flag waving was all over. For Stoker Arnold, however, the end of the conflict did not mean the beginning of peace. Churchill had warned that the runaway victories of the Red Army might not stop at Berlin. Hungary, Czechoslovakia, The Balkan Stakes all fell to Stalinism, and it was touch and go whether Italy and France would go the same way. To make sure that they didn't, a strong naval force was sent to the Mediterranean by the British and American navies to show the flag around various ports.

Among the crew of the British Flagship, the Battleship HMS Duke of York, was Stoker Arnold making the final voyage of his naval career.

During twenty-two years service he had survived a subsmash, torpedo, bombing and machine gun attacks and a ramming. He had served in the Atlantic, North Sea, Mediterranean and Pacific Campaigns. In addition, he lost a brother in the submarine HMS Olympus, another in the submarine HMS Thames, a brother-in-law in the submarine HMS Utmost, had another taken prison of war when the submarine HMS Seal was captured off Denmark, and yet another left with a fractured spine following the loss of HMS Laforey off Anzio.

Throughout all his trials and tribulations he neither sought nor was awarded any medals in recognition of his efforts.

One memorable moment of recognition occurred in 1990, when the Royal Navy built five new accommodation blocks at the submarine base at Gosport. It was decided to name each one after a famous submariner, normally VC holders. Mainly through the protestations of Gus Britton of the Submarine Museum, Gosport, one of these blocks was duly named Arnold. Gus argued that the Arnold family had given the service their all, what more sacrifice could be expected? As I conclude this foreword in the summer of 1997, the news of the death of Gus Britton has reached me. He was a fine man who will be greatly missed.

Sadly, the Arnold block and the others were to be closed after two years when the end of the cold war signalled a reduction in naval personnel.

Walter Charles Arnold, Petty Officer Stoker Mechanic, would inwardly have been proud to at last have been recognised but outwardly would have shown a modicum of embarrassment at the gesture, a reflection of the gentle, inoffensive man that was my father, 'Stoker Arnold of the Thetis'.

Derek Arnold September 1997

Preface

THIS book is respectfully dedicated to the memory of the 162 men who lost their lives while serving in or in connexion with His Majesty's Submarine *Thetis* or, as she later became, His Majesty's Submarine *Thunderbolt*.

Those parts of the book which represent our personal opinions can be clearly seen as such. Those parts which are written as fact are so to our best knowledge and ability—and thanks, very largely, to the generously given assistance of all those people whose names are listed below. A brief reference should be made to Chapter 11, however. By the nature of this chapter, much of its contents must be a reconstruction of what happened, arrived at on the basis of official evidence and in the light of available experience.

We wish gratefully to record our indebtedness to all the following, who, by supplying information, advice, photographs, etc., have helped in the production of this book. We would emphasize, however, that we are solely and jointly responsible for all opinions expressed, for any factual errors contained in the text, and for any shortcomings.

Apart from all others, we should like to thank Captain W. O. Shelford, R.N. (retd.), who is probably the greatest living authority on the problems of Submarine Escape and Salvage and who is the only submarine officer to have become the Royal Navy's Superintendent of Diving. His sound judgment and expert knowledge have been generously placed at our disposal, and he has carefully checked the manuscript. Without his help it is very doubtful if this work would have been completed.

Next, we are sincerely grateful to Stoker Petty Officer W. C. Arnold and to Mr Frank Shaw, two of the original four survivors of *Thetis*, for their most ready, kind, and detailed help; and similarly to Mrs Joyce Watney, Mrs Helen Woods, and Major F. M. Woods, R.M., respectively widow, mother, and brother of the late Lieutenant-Commander F. G. Woods, D.S.C., R.N.

Thereafter, in respect of H.M.S/M. *Thetis*, we wish to thank the Secretary of the Amalgamated Engineering Union; Mrs W. C. Arnold; Chief Petty Officer Telegraphist J. H. Barter, D.S.M.; Commander J. W. F. Bennetts, R.N. (retd.); Mr C. Brock (Wreck Master, Mersey Docks and Harbour Board); City Caterers (Liverpool), Ltd; the late officers of s.s. *Delambre*; the Secretary of the Electrical Trades Union; Mr C. Felcey, D.S.M., Bos'n

R.N. (retd.); Mrs M. Glenn, widow of the late Mr R. E. Glenn, Commissioned Engineer, R.N.; Captain A. E. Godfrey; Professor J. B. S. Haldane, F.R.S.; Captain H. V. Hart, O.B.E., R.N.R.; the Secretary of the Institute of Engineers and Shipbuilders in Scotland; the Secretary of the Institution of Naval Architects; Mr F. Jenner, Bos'n R.N. (retd.); the Marine Superintendent of the Lamport and Holt Line; Mr W. Linton; the Liverpool Towing and Lighterage Co.; the Secretary of the Lord Mayor of London's Appeal Fund; Dr A. Maddock-Jones; the Mersey Docks and Harbour Board; Metal Industries (Salvage), Ltd; Commander R. H. Mills, O.B.E., R.N. (retd.); Chief Petty Officer R. Oliver, A.M., B.E.M.; Lieutenant (E) R. Ostler, D.S.C., R.N. (retd.); Mr J. G. Passey, M.B.E., Commissioned Bos'n, R.N. (retd.); Mr H. Rowkins, Bos'n R.N. (retd.); Lord Somervell, P.C., O.B.E.; Mr T. Webster, D.S.M., Gunner (T) R.N. (retd.).

Unfortunately Messrs Cammell Laird and Co., Ltd, and Messrs Wailes Dove Bitumastic, Ltd, felt unable to assist us.

Then, in respect of H.M.S/M. *Thunderbolt*, we wish to thank Lieutenant-Commander R. L. Bird, R.N.R.; Rear-Admiral S. Brengola, Italian Naval Attaché, London; Admiral Aldo Cocchia, Italian Navy; Mr and Mrs C. B. Crouch, senr; Lieutenant A. Frattura, Italian Navy; Lieutenant-Commander (E) W. R. Glass, D.S.M., R.N. (retd.); Lieutenant-Commander M. Hutley, R.N.R.; Mr C. S. Jones, D.S.M., Bos'n R.N. (retd.); Mr E. Jones; Mrs M. Maughan, widow of the late Petty Officer T. Maughan, D.S.M.; Lieutenant-Commander A. Migliorini, Italian Navy; Mr F. C. Monnington; Lieutenant-Commander (E) J. W. Northwood, M.B.E., D.S.C., R.N. (retd.); Mr J. G. Passey, M.B.E., Commissioned Bos'n, R.N. (retd.); Captain J. S. Stevens, D.S.O., D.S.C., R.N.; Captain T. Trattles; Mr W. M. Turnbull; Petty Officer E. Webb, D.S.M.; Mr T. Webster, D.S.M., Gunner (T) R.N. (retd.); Mrs M. Yeates, widow of the late Petty Officer Telegraphist T. Yeates, D.S.M.

Acknowledgment is also made to Their Lords Commissioners of the Admiralty for their assistance in that part of this narrative which deals only with *Thunderbolt*, for which we are duly grateful.

Finally, we wish to thank our wives for all their help, tolerance, and encouragement over what must often have seemed an inordinately long period of time.

C.E.T.W.
J.B.

Contents

Illustrations

9

Another View of the same Jolly Roger

Thunderbolt returning from Patrol

Thunderbolt's Control-room

" Charlie " Jones

The beached *Thetis* on the small Traeth Bychan, Moelfre, Anglesey.

Mine Rescue Team, being briefed to recover the bodies from *Thetis*.

The crew of *Thetis* marching along Conway Street in Birkenhead.

Thetis leaving the River Mersey in 1939.

Telegrams that flashed between the Admiralty, the Merseyside home of Walter Arnold and Submarine HQ at Fort Blockhouse.

Thetis in Traeth Bychan, Moelfre, Anglesey where local men and Navy personnel are working on her

Walter Arnold, his wife May, and Cammell Laird Fitter Frank Shaw on their way to the Court of Inquiry in London.

Extract from the Daily Sketch June 8 1939.

Maps and Diagrams

Liverpool Bay : Nine Charted Positions of *Thetis*, June 1 and 2, 1939

Nos. 5 and 6 Mechanical Indicators

Bow-cap Operating Lever

D.S.E.A. Escape Chamber

Maps showing Positions of Various Units at 8 A.M. and 3 P.M., June 2, 1939

Sectional Drawing (simplified) of a " T "-class Submarine (1939)   *endpapers*

1

December 1936 to
Tuesday, May 30, 1939

The Beginning

I KNOW how you feel—I've got it myself. I hate the damned boat."

There was silence as each man realized that at least one other person felt the same as he did.

" Well, I can settle it as far as you're concerned. You have a direct order from me not to go out in *Thetis* to-morrow."

Warrant Engineer Robert Ostler, of the new submarine *Taku*, still under construction at Cammell Laird, looked at his commanding officer. Unsure of what to say, he maintained for a moment his hesitant silence.

" I'm only sorry that you're going out with her, sir."

Shortly before 10 A.M. on the following day, June 1, 1939, His Majesty's Submarine *Thetis* left Birkenhead under the command of Lieutenant-Commander G. H. Bolus, Royal Navy, for Liverpool Bay. The principal purpose of the day was to make a diving trial at sea. This was to be *Thetis's* first venture as a submarine proper. She had on board a complement of 103, fifty more than her normal crew.

Five hours later she was lying, sunk, 160 feet down, with her bows in the mud. She was only 38 miles from land. But of the 103 men who sailed in her a mere four survived.

Guy Bolus—" Sam " to his friends—had joined his command almost twelve months previously, a few days before she was launched on June 29, 1938. *Thetis* was the third of the new " T " class of submarine, ordered under the Navy Estimates of 1936. But she was the first of the class to be built at Birkenhead.

She had been laid down in December 1936, and had been budgeted to cost approximately £350,000. Her job number was 1027; and all the plates and ribs and bits and pieces that had first accumulated around the slipway and then been assimilated into her anatomy had been boldly marked with the four proud numerals.

Her class was designed to provide a general-purpose submarine, capable of operating over long distances and, if necessary, in tropical conditions, but yet not as large as the " O," " P," and " R " classes of the 1920's and early 1930's. She was 270 feet long overall, displaced 1575 tons submerged, had a maximum speed of 16 knots on the surface and 9 knots dived, and a range of 8000 miles. She carried one 4-inch gun and six 21-inch torpedo tubes.

In addition to Bolus, two other officers and four ratings stood by *Thetis* during the whole period of her fitting-out—that is, from launching to final acceptance trials. Without exception they all rejoiced in their good fortune. For the appointment to a " new construction " meant for all who joined her early a long period of that sort of domestic routine—off to work in the morning and back in time for supper—which is seldom part of a sailor's life.

A second party, of twelve senior ratings, arrived two-thirds of the way through fitting-out, immediately after Christmas leave. And shortly before the end of February 1939 Bolus was able to tell Submarine Headquarters at Fort Blockhouse, Portsmouth, that he was ready for the rest of his crew.

For these final 34, travelling up from Portsmouth by train, Birkenhead was first of all a confusion of kit-bags and hammocks. Then a meeting with a pre-arranged landlady in civilian digs.

When they first caught sight of *Thetis* the next morning she lay below them in the fitting-out basin. She was still finishing painting, and patches of red lead stood out from among the uniform grey and the uncovered rust. A spider's web of electric leads sagged between the boat—all submariners refer to their craft as " boats," not " ships "—and the side of the yard. She was still largely characterless, a piece of grown-up Meccano. Her heart was beating firmly enough, but it was still located in a bare, dusty office near by.

Her first metamorphosis did not take long. On March 4 she was commissioned as a unit of the Royal Navy and placed on the books of the Portland submarine flotilla, which she would eventually join.

The series of trials and inspections began to take their normal course. First, there was the ' trim dive ' in the fitting-out basin. This was an experiment in extra-slow time to calculate the correct amount of compensating ballast the submarine should carry to enable her to be buoyant on the surface, but capable of immediate diving once her main tanks were flooded.

During the trim dive the newly arrived ship's company worked the necessary mechanism—in particular the telemotor, or oil-pressure, controls to the flood valves, allowing the sea to enter the various tanks, and to the vent valves, through which the air escaped as the water took its place. The direction of the experiment, however, remained in the hands of Mr A. B. Robinson, Cammell Laird's foreman engineer, and Mr A. A. F. Hill, the Admiralty Principal Ship Overseer, who shared the control-room with Sam Bolus. Trimming responsibilities were not yet in the hands of the ship's officers.

In *Thetis's* fore ends Lieutenant Frederick Woods, the torpedo officer, was checking the carrying out of the orders relayed from the control-room. During one of the dives—several always took place to corroborate the calculations—he thought he remembered numbers 5 and 6 torpedo tubes being filled to compensate for the torpedoes she would normally be carrying.

On March 31 a Submarine Escape apparatus inspection was carried out by Lieutenant-Commander E. R. C. MacVicker, the Submarine Command Escape Officer. With one small technical exception, he gave the boat a clean bill of health. In accordance with normal practice the actual ' sets ' of escape breathing apparatus for the crew were installed in the submarine by the D.S.E.A. staff and the lockers sealed. The sets for the passengers that *Thetis* would be carrying on trials were in boxes of 28, sealed and left in the stores until the boat was ready to go to sea: they took up too much room to be put on board any earlier.

Thetis was now ready to become a submarine in the full sense of the word. She had her crew, and all her apparatus and gear had been installed. She had carried out a series of searching dockside tests and trials. The next step was to co-ordinate the men with the machinery, and the only satisfactory way of doing this was to go to sea. A certificate, dated April 12, and stating, as the contract expressly required, that the vessel was in a proper condition to undertake sea trials, had been issued by Cammell Laird and countersigned by Bolus and several Admiralty officials.

Accordingly, on April 30, *Thetis* sailed for her official sea trials for engines and steering. She was also to undertake her first dive under way in the open sea.

" Starboard ten, half ahead," called Bolus from the side of the bridge to his Coxswain at the upper steering position.

" Starboard ten, half ahead, sir," came Chief Petty Officer George Cornish's voice in reply.

Slowly, but quite steadily, the submarine's head paid off to port.

" Starboard twenty," called Bolus.

Surely enough, she continued swinging to port.

" Midships, port twenty." As Bolus had realized, the steering gear had been connected up incorrectly, and the contrary direction had the required effect.

This state of topsy-turvydom became, for the duration of the trial, a fixed hazard for officer-of-the-watch and helmsman to negotiate between themselves. While at the outset it caused unbelievable merriment among the crew, the incident did not pass unnoticed by the more sober-thinking persons on board. It seemed strange that acceptance machinery tests, supervised by Admiralty overseers, should have failed to detect so obvious a mistake.

Leaving the Mersey, *Thetis* headed north through the Irish Sea for the trials ground in the Clyde Estuary. The days away were strenuous. The crew were busy finding out how their new boat behaved, as well as getting to know one another. Conditions were crowded. Every day the visitors—Admiralty staff, Cammell Laird men, and extra naval personnel—came out to the anchorage from the hotel at Arrochar, where they were staying. Right from the start one thing became apparent. *Thetis* was a happy boat, and under Sam Bolus's benign guidance her ship's company immediately began shaking down into an efficient team.

It had been intended to make the diving trial in the Gare Loch, the traditional site for all such proceedings in the Clyde area. In preparation for this initial tests were ordered on the hydroplanes. (These are like horizontal rudders, which act in concert with the movements of a submarine through the water to drive the vessel downward or upward, in much the same way as the angle of a diver's hands controls his progress through the water.) As the for'ard hydroplanes were being run through their full compass they jammed at ' Hard to Dive,' and, despite the united efforts of *Thetis*'s crew and the Cammell Laird staff, they could not be shifted. So the diving trial was postponed, and Admiralty approval was subsequently obtained for it to be carried out at a later date, in Liverpool Bay.

During early May came the torpedo equipment trials. *Thetis*'s six tubes were all situated for'ard. They were arranged in two vertical rows of three each, numbers 2, 4, and 6 to port and numbers 1, 3, and 5 to starboard. Each tube was just wide enough to admit a 21-inch-diameter torpedo and was fitted with two doors. The ' bow-cap,' the one at the for'ard or seaward end, was opened after a torpedo was in the tube prior to firing; the ' rear door,' inboard, opened to allow a torpedo to enter the tube. Obviously a bow-cap and a rear door should not be open simultaneously !

Each rear door was fitted with a test cock. This was so constructed that when a small lever was operated two narrow holes moved adjacent to each other, making a continuous hole through the rear door. An opened test cock thus served as a check on the presence of water in a tube.

A few days after the torpedo equipment trials a painter and an enameller arrived from a Cammell Laird sub-contractor (Wailes Dove Bitumastic, Ltd) and commenced work on the insides of the tubes. Unfortunately, when he was applying the bitumastic solution to the insides of the rear doors, the enameller took no steps to prevent the solution choking the test-cock holes. At the enamelling stage, later, he did in fact twist some cotton waste into spools, soak them in oil, and use them to plug all the test cocks, keeping them there until after he had finally smoothed off the top surface with a blow-lamp. But the damage, if damage it was, had already been done.

There remained a last inspection of the Davis Submarine Escape arrangements and the re-installation of the D.S.E.A. sets themselves. Up from Portsmouth, a few days before the postponed diving trial, came Chief Petty Officer Harry Rowkins, the Submarine Service's senior D.S.E.A. instructor. With the help of Leading Stoker Walter Arnold, who had been standing by *Thetis* as Engineer's Writer and Storekeeper for almost a year, he set to work. Under Admiralty instructions any submarine proceeding to sea had to have one set of breathing apparatus for each person on board plus a one-third excess. On the expectation of 98 persons being carried on the trial, this meant that Rowkins had to check a total of 131.

In addition to Rowkins and Arnold, Lieutenant Woods took part in the work. In fact, in his final report to *Thetis's* First Lieutenant, Lieutenant Harold Chapman, Rowkins felt moved to remark on the considerable interest which both Woods and Arnold had shown in every detail of the escape arrangements: just as he was leaving the submarine Woods had even asked him to run through the escape drill once again. This attitude was in direct contrast to the usual submariner's opinion of D.S.E.A. Almost invariably the whole idea of ever having to get out of a boat was received with unprintable expressions of disfavour.

As it happened there was a lot of gossip about submarine escape when Rowkins arrived in Birkenhead. On May 23 the U.S. submarine *Squalus* had sunk in 220 feet of water. Thirty-three officers and men had remained alive after the initial disaster, and all these were rescued within forty hours by the use of a new type of escape apparatus. This was a rescue chamber that was lowered from the surface and clamped over one of the hatches of the sunken submarine.

Among the submariners at Cammell Laird this *Squalus* episode was very largely treated as just another example of American 'bull.' The American practice of making submarine trainees undergo an ascent from the bottom of a 100-foot tower—the Royal

Navy's tank at Portsmouth was, until 1954, only 15 feet deep—
also received perpetual scorn. It was with this sort of comment
ringing in his ears that Rowkins returned to Portsmouth.

Once this stage of the proceedings had been reached, *Thetis's*
time at the builders was nearly at an end. So far, with the exception
of the steering and the hydroplane episodes, everything had gone
swimmingly. It was difficult to know how much importance to
attach to these mishaps. One man at least viewed them quite
seriously. Lieutenant-Commander Richard Garnett was standing
by at Birkenhead in command of the submarine *Taku*. To get as
much experience as he could of the new class of boat, he had gone
with *Thetis* on her Clyde trials. And he had not been impressed.

As the date of the revised diving trial drew near the traditional
' passenger list ' appeared again. Whenever a new class of submarine is undergoing trials, whether surface or submerged, as many
interested officers and men as it is possible to take go out in her.
This procedure helps to cut down the teething troubles of the boats
that follow. The responsibility for making up this passenger list
is always that of the engineer officer of the submarine conducting
the trial. So it was that on the Tuesday before *Thetis* was due to
sail on the Thursday, Roy Glenn walked into the office marked
" Engineer Officer, *Taku*."

" I've got your name on the list, Bob. Do you good to see how
a real submarine works."

Glenn had a way of putting an inflection in his voice that could
quickly get a man's back up.

" Well, you can take it off, then, Roy," the Yorkshireman's
reply came back bluntly.

The two engineers looked at each other. They were really the
best of friends. When Ostler had arrived in Birkenhead in the
January Glenn had taken him to his digs, and they had stayed
together until Ostler's family arrived to join him. Glenn was
undeniably an outspoken man. An outstanding engineer, he was
not averse to expressing his opinions about the workmanship that
was going into *his* submarine. And his comment was seldom ill-
informed. He had in fact found that the fuelling system could
be improved, his drawings had been sanctioned, and the modified
design was incorporated in the remainder of the class.

Although he was a Commissioned Warrant Officer, which meant
that he had risen from the lower deck, he had never been invited
with his brother officers to the daily luncheons given by the Cammell
Laird management. This rankled very sorely with Glenn, and also
among all the submarine officers at Birkenhead, for practical as
well as social reasons; for in a friendly and informal luncheon

atmosphere much useful technical discussion could take place. As far as Glenn was concerned, he set out to make sure that *Thetis* should in no way suffer from this circumstance, and his routine ' driving ' of the Cammell Laird foremen and Admiralty overseers was intensified.

This distinction between wardroom and warrant officers was not, of course, of Cammell Laird's making. In the pre-war years the Navy's own demarcation line had to be strictly observed. The only exception to the rule was the Submarine Branch. And a shipbuilder's conception of Service protocol could not be expected to comprehend the numerous minor divergences between branch and branch.

What made the whole matter so much more unfortunate was that the more Glenn chased the senior Cammell Laird and Admiralty representatives, the more they did what they could to let him know that they were taking as few orders as possible from a Commissioned Warrant Officer, and the more they avoided him. To get away from his tongue they were even prepared to wait to carry out tests until after he had left the yard in an evening. And although during construction and fitting-out the responsibility for all material and for the working of all machinery was the appropriate Admiralty overseer's and not the Engineer Officer's, any neglect of experience as wide as Glenn's was obviously unwise.

Glenn had been furious about the wrong connecting of the steering gear, and when later on the same trip the hydroplanes stuck, tempers got completely out of hand. The hydroplane mechanism was admittedly the responsibility, not of Cammell Laird, but of Vickers Armstrong, and the steering gear of yet another subcontractor, but, said Glenn, this did not mean that they should not have been checked by some one.

Each time *Thetis* had been due to go to sea on trials Glenn had confronted Ostler with his list. Each time Ostler had refused. This time it was different. This was certain to be the first sea dive. *Thetis* was to stay down for three hours and would carry out underwater manœuvres. It would be an ideal opportunity for Ostler to see how his boat should operate. But he felt he could not go out in *Thetis*.

For him, she had an inexplicable atmosphere. Inside her, even in a dry basin, his confidence drained completely, with the result that he felt he would never make a success of building *Taku*. But as soon as he set foot back on the side of the basin the feeling disappeared. He had never tried to explain any of this to Glenn— it would have been impossible—and his continued refusal was badly received.

" Your Skipper will be impressed by your keenness."

Ostler shrugged his shoulders.

" I suppose you know that you will be the only submarine officer in Cammell Laird's not coming ? Anyway, why don't you want to come ? "

" Look, Roy. You know there are too many going if all goes well—and far too many if you have any snags. If I go and see my Captain, will that satisfy you ? "

Glenn nodded and left in silence. So the next day Ostler spoke to Dick Garnett and received a direct order not to go out in *Thetis*.

" I envy you, Chief," Garnett had said. " You know she should have gone out last week. Well, I made the excuse that as it was my wedding anniversary and as I was giving a party I wanted to stay behind. Do you know how many came to the party ? Two. My wife and me. And I can't use the same excuse to-morrow."

Ostler made his way to Glenn's office and reported that his captain had ordered him not to go out. Glenn was patently displeased and the two engineers parted coldly. They never saw each other again.

2

*Tuesday, May 30, to
Thursday, June 1*

Preparations

DURING the forty-eight hours immediately preceding *Thetis's* sailing on her final acceptance trials the usual preparations were taking place. A tug had been chartered to act as chaperone, and a number of last-minute checks were being carried out inside the submarine.

In the course of one of these Mr Thomas Wolfe, the assistant foreman ship fitter of Cammell Laird, and Mr H. Horsman, the Admiralty ship-fitting overseer, were working on the torpedo tubes. When they had finished they left each of the six bow-cap operating-levers in a vertical position, which meant that they were at Neutral.

Here the first misunderstanding of the trial occurred. When a submarine is in deep water there is considerable pressure on any one bow-cap: not only the pressure consonant with the depth (roughly half a pound per square inch for every foot), but also the resistance set up by the way that the submarine is making through the water. To overcome this the bow-caps are opened by rams which in turn are powered by telemotor pressure.

The levers controlling the supply of telemotor power to *Thetis's* bow-caps had three positions: Open, Neutral, and Shut, with a travel of some 90 degrees between the two extremes. Other than being the central position through which the lever passed while moving from one limit to the other, the neutral position served to lock the telemotor power in whatever direction the lever had previously indicated.

This was theoretically fine, but there was a feeling among submariners that there was nothing quite so shut as 'Shut.' In support of this the ignoring of the neutral position was firm and established submarine practice. This point had been emphasized at the time of the torpedo equipment trial early in May, when the officer in charge of the trial, a Commander A. Maguire, seeing a control-lever at Neutral, had given instructions that only the Open and Shut positions should be used. On this occasion, however, contrary practice, on what might at the time have appeared a matter of detail, had still persisted.

On the same day the watertight doors between the six main compartments of the submarine were vacuum-tested. The mechanism of the two indicator-buoys was examined and so was the rather complicated 'smoke candle' signal apparatus, or underwater gun, as it was more familiarly known to submariners. This was used to eject flares which would ignite on the surface and mark the submarine's position in the event of an emergency or when she was being 'hunted' during an exercise. It was, incidentally, the only gun in the Navy that was fired by stokers.

Each test found everything completely in order. There remained only the various calculations involved in the putting on of *Thetis's* 'main ballast' trim before she sailed. The figures that had been obtained from the basin dive early in March had to be adjusted by the Admiralty overseers—they would not become the responsibility of the First Lieutenant until after the trial—for any difference in weight: extra complement, additional stores, a greater amount of fresh water for drinking, more food or rum, and so on. Very roughly it averaged 15 gallons per man.

When a submarine is designed various trimming calculations are made. It cannot be guaranteed on the drawing-board, however, that these will be absolutely correct, as a certain margin of error has to be accepted until the submarine is tried out. If she is then still light—and all margins are on the safe side—the builders place ballast in the form of pig iron along her keel until they arrive at the ideal basic trim. This was the stage that *Thetis* had reached some months previously.

The division of labour involved in putting on the actual trim for the day's trial was a little complex. Later the First Lieutenant would simply tell the Chief Stoker how much water he was to put into each of the various tanks. On this occasion one of the Admiralty overseers handed the trim statement to the Cammell Laird foreman engineer. He passed it to one of his fitters, a Mr H. Eccleston, who finally manipulated the valve controls and put the trim on under the supervision of one of the assistant Admiralty overseers.

A few minutes before *Thetis* was ready to leave the basin Mr John Rowe, a Cammell Laird assistant yard manager, took the draught of the hull in the water, for'ard and aft. The submarine was still four inches higher out of the water—*i.e.*, lighter in weight—for'ard than she had been at the time of the basin dive in March. It was at this point in the proceedings that *Thetis's* Chief Stoker

Dillon-Shallard was heard to remark that he had his doubts about the final trim being correct.

When Rowe handed his draught figures to the Admiralty constructor, Mr Bailey, he pointed out that both sets of draughts he had taken that morning showed *Thetis* to be three and a half inches deeper in the water to port than to starboard. In the ensuing conversation between the two Admiralty officials Bailey and Hill, Rowe heard a remark to the effect that they would have to fill, or else that they could fill, one or more of the starboard torpedo tubes. If this were necessary the chain of communication would be the same complicated one employed for putting on the trim.

The filling of a torpedo tube with water is normally carried out, other than for practice shoots, only as trimming compensation for a torpedo. At all times the tube is either completely full or completely empty. In other words, it is never used like an auxiliary, or compensating, tank, with varying amounts of water in it.

The orthodox submarine method of filling a tube is from the ' main line '—*i.e.*, from the internal pumping system. It is admittedly physically feasible for a tube to be filled by opening the bow-cap, but, because of the difference this would make to a boat's trim, as well as on account of the risk of flotsam fouling the mouth of the tube, this method is avoided.

In addition it was also possible to flood up with water from a small tank beneath the tube. This method was most probably the one that any Cammell Laird representative would use, particularly as he would be accustomed to working in the submarine at times when there would not be sufficient people on board to operate the rather complicated ' main line.' But there was still a chance, as one of the firm's spokesmen was to admit later, that on any urgent occasion a tube would be flooded through the bow-cap.

There was, however, on that bright Thursday morning, no suspicion at all that this possible divergence in practice could prove dangerous in the extreme.

Some time before all the calculations and trim adjustments had been completed the full company of 103 persons sailing in *Thetis* had reported on board. What sort of a craft had they come to test ?

Thetis was divided into six main compartments by five watertight doors all designed to close towards the control-room in the centre of the boat. Except for the door farthest for'ard—the one between the tube compartment and the torpedo stowage compartment—they were all circular and secured in their shut position with a ring which moved over their outside circumference. The one farthest for'ard was really four separate doors, two port and two starboard.

This arrangement was made necessary by the fact that the lower torpedo tubes were below deck level. Each of the four doors were secured by butterfly bolts which fitted into clips hinged to the door. The two large doors—the upper ones—each had eighteeen pairs of bolts and clips.

With exception of the stokers, the crew of *Thetis* lived between the second and third watertight doors (see diagrammatic end-papers). Beneath this living accommodation were the main battery tanks. Normal entry into the submarine was by the for'ard torpedo loading hatch and down the steeply slanting steel ladder to the torpedo stowage compartment, where the spare ' fish ' would normally be housed along the boat's side. In addition to the tor-pedoes, extra stores and food, the crew's kit, and any odds and ends that were being carried would find their way into this compartment. It was also a reserve living space.

To get to the living accommodation proper, the messes, one turned aft and ducked through the circular watertight door, taking care to step well clear of the coaming.

The main companionway from the for'ard hatch to the control-room was on the starboard side, the messes being built on the port side and separated from the companionway by curtains. By normal civilian or even by normal surface ship standards living space was restricted in the extreme. For most submariners the first criterion of a new class of submarine is, not surprisingly, the comfort it has to offer. With the exception of a few large mine-laying submarines no British boat had ever provided enough bunks for the whole of her crew. *Thetis* came very near to it, but even so some of the seamen would have to sling hammocks in the fore ends, as the torpedo stowage compartment was usually known.

Going aft along the companionway one passed the Seamen's Mess, the Petty Officers' Mess, the Engine Room Artificers', or E.R.A.s', Mess, and the Wardroom—the latter butting up to the third water-tight bulkhead. Then, adjoining the control-room, there was the little box that was the Captain's cabin. Here he would work and sleep, but with only one eye shut, a split second's notice from the periscope. He would be the only man with any privacy at all.

The control-room, with its mass of pipes, wheels, levers, dials, and electric cables, would cause consternation to anybody but a submariner. Dominating the whole of its area were the two periscopes which, when housed, were lowered into two wells in the deck and very nearly rested on the keel. At the after end of the control-room were the wireless and Asdic offices and, finally, the galley, just inside the fourth watertight bulkhead, separating the control-room from the engine-room.

The first impression of the engine-room was one of comparative space—a rarity in submarines. In the new " T " class the engine-room proper, with—in the case of the Cammell Laird boats—its two huge Sulzer diesels, and the motor-room had been combined. Through this twin compartment the companionway ran amidships, in between the diesels and the main electric motors and their switchgear. The diesel engines powered the submarine when she was on the surface. With the vast amounts of air that their internal combustion process demanded it was impossible for them to be used for underwater propulsion, for in 1939 the Schnorkel had yet to be developed. Once the submarine dived, she switched to her huge electric motors. These were sometimes used, too, for surface manœuvring and also, when geared to the diesels, acted as dynamos for charging the main batteries.

Beyond the fifth watertight door the companionway reverted to the starboard side. There, away from the rest of the ship's company and in comparative comfort, lived the stokers, surrounded by and above the machinery between which and the engine-room their responsibilities were largely divided. All that remained of the submarine was the steering mechanism that transmitted the helmsman's wheel-movements in the control-room to the boat's rudder, the after hydroplane machinery, the air compressors, and the two underwater guns.

Thetis's two escape chambers were situated right for'ard and right aft: the one between the torpedo stowage compartment and the mess-decks and the other between the motor-room and the stokers' mess. Each chamber was in the form of a cylinder, three feet in diameter and six feet nine inches in height. The hatch at the top opened direct to the sea.

As the submarine's passengers settled down in what space they could find, many of them produced copies of the morning's papers. They read that Lancashire had batted all day for 488 for six wickets and that Surrey had made 345 at the Oval and then taken four Sussex wickets for 75.

The first of a new series of cruisers had been launched on the Clyde—the 8000-ton *Fiji*. And in their own Cammell Laird yard at Birkenhead the keel plates of the largest ship ever to be scheduled for Merseyside were to be laid down that day. This was to be the 40,000-ton battleship *Temeraire*. She was planned to cost 10 million pounds and it was reckoned that she would provide employment for 2000–3000 men for at least three years.

Thetis's ship's company were interested in the day's ' Movements of Warships,' particularly in the submarine arrivals and departures to and from Portland and Shanghai, Alexandria and Malta. And of perhaps wider appeal was a speech made by M. Molotov, in which he stated that Anglo-Russian negotiations for a non-aggression pact were progressing.

King George VI and Queen Elizabeth were on their Canadian tour and had left Victoria for Vancouver before starting their return journey east. And the Labour Party Annual Conference at Southport spent nearly the whole day debating the Government's military policy, with Mr Hugh Dalton as the principal speaker.

The Military Medal had been awarded to a corporal of The Queen's Royal Regiment for gallantry in Palestine. The Royal Counties' Show had opened on Southsea Common. And the weather forecast for Thursday, June 1, read, " Good, with high or moderate East winds over Irish Sea; visibility good and sea slight."

It looked a very ordinary day.

" Main engines ready, sir," reported Roy Glenn.

" Thank you, Chief," replied Bolus.

The engines were ready, the shipyard staff not coming out on the trial had already gone ashore, the official pilot was on the bridge, and the gangplank was up.

" Obey telegraphs," called Bolus down the voice-pipe connecting the bridge with the control-room.

" Let go aft."

He watched the seamen cast the wires and ropes away.

" Let go for'ard," he almost nodded to Lieutenant Chapman, who in his turn passed the order to *Thetis's* second coxswain.

And, as the hawsers slipped heavily into the greasy dockyard water and were heaved up over the brim of the basin wall by the shore berthing party, the first manœuvring order of the final trial was given.

Thetis, impatient to become properly part of the Navy, was under way.

3

First of June

IT WAS 9.40 A.M. when *Thetis* slipped and proceeded out of the basin. She was, of course, His Majesty's Submarine *Thetis* and was wearing the White Ensign. Paradoxically, a new construction always assumed naval status for the last weeks or months of her dockyard existence and before the final sea trials were commenced.

She had, all told, 103 men on board. Besides her crew of five officers and 48 ratings she had as passengers nine other officers, either from Submarine Headquarters or from the two other submarines at Birkenhead, as well as seven Admiralty civilian staff and 26 employees of Cammell Laird, who, perhaps, could hardly be called passengers. Of the remaining eight, five came from other shipbuilding companies, principally Vickers Armstrong of Barrow, two were from a Liverpool firm of caterers who were supplying the luncheon, and last, but by no means least, the total was made up by a Mersey pilot.

For the 26 Cammell Laird employees there was no question of volunteering. A list was put up in the shipyard and every one named on it was expected to go. The extra pay involved depended on the length of time at sea, but a fitter could expect to pick up anything from an additional 10 to 30 shillings a day, no small sum in the late 1930's. And, since the last submarine to be lost on trials had been *K* 13 during the 1914-18 War, there seemed to be no reason for looking forward to anything other than a very pleasant day's outing.

There were a few people aboard who might not normally have expected to go out in her, but the much larger Cammell Laird new construction, the liner *Mauretania*, was on trials in the Clyde, and the heads of many of the yard departments were away in her. Accordingly their deputies were sailing in *Thetis*.

Within 20 minutes of slipping she was slowly edging out of the entrance to the Cammell Laird yard and into the river to catch the high tide. A few of the yard men caught sight of her as she manœuvred through the lock. Some of them—perhaps because not all of the occupants of her bridge wore white-covered uniform caps—gave her a casual wave before turning back to their work. One man stood on his own, half hidden in the shadows, and watched as *Thetis* changed from her electric motors to the powerful diesels. Bob Ostler—for it was he—waited and gazed until not even the water showed where the submarine had passed. Then, when there was nothing more to see, he shrugged his shoulders and slowly returned to the Submarine Offices.

One other submariner should have been aboard *Thetis* that morning. Chief Petty Officer Telegraphist J. H. " Egg " Barter, who was attached to the almost-completed *Trident*, shared digs with Petty Officer Telegraphist J. A. Hope of *Thetis*, and had intended to come along with his opposite number " just for the ride." The previous evening, however, had seen a rather heavy alcoholic party, with the result that when Hope shook him Barter could only bury his head back in the pillow and murmur, " There'll be plenty of other occasions."

The Liverpool Screw Towing and Lighterage Company's tug *Grebecock* had left Birkenhead before *Thetis*, for whom she was to act as escort during the trials. The submarine had been lying in a position easily accessible to the entrance of the yard, and the pilot had told the master of the tug, sixty-year-old Mr A. E. Godfrey, that he would not need any help in getting out. As *Thetis* would be proceeding at 16 knots for part of the way out to the trials ground, and as *Grebecock's* maximum speed was a puffing and blowing 12, it seemed a good idea to take the opportunity of starting off in advance. Bolus had agreed, too, to accommodate his speed to that of the tug wherever necessary. Even though much of the submarine's advantage would be lost by her wandering off course on steering trials and on checking compasses, Godfrey wanted to be on the safe side.

Over and above his crew of seven Godfrey had four passengers on board. Two of these, Lieutenant R. E. Coltart and Telegraphist V. J. Crosby, were submariners attached to the other submarines building at Birkenhead. The other two were from Cammell Laird.

Coltart had had five years' experience in submarines and had not long been appointed to *Taku* as Garnett's First Lieutenant. On the previous day Bolus had asked him if he would go as liaison officer in *Grebecock*. A trifle disappointed, for he had been looking forward to seeing one of *Taku's* predecessors in action, Coltart had cheerfully agreed.

Bolus and he had had a discussion on how they should keep in touch with each other while *Thetis* was dived, to enable *Grebecock* to warn the submarine if another vessel came near. "I asked him," Coltart said afterwards, "what sort of underwater communication we should have, and we came to the conclusion that there were only two methods that could be used—by tapping on the hull of the tug and by dropping explosive charges overboard. Commander Bolus decided to dismiss the idea altogether. He said he would have a good look round through the periscope before going down below periscope depth."

It was also agreed that *Thetis* would not stay long enough below periscope depth for a ship to be allowed to approach close enough for any warning from *Grebecock* to be necessary.

To make it easier for those aboard *Grebecock* to see her when she was at periscope depth it was also arranged that *Thetis* would wear a red flag. *Grebecock* was similarly attired, for this was the customary signal from a surface vessel escorting a dived submarine.

As *Thetis* manœuvred into the river twenty-five-year-old Norman Willcox checked his bearings and gave the order that would swing her stern round and bring her bows to face the open sea. Willcox was young for the important post of Mersey pilot, but he had more than his own experience behind him, for both his father and his brother were Mersey pilots too. Neither of them had ever handled a submarine, however, which made him doubly pleased with his assignment.

The squat, self-important river ferries eased their speed as *Thetis* came towards them through the dirty Mersey water. One or two stopped and let their passengers watch the spectacle of this latest of warships going off to the sea. A submarine was not all that common in the great trading port of Liverpool and there must have been many people on the ferries that June day seeing in *Thetis* something new. A few, at least, would surely have uttered the layman's stock comment, "They'd never get me in one of them things."

At 10.45 A.M. one of the New Brighton Coastguards saw *Thetis*:

> . . . when she crossed the Liverpool line for the open sea. Three or four men were standing in the conning-tower. Another was up on her bow. She was proceeding at a good pace—about 7 or 8 knots —and all seemed well.

All was well. Life was settling down to a normal day's submarine exercising. With so many of their functions being performed by the Admiralty civilians or the Cammell Laird staff the ship's company were finding ample time for gossip and reminiscence.

The strong China-flotilla element meant that much of the conversation centred around the relative merits of Hongkong and Birkenhead local-brewed beer.

The large numbers on board gave the trip a feeling all of its own. There was always a slight party atmosphere about the first sea trials of a new submarine, the high-spot of which were the ' big eats '—the festive luncheon traditionally provided by the builders. There was keen rivalry among the big firms to do each new submarine well on these occasions, and ' Jack ' was not slow to realize that he was the principal beneficiary.

The ' top brass ' was sitting cramped together round the wardroom table.   Captain H. P. K. Oram commanded the flotilla in which *Thetis* would serve for a brief ' shake-down ' period after her trials. He had come on the trials for the purpose of getting to know the boat's officers and seeing them at work.   On the stokers' mess-deck it was being said that he was on board, too, as a direct result of Glenn's adverse report at the time of the first trial in the Clyde.

Almost ten years previously, in July 1929, Oram had had the misfortune to be in command of the submarine *L 12* when she was in collision with another submarine, the *H 47*, off the Pembrokeshire coast.   *H 47* had sunk with the loss of 21 lives, and, in the confusion, Oram had been swept off the bridge of *L 12*, to be picked up by another submarine exercising in the area after some 15 or 20 minutes in the water.

One of the most popular figures on board, and certainly one of the easiest to pick out on account of his huge size, was Engineer Captain S. Jackson.   A kindly man, " Daddy " Jackson, as he was known to all in submarines, was very much the veteran of the party, being able to look back to Baltic Flotilla service in 1919.   He was attending *Thetis*'s final trial in his capacity as Engineer Staff Officer to Flag Officer Submarines and, as he had just completed four years as Engineer Overseer at Vickers Armstrong's yard at Barrow, trials were very much a part of his regular life.

Also squeezed into the wardroom were three other uniformed and seven civilian Admiralty officers and four Cammell Laird managers.   As accommodation had been designed for a maximum of six, conditions were a little cramped.   Partly in order not to aggravate this over-crowding, and partly because the technical business of the trial was none of their concern, the officers from *Trident* and *Taku* tucked themselves away wherever they could and prepared to make notes.

Meanwhile, a normal day's existence was developing for a number of people shortly to become intimately involved with *Thetis*.   A team of civilian divers under the leadership of Mr Thomas McKenzie,

Chief Salvage Officer of Cox and Danks, Ltd, was at work at Scapa Flow, engaged on the raising of the scuttled First World War German battle-cruiser *Derfflinger*. The crew of the deep-diving vessel, H.M.S. *Tedworth*, were looking forward to a trip ashore from their anchorage at Inveraray for a long-planned game of football. The divers among them were on their last week of a three months' deep-diving course. A fitter crowd of men it would have been hard to find anywhere in the world. At an R.A.F. station, also in Scotland, Acting Flight Lieutenant John Avent was contemplating another day's boredom as ' Duty Flight.' And in the back of the Post-office building at Gosport, some two miles by road from Submarine Headquarters, the telegraph boys were idly seeking some sort of amusement to pass the time.

Thetis, now accompanied by *Grebecock*, cleared the Bar Light Vessel, at the entrance to the main channel some 14 miles out of Liverpool, at about noon. Once this position had been reached the pilotage contract ended and the pilot's duties ceased. Willcox, however, chose to remain with *Thetis* and complete a day full of new experience, rather than leave via either *Grebecock* or the pilot cutter. When the master of the latter hailed *Thetis* he was waved away.

Leaving the Bar Light, Bolus signalled to the tug, " Follow me, speed 9 knots." The weather was fine and clear and, as she had reached open water, *Thetis* started her steering trials. During the course of these she blew high-pressure air through all her main ballast tanks to test them for diving.

Lunch was served as the submarine continued steaming slightly north of west—a course designed to take her to the deeper waters of Liverpool Bay. By all accounts City Caterers (Liverpool), Ltd, who then held, and still hold, the Cammell Laird contract for such occasions, put on a spread that exceeded even the wildest expectations of the mess-decks. Their two representatives, Messrs. Dobells and Bath, were soon the toast of the hour.

Partaking in the generous selection of cold meats, pies, and all that went with them, not to mention the accompanying bottle of beer, was the Cammell Laird charge-hand engine fitter, Frank Shaw. He was lunching in a corner of the control-room, seated on a D.S.E.A. chest which he shared with either Dobells or Bath. He did not know which was which.

" How are the engines running ? " the caterer asked Shaw.

" Fine," he replied, " as sweet as a couple of sewing machines."

" Good," came the comment, " we have nothing to worry about now, then."

There was a certain general sorrow, therefore, at the end of the repast, when *Thetis* reached her diving position just before 1.30 P.M. She was by this time 38 miles out of Liverpool and 15 miles slightly west of north from Great Ormes Head, the prominent landmark at Llandudno, on the North Welsh coast.

Bolus was on the bridge. On his instructions word was passed through the boat that anyone who wanted to disembark should come up topsides. Nobody appeared. There had probably not been any fixed number expected to leave at this stage, but it would certainly have been usual for at least some of the passengers to transfer 'o the escort before the dive. Still nobody appeared, not even the two caterers' representatives—the people with the smallest possible technical interest in the trial.

Any question of whether it was wise for a submarine to dive at any time overcrowded to the extent of double its normal complement, and particularly as probably the only time in a pre-Second World War submarine's career at which this would arise would be the occasion of her first-ever dive in the open sea, depended ultimately on the tightness of control that had been exercised over her in the immediately preceding period. It may now, in retrospect, be open to considerable doubt. In June 1939, however, no such doubt appeared to exist in anybody's mind, and there can be no justification for thinking that Bolus should have compelled as large a transfer to *Grebecock* as could be warranted.

So it was that, perhaps surprised, but beyond doubt in no way dismayed, that *Thetis* would be diving with as many as 103 souls aboard, Bolus signalled the tug to close. As she approached he hailed her through a megaphone.

" I shall not be disembarking anybody. Take station half a mile on my port quarter. The diving course will be 310 degrees."

One minor matter had gone wrong in *Grebecock*. On leaving the Bar Light Godfrey had streamed the log—a piece of distance-measuring equipment towed at the end of a length of line. But the manœuvres that the tug had had to execute while *Thetis* was adjusting compasses and undertaking large circling movements during her steering trials meant that at times the log was on the bottom. The dead-reckoning position taken from its reading could not, therefore, be entirely accurate, and there was the risk that it might have fouled the propeller. So it was hauled in.

Apart from this Godfrey had enjoyed the trip out during the forenoon. He knew and loved the stretch of water on which he was operating as well as any person alive; it was a lovely sunny day and he had agreeable company on board. The time passed quickly and soon they had approached the diving ground. Lunch was the order of the day and, while Godfrey regaled himself in the wheelhouse with a Lancashire hot-pot he had brought from home and had had warmed up in the galley, Coltart and Crosby basked in the sun and devoured sandwiches and mugs of tea.

When the time came for disembarking some of the people from *Thetis* there was general surprise that every one had elected to stay in the submarine during the dive. Mr Randles, from Cammell Laird, had been told off to sail in *Grebecock* for the very purpose of superintending the transfer, and he had expected—although it had been by no means fixed—that between 25 and 30 would be the number involved. On his instructions the tug's two lifeboats had been swung out ready for lowering some time beforehand. But Godfrey was glad not to have to put them down.

" I confess I'm feeling a bit anxious, now she's come to the point of diving," he told Coltart. Although he had been on anti-submarine patrol during the 1914-18 War he had never seen a submarine dive or break surface.

" Will she leave any track if she goes below periscope depth ? And what will be her speed underwater ? " he asked.

" Don't worry. Don't worry. Everything will be all right," the young submariner smilingly reassured him.

By this time *Grebecock* was lying stopped some 200 yards from *Thetis*, and through the pair of binoculars they shared between them Godfrey and Coltart could see the conning-tower being cleared. As the submarine moved slowly ahead, picking up speed only very gradually to about 4 knots, the tug remained still for a while, until the distance between them should be a little more like the requisite half-mile.

Aboard the submarine there had come the long-anticipated order, " Open up for diving." In deliberate slow time—a direct contrast to the speed of operation with which diving orders would ultimately be met—*Thetis* was brought to a state of readiness. Cotter-pins were removed; depth and pressure gauges opened; flooding, blowing, and pumping controls checked. Ten minutes later, at 1.40 P.M., Bolus despatched his formal diving signal:

> From H.M.S. *Thetis* to Captain *S* 5 and Admiralty C.-in-C. Plymouth ASCB.S—Important. Diving in position 5335 North 0400 West, for 3 hours.

The acknowledgment from the Naval Wireless Station at Plymouth arrived at 1.56 P.M. Bolus left the bridge immediately and shut and clipped the conning-tower hatch. Together with Captain Oram, he took up position in the control-room and gave orders for flooding the main ballast tanks in pairs—again in slow time. The diesels had already been stopped (with their huge consumption of air they could never be used other than on the surface), and the main electric motors had been ordered Half Ahead. *Thetis* was diving.

The manner of her diving reflected the anomalies that surrounded every new naval construction at this stage of its career. In the same way that she was wearing the White Ensign and carrying the prefix "His Majesty's Submarine" before having finally been signed for and accepted, so the contract between the Admiralty and Cammell Laird provided that:

> diving trials will be carried out by naval officers and crew, but the contractors shall work the main and auxiliary machinery.

This apparent contradiction was intended to indicate the division of responsibility. In addition there was the complication that the Chief Admiralty Overseer, in collaboration with Cammell Laird, had prepared the trim statement on which the ballast condition immediately prior to diving was based.

It would be easy to see in all this series of arrangements a straightforward case of too many cooks potentially spoiling the broth. It would in fact be tenable that the officers and men of *Thetis*'s ship's company were the only real professionals in the business and should have been left alone to prepare and dive the submarine themselves. But there were a number of excellent legal and procedural reasons why the operation should have been conducted the way it was. Nor was there any precedent to suggest that the system contained or concealed any flaws. First dives had the reputation of being tedious rather than terrifying.

Thetis, then, was diving on her first dive. Back at his desk in the Submarine Offices in Birkenhead, Bob Ostler had noted the time and was doodling meaningless diagrams on a pile of scrap paper, while recalling every word of his previous day's conversation with his commanding officer. And, folded away in a corner of *Thetis*'s control-room, Dick Garnett was probably the only man aboard faced with any persistent doubts about what lay ahead.

At about this time, too, the libertymen were being inspected by the Officer-of-the-Day of H.M.S. *Somali*, flotilla leader of the Sixth Destroyer Flotilla at Portland. Another destroyer, H.M.S. *Brazen*, was returning to Plymouth from the Clyde, where she had been attending the cruiser *Belfast* on gunnery trials. And the telegraph boys at Gosport Post-office were finding the First of June to be very much just another day.

Also at Gosport, routine activity was proceeding at Fort Blockhouse, where, it being a Thursday, there would be the usual submarine officers' Guest Night dinner. A daily record was always kept of the time at which every British submarine dived and of proposed and achieved times of surfacing. *Thetis's* 1.40 P.M. diving signal, being transmitted in the first instance to Plymouth, did not reach Blockhouse until 2.5 P.M. As the signal had not come there direct it was not known at what precise moment the acknowledgment from Plymouth had been received by *Thetis* and at what precise moment, therefore, she would be starting her dive. It could be reckoned, however, that she should surface not later than 5.5 P.M. and that her signal to this effect should reach Blockhouse not later than 5.30 P.M.

In accordance with normal practice the Duty Chief Yeoman of Signals at Blockhouse had noted all these times.

Sharp at two o'clock Coltart knew that *Thetis* had opened her main vents. The ' whoosh ' of the air rushing out of her tanks could be clearly heard aboard the tug. Then, for 50 minutes or more, all of them on *Grebecock's* bridge watched her submerging slowly and on an even keel. It was quite definitely ' a dive in slow time,' as had been planned. Both the submariners felt certain that she had too much buoyancy when she started her dive. According to Crosby:

> She appeared to be light. She got her bow down at a slight angle and remained in that position for approximately 20 minutes. Then she levelled off until the top of her guard rails for'ard and aft were just showing above the water. A short time later she went down until her gun was awash and half her conning-tower above the water.

Their surprise at her excess buoyancy grew into astonishment as she continued to remain above the surface. Then, at about two minutes to three, just as they were thinking that she would never disappear, she went down suddenly. Coltart saw her bow come up:

> She just broke the surface and I saw a splash of air just for'ard of the bow. She dived horizontally and fairly fast.

She had completely disappeared within a minute. The ' splash of air ' for'ard had caught all their attentions. It was rather like a lot of foam, a sort of air bubble that could have been caused by the bow breaking surface. Thinking back later, Coltart described it as the water turning white. There was a very slight wave, he said, very like the disturbance aft caused by the working of the propellers.

None of the three observers had liked the look of the dive. Crosby was the first to speak.

" She went down very quickly."

T.A.R.—3

" I think she was in trouble," added Godfrey.

" Don't worry," counselled Coltart. " This is her first dive and they are probably having trouble over the trim, with so many dockyard mateys aboard."

He was rather worried in his own mind, despite what he had said, about *Thetis* obviously having become heavy so quickly after having been so light. This *could* have been caused by a main ballast vent sticking, thus retaining the air and accounting for the undue lightness. Extra water would have been taken into the compensating system to counteract this and, while this was being done, the vent could have come open and the main ballast tank flooded, making the submarine suddenly too heavy. But, he reasoned to himself, she would still be quite manageable. She would speed up to give her hydroplanes greater effect and pump out or blow some of her auxiliary tanks. There seemed to be no sufficient reason for deciding that a serious accident had taken place. And, if anything disastrous had by any mischance occurred, there would be some immediate sign on the surface—a smoke candle or an indicator-buoy.

At first Coltart found it difficult to decide upon his proper course of conduct, but within a couple of minutes of *Thetis* having disappeared he gave orders for the tug not to proceed along the course ordered for fear of overrunning the submarine. It was this remarkably quick and completely correct reaction that was, in the cussedness of events, to be one of the causes of *Grebecock's* position eventually differing so much from that of *Thetis*.

Grebecock stopped engines, going ahead again at intervals to stem the 1- to 2-knot tide and trying to maintain the position in which *Thetis* had dived. Unfortunately she was not in a depth of water in which she could anchor; not, at least, unless she went to the comparatively lengthy rounds of shackling her two anchor cables together. Having been chartered solely as a chaperone and not as a fully fledged escort, she had, moreover, no marker-buoy she could use to fix the submarine's last position.

All available eyes were immediately ordered on lookout. With the exception of one man in the engine-room the whole complement of 12 was searching the surface, seeking the slightest sign. The day was fine and clear, with a smooth sea, but no signal of any kind appeared. For a while this allayed Coltart's anxiety. He continued to expect *Thetis* to reappear at any moment, and was reluctant to report to Fort Blockhouse that the submarine was in distress, if a little while later she were to turn up on the surface none the worse for her rapid dive.

As the minutes dragged by it soon became apparent, though,

that *Thetis* was not adhering to the programme for the dive that Bolus had given Coltart. She was due to submerge to check trim, surface and blow main tanks, dive again to periscope depth, lower periscope, dive to 60 feet, and then fire smoke candles. None of what had so far happened could be said to correspond.

Coltart realized this and appreciated that some minor mishap, at least, had occurred. He expected, however, that *Thetis* would be able to correct her trim by increasing to maximum speed. This might well mean, particularly as *Grebecock* had stopped engines, that she would break surface—quite possibly without surfacing completely—at such a distance away from the tug that her periscope and red flag would be invisible. But when, a little while later, there was still no sign of any kind from the submarine, this all seemed rather cold comfort, and Coltart decided to take further action. A fair amount of time had elapsed since *Thetis* disappeared, but in the hustle and bustle of the circumstances in which *Grebecock* found herself the minutes had passed unconscionably quickly.

"I sent a signal by Seaforth Radio [at Waterloo, just outside Liverpool]," Coltart recalled later. "The intention of the signal was to convey my anxiety without causing alarm, which I did not feel."

The signal ran:

Captain S5 Fort Blockhouse Gosport Hampshire
From tug attending on *Thetis*
What was duration of *Thetis* dive?
Coltart
ToD (Time of Despatch) 1645

Grebecock's radio-telephony equipment had an official range of 75 miles, although in Godfrey's experience its performance varied tremendously in different atmospheric conditions. On the credit side he had on one occasion spoken to another of his company's vessels as far as 150 miles away. But, Crosby decided, he had found it on one of its bad days. Although they were only 38 miles away from the shore station, he could not make contact until the pilot vessel, from somewhere between the Bar Light and the river, told Seaforth that *Grebecock* was calling her. Seaforth kept complaining of weak reception and on more than one occasion asked Crosby to try an alternative wavelength. Eventually, by 4.56 P.M., the message was finally received and acknowledged.

Immediately he had sent the signal Crosby returned to lookout duties on the bridge, from where it was possible to hear the R/T loudspeaker, should a reply come through. Meanwhile the message was proceeding on its weary way to Fort Blockhouse. It left

Seaforth for Gosport via Liverpool and London at 5.03 P.M. It arrived at Gosport at 5.38 P.M.

It was unfortunate, to say the least, that by this time the duty telegraph boy at Gosport Post-office should have been otherwise engaged. He was at the Post-office, but he was in the process of mending a puncture that his recalcitrant bicycle had seen fit to acquire. Since the telegram appeared to the senior staff in the Post-office not to be urgent, nobody hurried him. He was not ready again until half an hour after Coltart's message had arrived at Gosport, and it was not, therefore, until 6.15 P.M., an hour and a half after its origination, that the orange envelope was handed in at its final destination.

Back in *Grebecock* Coltart had asked Crosby to send a further message to Fort Blockhouse about 10 to 15 minutes after the first one had got through to Seaforth. He wanted to strengthen his original signal somewhat and decided to say that *Thetis* had dived and failed to reappear. Try as he might, Crosby was unable to make any contact at all, and the second message was never sent. And in the circumstances it was quite impossible for *Grebecock* to close the shore to make sure of the message being received, since there was always the hope that *Thetis* would suddenly surface and might need help. Coltart was also constantly expecting to receive over the radio-telephone some sort of reply to his first signal.

All this time *Grebecock* was still trying to maintain the position in which she had stopped at the moment of *Thetis's* disappearance. Godfrey would let her drift to the west for about 10 minutes and then steam back eastward at dead slow speed for about five minutes. As far as the strength of the ebb-tide could be estimated, this was, Coltart and he decided, a reasonably exact procedure.

At about 5 P.M., under pressure from Godfrey, which he had resisted earlier out of regard for the depth of water, Coltart agreed to anchor. This proved rather a lengthy business. The bottom was some 22–23 fathoms (around 135 feet) beneath them; and, in order for an anchor to hold, cable to the tune of three or more times the depth of water has to be paid out. As each of *Grebecock's* cables was 40 fathoms long, this meant unshackling the second anchor and introducing the free cable to the first so that the tug was finally lying to one anchor on 80 fathoms of cable. It took an hour's back-breaking, hand-tearing work before the manœuvre was completed.

Once it was completed there was firm conviction in both Coltart's and Godfrey's minds that *Grebecock* was anchored in *Thetis's* last-known position. But, in actual fact, during the three hours that had elapsed since the submarine's disappearance, the tug had shifted some four miles. The process of stemming the tide had been less exact than they had thought—or so it was later to transpire. This loss of position, although largely unavoidable in the given circumstances, was to have the most unfortunate consequences.

It should be made clear, of course, that *Grebecock* was engaged solely to keep other ships away from *Thetis* and therefore was not specifically in need of signalling or navigational aids. As it so unfortunately happened, in the impossible situation in which they found themselves, Coltart and Godfrey felt the lack of equipment keenly. And even the small but important fact that Coltart did not have a watch with him had an ironic connotation. The Navy did not recognize a watch as a necessary everyday instrument—or so it was always assumed from official refusals to compensate officers and ratings who lost watches in the course of their duties.

At 2.5 P.M. that afternoon the Duty Chief Yeoman of Signals at Fort Blockhouse had received *Thetis's* 1.40 P.M. signal that she would be diving for three hours. At 4.45 P.M. he reported to the Duty Commanding Officer of the Fifth Submarine Flotilla, in the absence of Captain Oram, that *Thetis* had been due to surface by between 4.40 P.M. and 5.5 P.M., but that so far no surfacing signal had been received.

If *Thetis* were in trouble one man at least had been able to act quietly, efficiently, and within a matter of moments from the time that any necessity for his action first arose. It was soon to prove tragic that the Chief Yeoman's polished competence was not reflected on more sides.

4

4.45 P.M., *Thursday, June 1, to*
7.54 A.M., *Friday, June 2*

Up Top

WHEN Captain I. A. P. Macintyre, Chief of Staff to Flag Officer
Submarines, heard what the Chief Yeoman had to say he immediately set to work. From 4.45 P.M. onwards Fort Blockhouse
called *Thetis* on W/T every 10 minutes. Culver Wireless Station
and the Admiralty were contacted, but neither could report any
communication with the submarine. No news came from
Macintyre's telephone call to Cammell Laird, and a signal to the
Bar Lightship produced just one more nil return. All was silence;
silence and speculation.

Around *Grebecock* meanwhile the sea continued calm and
smooth. All aboard the tug were showing unrelieved anxiety.
Their earlier ideas about a happy outcome were fast becoming
mere wishful thinking.

"Perhaps there'll soon be a naval vessel turn up," said Godfrey.
"With an underwater search by Asdic they'll surely not be long in
finding her."

But no naval vessel appeared, and all Godfrey could do, albeit
with decreasing confidence, was to order the all-round scanning
of the surface to continue and to plan for a long night's vigil.

"We must get information back to the authorities somehow,"
he told Coltart. "It seems we're outside radio-telephone range
and we're well away from the normal routes for ships crossing
Liverpool Bay. We mightn't get anyone come within visual
signalling distance all night. I reckon we should stay in position
until nightfall, in case any of them come up by escape apparatus,
and then weigh anchor and run into Llandudno [some 16 miles
away], sound the alarm, and return. But, of course, there's the
danger that we wouldn't get so accurate a position again."

While Coltart and he were debating the pros and cons of their
dilemma, back at Fort Blockhouse there had been a marked
deceleration in the speed of action that had first greeted the report
that *Thetis* was overdue.

When no surfacing signal had been received from *Thetis* by
5.5 P.M. Captain Macintyre had evidence that for some reason she
had almost certainly been unable to surface. Yet the first order for
search by ship was not despatched until 6.22 P.M., and the first
request for search by aircraft was not sent until 6.50 P.M. This was
to mean that before either ship or aircraft could arrive on the scene
it was almost sunset.

Obviously, in retrospect, there was a delay of between an hour
and an hour and a half in organizing a proper search for *Thetis*;
and it was a delay that could well have been avoided. But what
were the contributing factors ?

During part of the time there was some difference of opinion
about when to put search proceedings in hand between Captain
Macintyre and the Duty Staff Officer at Plymouth, in whose area
Thetis was operating. At 5.50 P.M. Macintyre still thought it
premature, before there was any certainty that a casualty had
occurred, to set in motion the elaborate ' Subsmash ' procedure.

At that time no message had reached Fort Blockhouse from
Grebecock, and it could be said in justification of the ' wait-a-little-
while ' attitude that no one wishes to imagine trouble merely for
lack of news about a submarine. Similarly it could be said that it is
unreasonable at a later date to say that a man acting in the dark was
wrong, just because what was doubtful to him has since become
clear reality.

Both these considerations were advanced by the Report of the
Tribunal of Inquiry that was later to investigate the *Thetis* affair,
to be followed by these comments :

> At 5.50 P.M. the facts which were known or knowable were these.
> The *Thetis* was doing her diving trial in Liverpool Bay, in open
> waters and out of sight of land, and in an area of strong tides. She
> had a number of men on board largely in excess of her normal
> complement, and was therefore short of air reserve when submerged
> for a long time, and she had only the *Grebecock* standing by, a vessel
> without wireless and without the means of underwater signalling to
> the *Thetis* and with only a junior officer on board. It was late
> afternoon. Taking all these things into consideration, there was
> some delay in organizing a search for the *Thetis* by sea and air.
> This delay was not caused by any lack of vigilance and attention
> to the *Thetis* by the responsible staffs ashore. It was due partly to
> the absence of any reason to suppose that such a strange accident
> would happen, partly to a desire not to cause unnecessary alarm,
> and partly to a reluctance to set a number of ships and men in motion
> as required by the procedure laid down for such a case, if it proved
> to be a false alarm.

It was a contributing factor, too, that Rear-Admiral B. C. Watson, C.B., D.S.O., the Flag Officer Submarines, was away ill. His absence could possibly have made it more difficult for Captain Macintyre to treat *Thetis* as a casualty.

If she *were* a casualty, what *could* have happened to her ? The certainty was that more than one compartment must have been flooded, for her main ballast buoyancy was more than capable of coping with the weight of a single compartmentful of water. Secondly, something was obviously open to the sea which could not be closed from inside the submarine, otherwise she would have been able to pump out the offending compartments and resurface. Thirdly, the inrush of water, if two compartments had been filled, must have been so great that no time had remained for those inside to shut off the entries through the intermediate bulkhead.

What apertures could have admitted so much water ? What else could have happened ? There must have appeared to Captain Macintyre to be three possibilities.

There could have been a battery explosion, caused by sparking after a long charge without sufficient battery-compartment ventilation. A large enough explosion could well have killed all on board, and would have accounted for there being no signals and no escapes. But there had been no recent long charge.

Water could just possibly have come in through the battery ventilation trunking, and the flooding could have dispersed sufficient poisonous chlorine gas through the boat for the majority of the complement to have been incapacitated. In this case the battery tanks, and probably other compartments, too, would have been flooded.

Apart from these possibilities, she could have lost buoyancy through flooding pure and simple; and technical evidence would suggest that the necessary amount of water could have come in only through the torpedo tube compartment or the engine-room. In the latter event she would have gone down stern first, and all her signalling apparatus and listening gear would still be undamaged.

It must have been with thoughts such as these in his mind that Captain Macintyre was greeted, at 6.15 P.M., by Coltart's telegram from *Grebecock*. This immediately turned the scales in favour of new and dramatic action.

Admiralty Fleet Order 971/35—the then ' Subsmash '—was radioed at top priority. Telephone lines buzzed madly between Portsmouth and Plymouth, Portsmouth and Portland, Portsmouth and the Admiralty. Orders to report to the scene of the sinking " with utmost despatch " were flashed to a wide variety of units. Two submarines for underwater signalling (this pre-supposed that *Thetis's* underwater signalling gear was working); a mine-sweeping flotilla for sweeping the sea-bottom; a destroyer flotilla from Portland; H.M.S. *Tedworth*, the deep-diving vessel, from the Clyde; aircraft from various bases: all were given urgent, commanding, heart-tearing instructions.

The destroyer *Brazen, en route* through the Irish Sea to Plymouth from the Clyde, was not finding much of interest or excitement to while away the weary dog-watches. Her attendance on the cruiser *Belfast* during gunnery trials had been dispiriting in the extreme, and a 1939 economy ruling restricted her speed to a listless 13 knots, with only one boiler ' flashed up.' Life was dull, dull, dull, and they wouldn't get ashore in Plymouth until Saturday.

It was 6.22 P.M. when the Duty Signalman came doubling up on the bridge to where his captain, Lieutenant-Commander R. H. Mills, was standing. Mills read the signal.

Proceed to position . . . and establish contact with H.M.S. *Thetis*.

That was all: no indication of what type of vessel *Thetis* was—and she was a new name to him—and nothing about why she had to be contacted or any instruction to proceed with any sort of despatch.

Mills sent for his Navy List, but could not find the name ' *Thetis* ' anywhere (for, of course, she had not been finally commissioned). Fortunately the Signalman, a former submariner, spoke up.

" Excuse me, sir. *Thetis* is a new submarine. I reckon she must just about be on her acceptance dive."

So the essential information reached Mills. A junior rating's awareness of trade gossip had told him that which his superiors in Whitehall had omitted.

He was 55 miles to the westward of the signalled position. Immediately he decided that there was an urgency about the situation. He gave orders for maximum speed. Suddenly the ship sprang into life. Engine-room telegraphs clanged, another ' non-duty part ' of stokers was rushed below to raise more steam, lookouts were doubled, Asdic staff were alerted, and *Brazen* herself soon had the satisfaction of seeing her bow cutting through the evening sea until, in no time at all, her speed had risen to well over 30 knots, and the plumes of white water at her head were falling away and joining the white-and-grey corrugations of her wake, in a pattern of speed and fluency.

At three minutes after 9 P.M. she sighted *Grebecock*. Her Aldis lamp winked excitedly and evoked an immediate reply.

Brazen: Are you over position where S/M was last seen ?
Grebecock: No, position approximate.

Brazen: What was submarine's diving course ?
Grebecock: 310 degrees.
Brazen: What time did she dive ?
Grebecock: At 1500.

Then, at four minutes after 9 P.M., it was sunset.

Grebecock was unfortunately only too right in stating that her position was an approximate one, and both ashore and afloat the confusion about the likely whereabouts of *Thetis* was growing worse. Her actual position was 55.33 N. 4.04 W., which meant that she was 14 miles from Great Ormes Head on a bearing of 328 degrees. The position in which *Grebecock* had anchored, which was regarded for some time as the datum position for the search, was some four miles farther west. But a signal from *Grebecock* to Fort Blockhouse, after radio-telephony contact with Seaforth had been resumed, read:

> Am anchored in last position of *Thetis*. Position approximately 12 miles N.W. of N.W. Buoy.

Once this position was charted it could be seen to be some nine miles to the east of *Thetis's* diving position, and, incidentally, some 12 miles to the east of where the tug was actually anchored. This eastward deviation was all the more confusing to those ashore because of the knowledge that *Thetis* had dived on a westerly course, with no apparent intention of turning full circle. It was almost certainly not generally appreciated that, as *Grebecock* did not have W/T, she had not known the original diving position signalled by *Thetis*.

What had in fact happened was that Godfrey's and Coltart's initial dead-reckoning calculations had been almost exactly correct. Godfrey had marked his estimated position of the submarine with a cross. Coltart had put a small circle round it and written the name '*Thetis*' underneath. This position, had they had the full courage of their own convictions and had *Grebecock* still been occupying it, would have been much more nearly the one the authorities required. Instead, Godfrey talked on his radio-telephone with the pilot boat, allied the information thus received with his estimate of the limit of visibility at the time, and produced the second easterly and erroneous position. After dark, when he was able to pick up the loom of the Great Ormes Head and Point Lynas lights, he corrected his position back to that of his original estimate and reinformed Fort Blockhouse accordingly.

None of this, however, was known to Lieutenant-Commander Mills in *Brazen*, when the first signals with *Grebecock* had been exchanged. As *Thetis* had dived on a westerly course he decided to start by searching an area of about three miles to the westward of *Grebecock*. Had the tug in fact been lying more or less over the submarine's diving position, this would have been a most satisfactory beginning. But, as she was already four miles to the north and west of where *Thetis* was lying, Mills's chosen course of action, so patently correct in the circumstances as he knew them, was taking the destroyer even farther away.

An hour and a half earlier, at 7.40 P.M., Flight Lieutenant John Avent had taken off from the R.A.F. Station, Abbotsinch, in Scotland, 150 miles from Liverpool Bay, with a flight of four Ansons of No. 269 (G.R.) Squadron. He was told to look for a marker-buoy, oil, or air bubbles, and had been given an estimated position.

It was about 9 P.M. too, the same time as *Brazen*, that he arrived over the scene. His flight spread out in formation. The light was already going. Eyes were straining on the grey water. For five minutes, then for another five minutes, they patrolled, circled, turned, and resumed.

" There ! Can you see it ? " Avent himself had spotted something that looked like a buoy, with a long dark·object showing near it and under the water. " It's . . . it's like a shadow coming up from below. I'd put it at some 25 yards long by some two to three yards wide. God, it could be . . ."

Banking, he brought the Anson down to 50 feet above the surface and could see that it was quite definitely a buoy. It looked conical in shape and vaguely yellow in colour. " Look, there's a small flag sticking up from·it ! We've found her, we must have done ! "

Carefully he circled as his navigator first calculated his position by dead reckoning, then took a bearing of Great Ormes Head. And at 9.25 P.M. the first of the aircraft's two vitally important signals was despatched. It read:

> Important. Marker-buoy observed in position 322 degrees Ormes Head 13 miles.

This position was not much more than a mile S.W. of where *Thetis* was lying.

At the same time as it sent this signal the aircraft fired four green Very lights to try to attract the attention of a trawler some two miles away to the north-east, but without success. The flares were, however, seen by *Grebecock*, who reported them to *Brazen*. The destroyer steamed in their direction to investigate, sighted what looked like an oil patch, and remained in the vicinity zone-time-sweeping with A/S.

Avent and his navigator were still not satisfied. Men's lives were involved and the least one could do was to check and recheck the information one had sent. Slowly the aircraft circled the buoy. Carefully the navigator recalculated his position. Then, at 10 P.M., a second vitally important signal was tapped out:

Cancel my 2125 position of marker-buoy. 303 degrees Ormes Head 10½ miles.

This revised position lay fully seven miles S.S.W. of *Thetis*. The check calculations had been plotted incorrectly. Over-keenness and over-anxiety were to have drastically unfortunate results.

They were to misdirect *Brazen*, for a start. At 10.23 P.M. the destroyer received, relayed via Fort Blockhouse, the Anson's first marker-buoy signal. She shifted position and had only just started searching the new area when the second signal came through. Farther south and west she moved again, to patrol up and down, up and down. Without success. Throughout the night she swept the same area, keeping a non-stop Asdic watch and burning her searchlight and her two signal projectors. And as, with the earlier evening mist having cleared, it was now bright moonlight with a nearly full moon, it is inconceivable that, if *Brazen* had been in the area where the buoy was floating with the flag attached, she would not have found it.

All over the country ships and men were coming to *Thetis's* aid. The salvage vessel *Vigilant* sailed from Liverpool with Captain H. V. Hart, the Marine Surveyor and Water Bailiff of the Mersey Docks and Harbour Board. And in cinemas in Portland and Weymouth the evening house was interrupted by an announcement flashed on the screen.

Service Notice. SOS. All ratings of the 1st Anti-Submarine Flotilla and 6th Destroyer Flotilla must return to their ships immediately.

By buses and taxis and by running on foot the men streamed back to the harbour. Soon the eight new *Tribal*-class destroyers of the 6th Destroyer Flotilla, led by H.M.S. *Somali* (Captain R. S. G. Nicholson), left Portland. Speed was increased to their maximum 36 knots immediately they entered open water. It was not long before they passed the submarine *Cachalot*. She had also been lying at Portland, but, by dint of picking up any submariners he could find ashore, Lieutenant-Commander J. W. F. Bennetts had got together sufficient of a scratch crew to get under way an hour before the destroyers. By almost blowing every connexion on the main engines, the submarine had managed to make 17¼ knots—three-quarters of a knot faster than she had ever made before.

All these proceedings were being reported minute by minute to Fort Blockhouse, where Captain Macintyre was fast completing his mammoth task of organization. Eventually he felt free to leave his headquarters in order to take charge of operations in Liverpool Bay. His absence had been noticed at Guest Night but it was not until he dashed into the Wardroom to borrow a suitcase that the news about what had happened began to get around the base.

Somewhat incredibly—for so it surely must seem in the absence of any information to explain his decision—he travelled north to take charge of the operations over *Thetis* in the duty destroyer H.M.S. *Winchelsea*, a veteran lacking the high speed of the *Tribals*. She sailed at 10 P.M., which meant that it would be the following afternoon before she could arrive. In effect she took 19 hours. A car to Liverpool and then a boat—let alone the possibility of air travel—would have accomplished the journey in less than half the time. And on the evening of June 1, 1939, who was to know but that in *Thetis* every hour, every minute, counted ?

It should, of course, be made clear that Captain Macintyre travelled in the manner that he did with the full knowledge and, presumably, therefore the full approval of the Admiralty.

The first public announcement was given on the 11 P.M. news bulletin. It read, " The Admiralty regrets to announce that His Majesty's Submarine *Thetis* . . . has failed to surface."

Less than an hour later, at 11.56 P.M., *Thetis* had been shut down for 10 hours. With her known complement of 103 it could be calculated that, even if all her compartments were full of breathable air, the carbon dioxide content would have risen to approximately 5 per cent. of the atmosphere. Experiment would suggest that this would cause panting of the breath but no distress.

Undoubtedly just this sort of calculation was being made in the Cammell Laird offices during the late evening as the crowd of wives and relatives started to gather. At one o'clock in the morning Mr S. Woodward, the secretary of the company, spoke to the growing numbers who were waiting for news, assured them that all would be well, and urged them to return home.

Mrs Bolus, wife of *Thetis's* commanding officer, had been busy right from the start comforting all the other wives. She had been magnificent, all the more so because, as each hour ticked by and still no news came, she must have realized that she was the one woman virtually certain of becoming a widow. By the tradition of the sea her husband would be the last man out, and, even with her limited knowledge of submarines, she must have been able to guess that his chances were slim in the extreme.

After Mr Woodward's message she turned her energies to driving home all those who were prepared to go. Throughout the long night's work she hid her own sorrow.

It was around 3 A.M. when she drove the wife of Leading Stoker Arnold back to Tranmere. Mrs Arnold had been outside Cammell Laird's from immediately after the B.B.C. announcement. The waiting and wondering was no new experience to her. A submarine in which Arnold had been serving had been delayed 36 hours underwater two years earlier, off Malta.

The wife of Leading Telegraphist W. E. Allan—at six-foot-three the tallest man in the boat—was in digs at Birkenhead, and left her baby with the landlady to rush round to the shipyard as soon as she heard the news. She hated submarines and could remember quite clearly how she had shivered at her husband's cheery " Expect me when you see me ! " that morning.

A no less tragic kind of frustration during the early hours of the morning was being experienced by the divers of H.M.S. *Tedworth*. When the Subsmash signal arrived most of them were still ashore at Inveraray playing football. They hurried from the game and *Tedworth* hastily got under way. But instead of heading direct for Liverpool Bay she had to make course up the Clyde Estuary, over 70 miles steaming to Greenock, to replenish her empty coal bunkers. She arrived there during the early morning, but, for some reason or other, found she had to wait four hours before any civilian staff could be available to fuel her. This inability of *Tedworth* to proceed immediately to the scene of *Thetis's* disappearance meant that, during the whole of a vital period of 20 hours, the men in the submarine were to be deprived of the assistance of the ship and the ship's company more qualified to help them than any other in the country.

What aggravated the frustration among *Tedworth's* divers was the knowledge that some one in Admiralty must have been aware that she was nearly empty of coal, through the medium of the weekly fuel report, and yet no endeavour was made to send the divers south via any alternative transport. Only the week previously the U.S. Navy had sent divers to the scene of the *Squalus* disaster by air and road ; and a car from the Clyde to the Mersey could have arrived in good time for the morning tide. Faster still, of course, would have been a journey by air, particularly by flying-boat. And, while *Tedworth's* divers were fuming in a stranded ship, three R.A.F. flying-boats, ordered as part of the Subsmash organization, arrived at Holyhead. Their instructions were to be prepared to fly doctors and salvage experts to the sunken submarine and to help to maintain communications during rescue operations.

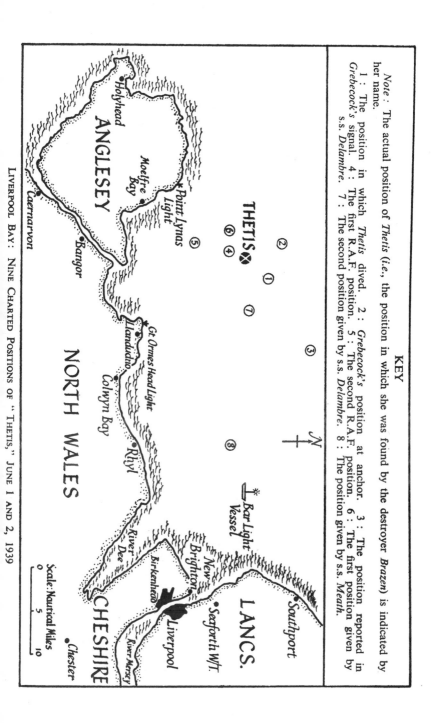

KEY

Note: The actual position of *Thetis* (i.e., the position in which she was found by the destroyer *Brazen*) is indicated by her name.
1: The position in which *Thetis* dived. 2: *Grebecock's* position at anchor. 3: The position reported in *Grebecock's* signal. 4: The first R.A.F. position. 5: The second R.A.F. position. 6: The first position given by s.s. *Meath*. 7: The second position given by s.s. *Delambre*. 8: The position given by s.s. *Delambre*.

LIVERPOOL BAY: NINE CHARTED POSITIONS OF "THETIS," JUNE 1 AND 2, 1939

Somehow, nobody associated them with the very need they could so ideally have filled.

By 3.56 A.M. *Thetis* had been submerged for 14 hours. Carbon dioxide content would by this time have risen to approximately $5\frac{1}{2}$ per cent. Panting for breath could be expected to have become more marked, and most, if not all, of the men in the submarine would be likely to be suffering from headaches, although these would not as yet be likely to be severe. But at this stage the greatest danger from carbon dioxide concentration was that a sudden change to pure oxygen—such as supplied by the Davis Submarine Escape Apparatus—would in many cases bring on acute vomiting. And this, in the mouthpiece of a breathing apparatus, could be dangerous in the extreme. This reaction to oxygen was a known factor, being regularly experienced in a milder form whenever a submarine surfaced and suddenly flooded her living-spaces with clean air after a long period dived.

Sunrise was at 4.48 A.M. During the next hour and a half the Irish steamer *Meath* and the British steamer *Delambre* reported sighting patches of oil and miscellaneous wreckage in three different positions in Liverpool Bay; but none of these could reasonably be connected with *Thetis*.

There were now, from various sources, some eight different positions marked on the charts ashore and afloat that were guiding *Brazen*, *Vigilant*, and the other searching vessels. In the midst of all these confusing directions Captain Hart decided to return to where *Grebecock* lay anchored and start sweeping again from there. It was 6.30 A.M. At 7 A.M. Lieutenant-Commander Mills came to the conclusion that, as all his searches to the south and west of *Grebecock* had been fruitless, he would steam to a position to the eastward and northward of her. *Brazen* was accordingly brought on to the new course to change position.

Shortly afterwards, at 7.50 A.M., Commander Mills himself thought he could see an object in the water two points on the destroyer's starboard bow and about three miles distant. He screwed his eyes tighter into his binoculars, held back his excited tongue until he could be sure, and then shouted. " There she is ! Green 25. Can you see her, Number One ? It's her all right ! " *Thetis* was found.

" Stop both," called Mills down the voice-pipe.

" Stop both. Both engines stopped, sir," came the quartermaster's reply. Slowly the destroyer glided towards the object protruding out of the water. As the distance closed, all on deck could see that some 18 feet of the submarine's stern was out of the water at an angle of about 40 degrees from the horizontal. Mills could see the small red, spherical indicator-buoy lying a few feet from *Thetis's* stern. The buoy had a flag and staff attached to it, but the flag was wet and wrapped round the staff. Nevertheless, cursed Mills, *Brazen's* searchlight would have picked it up during the night if they had only been in the right area.

" Carry on, please, Number One," he called down from the bridge to the fo'c'sle; and twelve underwater signal charges were hurled from the destroyer into the water alongside *Thetis*, to indicate to those inside the submarine that help was at hand and that escape could safely begin. *Brazen's* two whalers were already manned. Instantly they were slipped from their falls into the water, and a brief series of Morse symbols was tapped gaily on its way to announce the good news :

To Rear-Admiral Submarines; Admiralty; C.-in-C. Plymouth.
From *Brazen*. Immediate.
Have located submarine. Tail out of water. Position following : 328 degrees distance 14 miles Great Ormes Head. Time of Despatch 0754.

Thetis was found. And, with her tail being already out of the water, the waiting world could readily expect that the rescue of her crew would be a reasonably simple and speedy task.

5

Down Below

BOLUS had left the bridge and had shut and clipped the conning-tower hatch.   Descending into the control-room, he had started the necessary chain of activity that would cause *Thetis* to dive. Calmly and methodically the submarine's First Lieutenant, Lieutenant Harold Chapman (known to his brother-officers as " Bert "), had given orders for the main ballast tanks to be vented in pairs.

Intentionally, this would be done in slow time; and to control not only the submarine's buoyancy but also her fore-and-aft angle, the pairs of tanks would be selected from the amidships line—one pair for'ard, the next pair aft, and so on.   The electric motors were already running Half Ahead, at about 5 knots, and, on Chapman's instructions, use of the hydroplanes had been confined to a moderate angle of dive, certainly not more than 10 degrees.

" All main ballast tanks flooded, sir," reported Engine Room Artificer Jackson after what seemed, by normal submarine operating standards, an age; it was in fact five minutes after the order to dive. By this time the submarine should already have been below the surface and losing depth steadily.   As it was, she was still on the surface, and remained there in spite of increased use of speed and hydroplanes to drive her down.   Obviously her calculated trim had been exceptionally light.

This refusal to dive in the early stages of a trial, while possibly slightly inconvenient, was by no means abnormal.   In order to err on the side of safety it was often thought to be a good idea to make a submarine far too light on the first occasion of her diving.   This was certainly the Admiralty overseers' view; although if it had been left to *Thetis* herself she would probably have preferred to adopt the orthodox submarine technique of planning to be slightly heavy and then pumping out water while being held up by the hydroplanes.

The amazing thing was that, with none of the 25 to 30 people who had been expected to transfer to *Grebecock* having done so,

Thetis should not have been heavy even after having started out with a ' yard ' trim on her. For this excess complement represented some 400 gallons of water.

" Anyway, it should be easy to rectify," commented Bolus; and, as he was speaking, water was already being admitted to the auxiliary tanks in the compensating and trimming systems. Valve handles were spun open, solenoids clicked, pumps whirred.

" Not long now," one Leading Stoker muttered half aloud.

But ten minutes later *Thetis* was still on the surface. And twenty minutes later. And thirty minutes later.

" My God," muttered the Leading Stoker; and he spoke for all the crew.

Those in charge of *Thetis* had systematically attempted to shake off the positive buoyancy by flooding or taking in water into all the auxiliary tanks. Even so, with the planes at ' hard to dive ' and the motors at ' half ahead ' she could only with difficulty be forced down to 20 feet. The whole of the top half of her bridge would still be churning along above the water, creating a fine spectacle for *Grebecock* to see.

By this time it was clear to all the experienced submariners that the excess lightness was for'ard. This seemed the more extra-ordinary since it was comparatively easy to adjust the trim there, where there were so many tanks.

Chapman was dumbfounded. " But why ? " he asked aloud. " Damn it, most of the for'ard tanks are full. It just doesn't make sense."

His puzzlement stemmed largely from the anomaly that, while he had the task of controlling the actual diving of the submarine, the calculation of the trim on which the whole process of diving would depend had been undertaken, not as in a fully-fledged naval submarine by the First Lieutenant himself, but by the Admiralty overseers.

Suddenly an idea struck him and he turned to Bolus. " I wonder if Nos. 5 and 6 tubes are full, sir ? "

" I don't think they should be full," came a reply. Whose opinion this was it has never been possible to substantiate, but the likelihood is that was not Bolus's. The probability is that it came from one of the Admiralty or Cammell Laird staff who had put on the trim early that morning.

" Well, according to the trim statement they should be," countered Chapman. No one spoke up.

The slight hint of annoyance that had crept into Chapman's voice was echoed through the submarine. Regrettably it high-lighted the division of those on board into ' Navy ' men and ' Yard '

men. The one could hardly be blamed for feeling that the other
did not know his job.

"All this hanging around and messing about with pumps
shouldn't be necessary," ran the comment. "Vickers managed
to make *Triton* and *Triumph* dive without all this palaver. And,
anyway, this one has been down in a basin without planes or
power. Now she's got both and she's stuck on the surface."

So *Thetis's* earliest endeavours as a submersible were marked by
two connected circumstances, neither of which could be said to
assume the proportions of the tragic, although both should have
been avoided in conditions of reasonable efficiency: she was
incorrigibly light and she was diving with doubt and dispute
existing in her control-room as to the state of two of her six torpedo
tubes.

While all this was going on Leading Stoker Walter Arnold,
who had earlier taken part with Lieutenant Woods in the examination of the boat's D.S.E.A. equipment, was at his diving station on
the for'ard pump. He was squeezed into a tight little box which,
besides himself, contained only pipes and valves and gauges and
pumps and rams. It was called the for'ard pump room, or for'ard
machinery space, and lay down below the main deck, for'ard of
No. 1 battery tank and just abaft the trenches that extended from
the lowest pair of torpedo tubes—Nos. 5 and 6.

At the time of diving Arnold was feeling very satisfied with life—
in the short term, because he had managed to scrounge an extra
bottle of beer to help wash down the ' big eats,' and, in the long
term, because he felt that *Thetis* was going to be a very happy boat.
Nor was he deterred in this second reason by his knowledge of
current mess-deck gossip about the boat's being a Jonah, although,
as the delay in submerging continued, items from this gossip kept
circulating in his mind. He was still idly speculating on the pros
and cons when he first became aware of Lieutenant Woods coming
and going between the tube space and the control-room.

Woods had been a submariner for some three years previously.
He had joined *Thetis* in October 1938 and had been standing by
her during the later stages of her construction ever since that date.
As the boat's Torpedo Officer, his diving station during the trial
was in the torpedo tube compartment. There he had with him
Petty Officer E. Mitchell, the Torpedo Gunner's Mate, and Leading
Seaman W. L. Hambrook. Woods and Hambrook had served
together in another submarine, in an earlier stage of their careers,
and Woods, Mitchell, and Hambrook had been working as a team
in *Thetis* during several months of the stand-by period. They had
all taken part in the trim dive in Cammell Laird's basin in March,

and without doubt knew one another's actions, habits, and intentions in the performance of torpedo duties completely intimately.

About three-quarters of an hour before the diving trial started Woods had come down from the bridge to check that everything for'ard was in order. Passing through the control-room, he had noticed Chapman with the trim statement and had asked to see it. From it he had noted which compensating and trimming tanks were supposed to be partly or completely filled at time of diving, and saw that the statement contained an entry for Nos. 5 and 6 torpedo tubes. Alongside these was written the one word " Full."

He then went for'ard to the torpedo tube compartment, where he remained until after the dive had started. One of the first things he did when he got there was to order the starboard of the two main bulkhead doors between the tube compartment and the torpedo stowage compartment to be closed. The two lower doors were already shut. While Chapman was expressing his bewilderment in the control-room Woods was feeling equally surprised in the fore ends. In the tube compartment it was particularly obvious that the boat was light for'ard, because the vent valve to A tank, at the for'ard end of the compartment, was constantly being opened to allow increasing amounts of water to enter. Wood's mind began to work along the same lines as Chapman's. I wonder whether those two tubes are in fact full, he asked himself. I think I'll satisfy myself just what their real state is.

He decided first of all to use the test cocks set into the rear doors of the tubes. Starting with No. 6, he passed the test-cock lever slowly from the locked to the unlocked position. A small amount of water slopped out of the cock as he did this, giving him the impression that there was water in the tube at least up to the half-way mark, but that it was not under pressure. Whether more water would have appeared if, instead of moving the lever slowly through the whole of its travel, he had adopted the more correct procedure and stopped the lever in the middle of its travel (at the open position in which the two small test-cock holes would have been contiguous) is only an academic consideration.

Turning to No. 5 tube, he worked the test cock in exactly the same manner. No water came out at all. This enabled him to decide that, if this tube did have any water in it, the water was certainly below the level of the test cock. Having obtained a negative result from the test cock, he did not at this stage make use of the rimer, a pencil-like object provided for running through the holes of the test cock to remove grease, dirt, or other obstructions. With a brand-new boat he could well have expected no obstruction could have had the chance to accumulate. Certainly it did not occur to him that there was any risk of a hole being blocked with bitumastic enamel. Moreover, it had been his practice in previous submarines to instruct his Torpedo Gunner's Mate to rime the holes at frequent intervals, thus allowing him to assume that they were always clear. He had not yet given this instruction to Mitchell because the tubes were not at this stage his responsibility, and because he considered that Cammell Laird and the Admiralty overseers would have seen to it that the test-cock holes were clear.

But, due to the bitumastic enamelling, No. 5 was not clear, and, whether the tube was full or empty, Woods's test had in fact given him no evidence at all.

Puzzled as to the contradiction between his tests and the trim statement, he made his way aft to the control-room. " Are you sure those two tubes are meant to be full ? " he asked Chapman.

" Well, it appears quite definite that they should be," the First Lieutenant replied. " Isn't that so, Mr Robinson ? " He turned for confirmation to the Cammell Laird foreman engineer. To his surprise Robinson denied their having been filled—even though the Admiralty overseers may have thought that they had—and he would have been the man actually controlling the filling of any tubes back in the basin at Birkenhead.

" I think you'd better go back for'ard and check them again," Chapman told Woods. " Let me know what you find."

Back in the tube compartment Woods carried through the same tests in the same manner and with the same results. These he reported by telephone to the control-room. Very shortly after this he realized that A tank was almost completely full and that *Thetis* had still not succeeded in diving. Knowing that there might well be a call for further weight to be taken in for'ard, he went back to the control-room again.

" Well, as the tubes are empty, is there any likelihood of having to fill any of them to enable us to get down ? "

" Yes, there is," replied Chapman.

" Is power on the bow-caps, then ? " Woods asked Robinson.

" No, it's not."

" Then may I have it, please ? "

And so it was arranged with Robinson, with engine fitter Frank Shaw, and with engine fitter Eccleston that any power that was wanted for'ard by the boat's officers should be put on. This meant that a series of isolating and control valves had to be opened to allow the telemotor power access to the bow-cap control levers. When this had been done and, when the final valve in the tube compartment had been opened by Leading Seaman Hambrook, the latter reported to Woods that everything was correct.

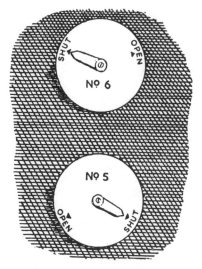

NOS. 5 AND 6 MECHANICAL INDICATORS

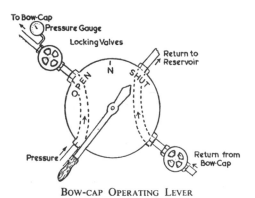

BOW-CAP OPERATING LEVER

Woods then—on what could only have been an impulse of the moment—decided to inspect the insides of the tubes. This was as much to see if they were dry and to verify whether or not there was any leakage round the seating of the bow-caps as it was to be able to report further to Lieutenant Chapman. On the earlier trial trip to the Clyde a small amount of water had come in at one of the bow-caps, and it seemed to Woods a good idea to make this inspection before *Thetis* went any deeper. He did not, however, inform the control-room of his intention.

Having decided to open the rear doors, Woods first went for'ard along the narrow alleyway between the two banks of tubes to inspect the bow-cap mechanical indicators. These were six five-inches-in-diameter circular dials set one above the other, and with pointers operated by the rams which actually opened and shut the bow-caps. There were numbered 1, 2, 3, 4, 6, 5. Not 1, 2, 3, 4, 5, 6. So that the fifth dial from the top actually indicated the state of No. 6 bow-cap and vice versa.

Moreover, the dial of No. 5 indicator—the lowest one—was extremely difficult to see because of a horizontal bar immediately in front of it. This meant that one had to scramble right for'ard and squeeze over the bar to bend downward.

Another complication about the bow-cap indicators was that the 'Shut' and 'Open' positions were in different places on different dials. On No. 5, for instance, 'Shut' was at five o'clock, while on No. 6 it was at eleven o'clock—in other words, exactly opposite.

In spite of all these complications Woods was able to satisfy himself that all the pointers were at the shut position on their respective dials. He immediately returned aft up the alleyway and proceeded to work the test-cock lever of No. 1 tube.

This was, of course, the same item of equipment that he had used earlier and completely correctly on Nos. 5 and 6 tubes. But on the earlier occasions he had been using the test cock purely to check whether the tube in question was more or less than half full. Now he was using it as a prelude to opening the rear door.

Technically speaking, he was no longer correct in relying on the test cock for this purpose. The procedure laid down at Torpedo School demanded that the state of a torpedo tube should be checked by the drain valve before the rear door was opened (the draining system being the normal method of emptying a tube). The rush of water coming through the drain valve from a tube with an open bow-cap is easily recognized.

Woods seemed to be content to use almost every check except the drain valve. He had sighted the pointers on the bow-cap indicator dials. He was going to use the test cocks. He also

ordered Leading Seaman Hambrook to sight the position of the
bow-cap operating-levers and received a report that was satisfactory,
not only to him, but to all the other four people who overheard
the answer and who knew what his next move would be.

But he had not used the drains. This meant that he was risking
putting something over 100 gallons of water into the tube space
bilges. While this would have been far from popular with the men
who would have to clean it up, and also with the First Lieutenant,
who would need to pump out before he could adjust his trim
(since bilge water cannot be kept in one place and so controlled
mathematically), this was categorically the worst that could
have been expected to happen. The evidence, as it appeared to
him, seemed completely to exclude any chance of a bow-cap being
open.

It was against this background of theory and what-might-have-
happened that Woods reached for the test cock of No. 1 tube.
Five people were near to him as he did so. Hambrook was standing
next to him beside the rear doors; another rating was right for'ard
between the tubes, watching the vents of the for'ard tanks;
Lieutenant Jamison, the engineer officer of *Trident*, was just inside
the tube compartment door; and Mitchell, the T.G.M., was with
Engine Room Artificer Howells at the telephone position just outside
the tube compartment.

A faint pressure of air came out of the test cock. Under Woods's
directions Hambrook opened the rear door. The tube was dry.
Woods examined it with a torch to verify that there was no small
leakage around the bow-cap and the rear door was then closed.

The identical operation took place with the rear door of No. 2
tube. The results were exactly the same.

Methodically Woods and Hambrook continued the procedure
with Nos. 3 and 4. Again the results were the same, except that
with each of these tubes no air pressure at all emerged from the
test cock. But both proved completely dry. By this time all the
men in and around the compartment were certain that the failure
or, at least, part of the failure of *Thetis* to dive was due to the
misunderstanding about the state of the tubes.

After Nos. 3 and 4 came, logically enough, No. 5. Woods pushed
up the test-cock lever as he had already done twice previously on
this tube. Just as before, there was no sign of either air pressure
or water. Hambrook then started to move the rear-door operating-
lever. It was the first of the five to be in any way stiff.

Hambrook paused for a second and then applied more weight.
Still somewhat unwillingly, as though *Thetis* was loath to betray
the men in her, the lever moved through the last part of its arc.

Suddenly, as it completed its travel, water started spurting out of the bottom of the tube. With a rasp and a crash the door was flung backward, out of Hambrook's hand. Within moments there was nothing but water, water, water—cold, fierce, dark, inexorable water.

No. 5 Tube

MITCHELL, tell the control-room to blow." Woods's reflex order was screamed out to his Torpedo Gunner's Mate the moment the force of the water had slammed back the door of the tube.

" Fore ends control-room: blow main ballast. We're flooding in fast through No. 5 tube." Even while Woods was still shouting his order the Petty Officer was repeating it on the telephone.

The water was pouring in faster and faster. Almost before any of the men for'ard had time to move, it had begun mounting up the sides of the tube space. Woods was so positive that the bow-caps were shut that, in the fragment of a second he could spare for an assessment of what had happened, he was sure there had been a fracture in the tube. " Had I realized, as I did soon afterwards," he recalled later, " that No. 5 bow-cap must have been open, I might possibly have been able to get at the bow-cap operating-lever." Certainly there was no possibility at all of a rear door being shut by hand against the full pressure of the sea.

Amid the tremendous weight of water lashing furiously in through the open tube Woods had to fight hard to make his way across the tube compartment to the port bulkhead door. The starboard door, immediately behind No. 5 tube, had, of course, been shut by his own orders at the time *Thetis* dived. As he struggled across he stumbled into Hambrook. The seaman seemed stuck between Woods and the bulkhead door and was obviously in trouble. The surge of water round his legs had thrown him off balance.

" Come on," gasped Woods. " Let me give you a push." He heaved the seaman over towards the door, where hands were already reaching through from the other side. For several precious seconds there was a confusion of arms, legs, helping hands, and fast-rising water. Then Woods, the last man out of the tube space, half scrambled and was half pulled through the bulkhead door into the temporary safety of the torpedo stowage compartment.

In the control-room Bolus and those around him had heard a

sudden dull *whoosh* and a muffled, metallic clang. These were
followed almost instantaneously by a sharply noticeable increased
pressure on the ears.

" Blow main ballast.   Full ahead, group up.   Hard to rise.
Surface."

Almost before there could be any real knowledge of what had
happened, and before even Mitchell's simultaneous telephone
message had come through, the aneroid barometer had risen three
inches.

The compressed air was hissing and spitting its way into the
ballast tanks, the motors were screaming ahead at full speed. But
within the first brief seconds *Thetis* had taken an angle down by
the bows and had begun to career deeper and deeper.   And fast
though the high-pressure air gushed through the manifolds, and
harshly though the motors screeched out their maximum revolutions,
Bolus and Captain Oram, standing beside him, immediately realized
that all their efforts were having no effect.

From his position down below and slightly aft of the tube compartment Leading Stoker Arnold's first experience of the disaster
was of a terrible rush of air coming from for'ard, followed by voices
shouting aft to the control-room to surface.

" Christ," he ejected as the wave of air hit him.

For a few seconds his mind stood motionless before it jolted into
action.   The air pressure had risen fast, and, to an experienced
submariner, that meant one thing only—the sea had come in.   It
must be a tube open, his thoughts tumbled over themselves.   That's
the biggest hole there is for'ard; and it must have been something bloody big to produce that effect.   A few seconds afterwards
he was up by the watertight door in the stowage compartment.

He found Woods and Hambrook just succeeding in fighting their
way out.   The moment they were clear and into the stowage compartment all of the several men up at the bulkhead turned their
attention to the door.

" Hurry, let's get it shut.   Swing it over," some one was shouting.
At least four hands started to swing it over on to its seating, but it
refused to budge.   It was a door that pivoted from for'ard to aft,
and it was held in the open position by a latch.   Before it could be
moved Lieutenant Jamison and E.R.A. Howells had to get round
behind it, half-way back into the water, and let the latch go.

" Now, she's free.   Swing her over quickly," ordered Jamison as
Howells and he moved clear.   Round the door swung under the
pull of several hands, with a small sharp clink of metal as it did so.
Round it swung, but it would not close.   One of the ' turn-buckles '
(the butterfly-nuts used for securing it when shut) had fallen out of

the spring clip in which it was housed and was hanging down between the door and the coaming, wedging itself in such a position as to stop the door closing completely. This had been the clink of metal that had scarcely been noticed.

" Blast, there's a turn-buckle jamming it ! Let her go back a bit." So the door was let swing partly back into the flooded tube compartment again while over-anxious hands pushed the turn-buckle back in its clip. More precious seconds had been lost.

" Now, let's have her back again—quickly." But every moment *Thetis's* bows were angling more steeply downward and the water was gathering on the door coaming between the two compartments. The angle and the pressure of water together were making it increasingly more difficult to pull the heavy door firmly enough ' uphill ' and into position. The half-dozen or more men were striving so to sort themselves out as to enable them all to exert an effective pull when—*sssssss*—the lights in the two for'ard compartments went out.

They continued to fight with the door. But in the blackness they were each fouling one another's efforts. The angle was still increasing and more and more water was coming over the coaming. They could get the door up to its seating, but not quite firmly enough to get any of the clips across. They were wet, cold, gasping for breath, and—in the sudden darkness—totally blind.

The water was coming quite fast into the stowage compartment. This meant that there was a new danger. The main batteries were in the compartment next aft of the torpedo stowage space. In no time at all there would be enough water in the second compartment for it to overflow the second watertight door coaming. And once the water reached the batteries there would immediately be vast clouds of poisonous chlorine gas dispersed over the whole boat. Unless the door at the end of the stowage space could be securely shut there would be no hope for a single man aboard.

Obviously losses had to be cut. " Evacuate the stowage compartment," came an order relayed from aft in the control-room. " Leave the for'ard watertight door."

Reluctantly, but resignedly, the small group of men clambered aft through the darkness. Last but one was Lieutenant Woods. As he started up the sloping deck he was almost swept back by a torrent of tables, stools, boxes, and other loose furniture, which the further steepening of the angle had caused suddenly to slide for'ard. To haul himself against this tide he had to pull himself hand over hand along the torpedo embarking rails.

The last man out was Mitchell, the T.G.M. He climbed over the stowage-compartment coaming a few seconds after Woods.

"I got one clip on the for'ard door, just at the last moment," he gasped.

"Bloody wonderful, chum," grinned Arnold, into whose arms he had stumbled.

"Well done, Mitchell," panted Woods. But all of them knew that this was only one clip out of a total of 18.

Further congratulations and any speculation about the holding-power of one clip were postponed in the need to close the door through which they had just come. This one was also heavy; it also opened for'ard; it also had to be pulled 'uphill' against the angle. But, fortunately, instead of having 18 turn-buckles, it was fitted with one circular, quick-acting lever. This was secured by Lieutenant Jamison and Arnold just as the water was beginning to lap over the coaming and into the fatal third compartment. And, as the dogs clamped shut into the door-seating, there was a jarring, reverberating impact felt throughout the boat as the submarine's bows hit the bottom. Right along the boat the jolt, allied to the angle, sent people flying off their feet. In the control-room a group of Cammell Laird fitters fell against the for'ard bulkhead and had to catch hold of things to try to stand up. There and in the engine-room tools and spare gear came crashing down.

From the group of men abaft No. 2 bulkhead there issued a mixture of quiet blasphemy and long, deep sighs. Then they turned to Mitchell. His action had been quite magnificent. He had deliberately stayed behind alone and in complete darkness, after having been told to abandon the compartment. And even though only one turn-buckle had been fastened, this must have meant, they told themselves, that at worst the flow of water into the stowage space had been substantially reduced.

As soon as he was sure that the second watertight door was completely safe Woods headed for the control-room. "Hambrook, were all the bow-cap operating-levers parallel to one another?" he asked before striding aft.

"Yes, sir, they were. Quite definitely."

So the mystery had already posed itself quite clearly—not that the answer to it would have helped those in *Thetis* at that moment. It was a threefold problem: Why was the bow-cap open? When was the bow-cap opened? Who opened the bow-cap? And, in spite of all the preoccupations of the moment, there were un-doubtedly many among those involved whose minds were pondering the Why? When? and Who?

In the control-room it had been a fight in vain to lift *Thetis's* bows and decrease the angle. Keeping a foothold on the sloping deck was a difficult business, and when the nose of the submarine smacked into the bottom, the gauge on the control-room bulkhead showed an angle of between 35 and 40 degrees from the horizontal. Calculating from the depth of the control-room, this meant that they had grounded at about 160 feet.

Bolus and Oram held a brief conference. They knew that so much water had been shipped aboard in so short a space of time that the lifting power of the air in the ballast tanks was being counteracted. In addition, the very angle that *Thetis* had been able to take up within a matter of seconds meant that the action of the high-pressure air in driving the water out of the holes in the bottom of the main ballast tanks was being diminished.

" Stop blowing," ordered Bolus.

" Stopped blowing, sir," he was told.

" Half astern both." He hoped to be able to withdraw *Thetis's* bows from the mud before she had time to get well and truly stuck, but, with no lifting power in the main ballast, it was a forlorn hope. In effect, all the main motors could do was slightly to increase the angle.

" Stop main motors," he called quietly. Temporarily, at least, the sea had to be given best.

After the main motors had stopped there was a silence that seemed, even to the uninitiated, to be a sign that things really had gone badly wrong. For a minute or so Bolus was occupied with taking telephone reports from all the other compartments of the boat. Then, with Oram, Chapman, and Glenn, he went for'ard to assess in detail what had happened, and to make up his mind what the current state of the boat actually was. It was very much a hand-over-hand progress against the steepness of the slope.

While the four officers were still for'ard the angle started slowly changing again. " Christ," whispered a hoarse, unidentified voice from the seamen's mess-deck, " she's levelling off."

So she was—slowly. Degree by degree the slope was reduced until by 3.40 P.M.—approximately three-quarters of an hour after No. 5 rear door had first been opened—*Thetis* settled on the sea-bottom at the insignificant angle of some six degrees bow down.

When the levelling-off process started Captain Oram was in the escape chamber that was built into the bulkhead leading to the flooded stowage space. In order to see what had happened since Jamison and Arnold had closed the second watertight door, he was shining a torch through the glass scuttle that looked on to the abandoned compartment. What he saw told him that Mitchell's one clip had provided only a temporary respite. There was a lot of water in the compartment: it looked about three-quarters full. And the level was still visibly rising.

Once *Thetis* had settled the for'ard indicator-buoy was released, and Chief Stoker Dillon-Shallard and Arnold fired a smoke candle from one of the underwater guns. With these signals of distress safely up to the surface it was possible for those in charge of *Thetis* to plan a course of action.

For several minutes Bolus, Oram, and Mr Bailey—the Admiralty Constructor—talked quietly together.

> We had a discussion about the best method of getting rid of the water [said Oram afterwards]. Two ways were talked over—blowing or pumping. The first was the simpler but, had it been adopted, there was serious danger that air would have bubbled out of a hatch used in harbour for taking torpedoes aboard. This hatch was designed to withstand external but not internal pressure.
>
> We feared that if we put a pressure into this compartment the air would bubble out of the hatch and so waste the stock of high-pressure air that we had remaining.
>
> So we turned our attention to the possibility of pumping the water out. The two pumps were both in an unflooded compartment, but before the water could be expelled it was necessary to close the hole through which it had entered.
>
> We proposed to do this by passing a man through the for'ard escape chamber so that he could get into the flooded compartments with his Davis escape apparatus on, close the rear door of No. 5 tube, and open the two main line suction valves.
>
> After that it would be possible for the ship's company to start the main ballast pumps and pump out the water.

Immediately they made the plan known to those around them in the control-room. " I'll go, sir," spoke two voices in unison. Chapman and Woods had both stepped forward, ready to advance their particular claims to the unpleasant task that lay ahead. Bolus chose Chapman to make the first attempt, thinking, perhaps, that Woods had already undergone a fair amount of nerve-racking and exhausting experience.

Arnold was in the control-room as Lieutenant Chapman started strapping on a D.S.E.A. set. He was already weighted down with heavy metal bolts to help him keep more or less upright in the water. Looking around him, the Leading Stoker was impressed by how little most of the people in the control-room seemed to appreciate the seriousness of the situation. " We'll get up all right," he heard. " The officers' plan will work; they know what they're doing." But when it became clearer what Chapman was expected to do there were a few dissentient voices. " Cor ! He's taking a one-way ticket, he is ! " Nor could Arnold find it in himself to believe otherwise.

It was a minute or two after 4 P.M. when Chapman climbed into the chamber. The door swung shut with a hollow clang. Oram and the others were watching through the glass scuttle and saw his thumbs-up sign. " Flood him up," came the order. In gushed the water, swishing and swirling first round his ankles, then up to his knees, then about his waist, and up, up over his chest. Bolus and Oram had decided to flood up fairly quickly—even though it meant that Chapman had to make a rather rapid adjustment to the new pressure—because at the depth at which he would be working his total endurance would not be more than about a quarter of an hour.

" He's going to make it," the running commentary was whispered back through the boat. And so it seemed, for the water-level had reached Chapman's face, and very soon the chamber would be completely flooded, and he would be able to open the door into the first of the abandoned compartments. Success—daylight, fresh air, and a warm bed back in Birkenhead—all seemed within sight.

Then, suddenly:

" He's signalling. Stop flooding. He can't make it. Let's drain him down. Quickly."

With a wave, a despairing shake of his head, and a prearranged signal, Chapman had had to give up the first attempt. And the whispers that accompanied the chain of buckets passed from for'ard to aft, emptying the flooded chamber, had already assumed a more anxious and ominous tone. There was a querulous element too. " Why the hell isn't this boat built so that it can be drained aft mechanically ? " some one asked. " All the other boats I've been in did."

It took a while before sufficient water could be drained out of the chamber by this laborious method to prevent any from slopping over the coaming and reaching the batteries. But, as soon as the door could be opened, Chapman was greeted with dry clothes and a steaming hot drink. He was pitifully upset and apologetic.

" I'm sorry," he gasped. " I'm sorry. I just couldn't go on any more. I was so faint and dizzy I just couldn't have carried out any of the plans."

The plans still seemed quite feasible, though. Woods pressed his demands to be allowed to try. Before agreeing, Bolus, Oram, and Bailey had another whispered conference.

" All right," he was told, " but let's be practical about this. It's not a good idea for you to try it alone. Let's face the unpleasant possibilities. Suppose you get through into the for'ard compartments and then collapse with oxygen poisoning or something. The for'ard door of the escape chamber would be open and the chamber would be out of action. We wouldn't be able to use it for any escape attempt."

"I'll go with Mr Woods." Mitchell had volunteered as soon as Bolus had called for another man to go for'ard. His offer was accepted, and it was agreed that Woods would have a rope around his waist which would be secured to the bulkhead into which the escape chamber was built, to enable him to find his way back. If he succeeded in shutting the rear door Mitchell could then deal with the two valves. But it was emphasized to him that he was to remain in the chamber throughout Woods's absence. If, after a certain interval, Woods failed to return from the fore ends, he would have the sad duty of closing the for'ard door so that the chamber could be drained down.

The crowded compartments were quieter when Woods and the Torpedo Gunner's Mate made their way for'ard and were fitted with their D.S.E.A. sets. The splashes that their feet made as they stepped into the water that had been left below the level of the coaming could be heard quite clearly farther aft.

"Now, remember," Woods whispered to the T.G.M., "if I don't come back into the chamber there are to be no heroics. No coming after me. There are all the others to think of. Understand?"

"All right, sir. I understand. But I reckon you'll make it."

Bolus and Oram were standing beside the chamber, ready to watch progress through the scuttle. "Good luck," called Bolus as the door was shut.

The mechanics of Chapman's attempt were repeated. Flood valves were opened and soon the water was rising up and up and up. Woods could feel its cold clamminess as it pressed his trousers close around his legs. It pushed and twisted the material into scores of tight creases, each one of which he could feel against his flesh. The regular *haw, haw, haw* of the oxygen flowing in through his mouthpiece had an almost hypnotic, comforting effect, and the slight tang of his returning exhalations, after they had passed through the soda-lime crystals in the container that absorbed the poisonous carbon dioxide, gave him an assurance that everything was working well. As soon as the water got up as high as his shoulders he decided to anticipate its cold creeping up his neck and over his face, and he ducked his head down into it, and let a few oxygen bubbles escape round the side of his mouthpiece. The resultant feeling of being in charge of the situation was psychologically very pleasing.

So far, so good. He jerked the heavy rope through his hands and fingered the electric torch, all wrapped round with insulating tape to improvise it for use in water, that hung from a loop on his wrist.

For the umpteenth time he pictured in his mind the exact layout of the compartments he was going to negotiate. Somehow, he hadn't time to consider that he might not get back to rejoin Mitchell in the chamber. It was then that he became aware of Mitchell gesticulating beside him. The man was indicating his ears and making signs that he could not continue. Impossible to ignore so impassioned a plea, so he added his signals to those of the T.G.M. But the people outside had already spotted Mitchell's frantic signs and had stopped flooding. Slowly the water level was reduced, and slowly the pressure eased.

It seemed an age before the door could be opened. Time for Woods to think and think again about what should be done. He had felt grand all the way through. He had been aware of the pressure on his ears, right enough. But he had been fortunate— he knew it was no more than that, no reflection of relative efficiency—in being able to clear the pressure by blowing hard down against his nose-clip and by swallowing hard against tightly shut lips. There was absolutely no reason why he shouldn't do just as well in another attempt. It only meant finding some one a little luckier with his ears than Mitchell had been.

Poor Mitchell was heartbroken. He had been trying not to give in ever since the pressure had begun to cause him pain, which had been before the water had got half-way up the chamber. In the end he just could not go on any longer.

The fact that Woods had survived quite happily and had no untoward signs at all seemed a very good argument for continuing the attempt. It seemed, too—though this went against the grain with Bolus—a very good argument for allowing Woods to play his part a second time. There had been a number of fervent applications to accompany him put forward while the chamber was still being drained down by the slow and tedious chain of buckets. One had come from Petty Officer C. E. Smithers, *Thetis's* second coxswain, who seemed to Bolus an ideal choice. And so a D.S.E.A. set was prepared for Smithers and another one for the wet, cold, and shivering Woods.

For this third attempt there was none of the silence that had accompanied Woods and Mitchell. Instead, there was a continuous murmur of tribute to the young torpedo officer. " Eeh, he's got some guts," a short, middle-aged Cammell Laird electrician remarked to Shaw. " He's already seen two men nearly flake out, and he's been through it once himself. I never did believe that anyone could do owt for'ard anyways."

Woods's only desire was to get on with things. He had scarcely felt the coldness of the water in the chamber, but as soon as he came in contact with the air he felt his body warmth, and, he feared, a little of his courage and confidence, draining away. Quickly and quietly he delivered himself to Smithers of the same lecture about remaining behind that he had given to Mitchell. The only difference this time would be that as soon as they had opened the door into the storage compartment both men would quickly try to screw down the fore hatch (with a view to subsequent ' blowing ') before Woods went on for'ard and Smithers returned aft.

Then, splash over the coaming, clang the door, and—*whoosh*— up with the water. One minute, a minute and a half, two minutes, two and a half minutes: the chamber was almost full. The water had climbed slowly up to, and then slowly past, the point it had reached when Mitchell had had to abandon his attempt. Good, thought Woods, Smithers is going to stick it. He himself could trace feelings of tiredness beneath his excitement, but he knew he could subdue them long enough to carry out the manœuvres he had now rehearsed so many times. It was just a question of shutting out all thoughts about not succeeding and not being able to get back. He was glad he had that sort of a mind.

In his impatience he had already started running his hands over the fastenings of the for'ard door to the chamber when he sensed a movement from Smithers that was different from the slight knee-flexing and arms-bending that the second coxswain had been using to preserve a feeling of mobility in the water. Woods turned, and, as he realized that Smithers was indicating that he, too, could not stand the pressure, there was a sudden snapping of something inside. He felt his shoulders sag forward, and his chest-wall seemed to deflate. It was nothing physical; only the mental admission of defeat. For he knew already that Bolus and Oram would regard this as evidence against any further attempt.

And so it proved. Smithers had managed to clear his ears the whole time, but he had suffered from the same dizziness as Lieutenant Chapman, and, in the latter stages of the flooding, he had felt a terrible pain around his heart. Once again Bolus, Oram, and Bailey conferred together.

> We debated among ourselves [recalled Oram, later] as to whether, having had three out of four cases of men who could not stand the pressure, it would be feasible to continue with our plan.
> We felt that under the ordinary conditions of escaping, where the pain or dizziness would only have to last a few minutes, it would be in order to go ahead. But in this case we required a man to work for some time under great difficulty and remain under that pressure for nearly a quarter of an hour, and unless he felt comfortable at the beginning there was not much chance of his success.
> So we decided to postpone that method for the time being, at least.

It was already 7 P.M. The three attempts to get for'ard had taken a total of three hours, although the majority of this time had been consumed by the process of hand-and-bucket draining of the chamber. Bolus and his advisers settled down to further discussion. The tempo of action inside *Thetis* had slowed. With the third failure to get into the fore ends, chances of a speedy outcome had diminished considerably.

7 7 p.m., *Thursday, June 1, to*
8 a.m., *Friday, June 2*

The Long Night

THE men who sat around the boat, fitters and seamen, civilian
electricians and uniformed stokers, soon assimilated the atmosphere
of speçulation. Small knots of them crouched together, talking,
asking, explaining, and occasionally laughing quietly.

There was a lot to think about, particularly if you looked at
things through the eyes of Bolus and the other officers. Theirs was
an unenviable situation. Not only had they their crew to save but
also a host of civilians, whose knowledge of submarines under such
circumstances was nil. Not one of them had probably ever put on
an escape apparatus before, and it was doubtful whether many of
them had remembered anything from the lecture on the subject they
had received on the previous day.

The sad thing was that *Thetis's* crew were little better off. As
soon as Chapman, Mitchell, and Smithers had failed to cope with
the pressure in the chamber it must have been all too apparent to
Bolus that, unless he could decrease the pressure considerably, there
would be a large number of people—probably nearly everybody—
unable to get out. The Submarine Service in the middle of 1939
had really very little experience in the art of escaping from a sunken
submarine. It was true that a few very gallant men had succeeded
in getting out of *Poseidon* from 125 feet, in 1931. But it was also
true that the Submarine Service's training in the use of the Davis
Submarine Escape Apparatus was confined to a tank only 15 feet
deep—not much more than the deep end of an ordinary swimming
bath—which was not constructed until after the *Poseidon* incident.

In *Thetis* that evening the epic of the American submarine *Squalus*
and American escape-training methods in a 100-foot tank (not
copied in this country until 1954) were widely debated. A number
of people cynically said that the whole story was one of finance.
The cost of equipping every member of the crew of a submarine
with an escape apparatus of the existing pattern was around £350,
they thought. The cost of training the same crew in the use of the

apparatus in closely simulated conditions and in something more than a token depth, and in giving every man the right sort of experience of operating under pressure, would cost, they calculated, anything up to £3500 a boat. And think what that would do to Navy Estimates, they told themselves.

There were doubtless others who were recalling in their minds Admiralty policy in incidents of this kind. In 1932, when the submarine *M 2* had been lost off Portland, the saving of life had depended, unsuccessfully, on long and dangerous salvage operations. Thereafter, Admiralty had rightly realized that any reliance on salvage to save life after a submarine accident was plain folly, and had directed that all submariners should be instructed in future not to rely on surface help but to use their escape apparatus, waiting, if possible, till they heard a ship on the surface who would signal her readiness to pick up survivors by dropping a succession of small explosive charges. It was these instructions that confronted those in charge of *Thetis* 150 feet down in Liverpool Bay.

It was this 150 feet of water that the Admiralty instructions would appear to have overlooked. There would seem to have been the impression that if a man could use an escape apparatus in 15 feet of water, then he was quite capable of using it in 200 feet; and if the pressure on his ears at 15 feet could be cleared by blowing down his clipped nose, then all he had to do at 200 feet was to remember the same drill. It was ironic that in the Naval Diving School, which had—surprisingly, perhaps—no connexion with the Submarine Service, this belief was not shared. The Diving School, with daily experience of getting people to reach 200 and 300 feet, knew the difficulties involved in getting even 20 per cent. of their intake to stand the physiological strain at great depths. In the light of this knowledge it must have seemed strange in *Thetis* that the submariner, completely inexperienced in the effect of depths and pressures on the body, should be expected to cope with their unpleasantnesses—to phrase it no stronger—together with the mental effect of an unknown and unnerving situation, and yet remain alert enough to manipulate correctly both the escape chamber and his apparatus.

With such speculations as these on the specialized nature of escaping from depth in front of him, Bolus must have found the go-it-alone policy a rather unhelpful one. Certainly the new plan of campaign, that was quietly announced by the small group of officers who had been deliberating around the wardroom table, showed clearly that they thought outside assistance to be essential to the survival of all those on board.

It was a neat plan. It appeared to be a workable plan. Partly

for their own peace of mind and partly with a view to eventually
getting it up to the surface, Roy Glenn wrote it down. It read:

> From *Thetis*.
> On bottom. Depth 140 feet. Six degrees bows down [this sentence
> was to be changed as the angle in the boat altered during the night].
> Tube space and fore ends flooded. No. 5 bow-cap and rear door
> open. Compartments evacuated. HP air required to charge sub-
> marine through either gun recuperator connexion or whistle con-
> nexion on bridge. Diver required to tighten down fore hatch, so
> that blow can be put on for'ard compartments without lifting hatch.
> Strongback required on hatch as soon as possible. Keep constant
> watch for men escaping through after Escape Chamber.

The idea was that when the fore hatch was tightened, and when a
supply of high-pressure air was being pumped into the submarine,
the men aboard would open certain valves, which would allow the
air access to the for'ard compartments and so force out the water.
It only needed a man to get the plan up to the surface.

By this time it was 8 P.M. There had been no sign of any vessel
having located them and sunset would be within the hour. It seemed
foolish in the extreme to send a man out into the open and un-
attended sea with darkness about to fall. Postponement seemed
a cheerless counsel, but in the circumstances it appeared that there
could be no other. If no signs or signals were heard during the
night they would make an attempt to get the plan up to the surface
soon after dawn, Bolus decided.

To make the most of the postponement it was also decided to
try to raise the stern of the submarine during the night, with the
hope of getting the after escape chamber as near as possible to the
surface, so as to reduce the pressure of water and make easier
the process of getting out.

So they started on the long watches of the night. The business
of setting up the pumping arrangements was largely an Admiralty
and Cammell Laird responsibility. It entailed a number of problems.
First of all, they set to pumping out 10 tons of fresh water, which
presented few difficulties. But when it became time to shift to the
fuel tanks several technical complications arose. Pumping systems
had to be adapted to purposes for which they had not been designed,
and the Cammell Laird fitters were kept busy for hours on end,
disconnecting and reconnecting valves and pipes all over the boat.

They undertook a monumental task. They had to work by hand
to rig jury pipes and junctions. Many of the pipes had to be
constructed almost from scratch. Lengths were cut out from
systems not likely to be used (principally the lubricating oil lines

of the main engines), flanges had to be made by hand, and the ends of adjoining pipes had to be beaten into the flanges. The whole job had to be completed without the assistance of a single blow-lamp.

In common with many of the naval personnel, Leading Stoker Arnold was not very busily employed. He had to find occasional tools now and then, but he spent most of the time talking to various men and idly speculating on their chances. The most frequently heard comment ran thus:

" Thank Christ they're getting the stern up. We'd never have been able to get out at that depth."

Nobody seemed very worried about their not having been found. They all knew that the Asdic and the underwater signalling gear had been put out of action when *Thetis* first hit the bottom. It was because of this that Petty Officer Telegraphist Hope took another telegraphist on one side and practised with him, to see whether short-range signals could be satisfactorily transmitted by hammering on the hull.

There was no sign of any panic as the hours passed. Food provided a welcome stimulus to morale, but it did not last very long. There had been some biscuits and cheese and a little chicken left in the control-room after the luncheon. These were shared out as far as they would go, and then supplies were exhausted. As luck would have it, the great bulk of the remaining stock of food was in the abandoned torpedo stowage compartment.

By midnight the air had started to get rather thick. The dehumidifier was run for about five minutes to see if it would improve the condition of the air, but without any noticeable success. Then the air compressors were started for a brief minute or two to try to take up some of the excess pressure inside the boat. The lack of oxygen had begun to get trying. Anyone who had to make physical effort of any kind rapidly became short of breath and needed frequent spells of rest and deep breathing before being able to continue. The temperature was quite warm, about 60 degrees, and there was a certain amount of dampness, but not enough to cause discomfort, due to a variety of very small leaks around pressure-hull glands. The electric-light system was working and the telephones were in order. In fact, apart from the for'ard two crippled compartments, *Thetis* was in perfect working order.

The raising of the stern was continuing steadily. By 4 A.M. the angle had increased from one of six degrees to one of 16. Over 50 tons of fuel, in addition to the 10 of fresh water, had been pumped outboard. But conditions were worsening, and some of the older men in *Thetis* were betraying signs of the ordeal. Engineer

Captain "Daddy" Jackson was at last showing some traces of fatigue. In order to keep out of the way—"I'm rather a large man, you know"—he had spent most of the night lying on Bolus's bunk, encouraging, and chatting away to all and sundry. He exchanged some words with Arnold on one occasion, and the stoker, somewhat irreverently, wondered how the huge senior officer ever got into an engine-room, and then, more soberly, how he could ever expect to get out of an escape hatch.

As the morning hours opened the stern rose more rapidly, and the angle within the boat changed from one that had only a mild nuisance value to people making their way from for'ard to aft, and vice versa, to one that made any sort of progress extremely difficult. By 7 A.M. it had reached 34 degrees from the horizontal, and Chapman and Glenn calculated that this meant that part of the stern must be out of the water. " Surely to Christ somebody will see us soon," gasped a voice from the for'ard accommodation spaces.

The condition of the air seemed suddenly to have got very much worse.

> The situation had deteriorated [Captain Oram was to recall later]. It was necessary to take deep and distressing breaths. Many men were retching and yawning, and watering from the eyes was continuous. One felt a great lassitude, and it required a distinct mental effort to co-ordinate mind and action.

Things were perhaps especially trying for the Admiralty civilians and Cammell Laird staffs. Not only did they number a far larger proportion of older men, and not only were they non-submariners, but they had also been busily occupied throughout the night on various tasks connected with the pumping-out of the tanks aft. Few of them even seemed worried about the outcome and there were certainly no signs of panic. Frank Shaw began, during the latter part of the night, to feel concerned for some of the men he saw around him, who were in bad shape; but he none the less shared what appeared to be the overall feeling of confidence.

" How are things going, do you think, Frank ? " one of his mates asked him.

" Fine," he found himself answering. " The officers have worked out a plan, and I reckon it's foolproof. As soon as somebody gets out the salvage people will start work right away."

It was some time just before seven in the morning when he first became aware of his reactions flagging.

" Shaw, what does that gauge read ? " One of the Admiralty overseers wheezed out the question at him.

He was conscious of some one having spoken, then, after an

appreciable time-lag—certainly, it seemed, one of several seconds—
he realized that he was the person being addressed.

They're talking to me. . . . what did they say ? . . . something
about what some gauge reads . . . this gauge, I suppose . . . let's
have a look . . . reads twelve pounds . . . must tell them what it
says. So went his train of thought, generously interspersed with
rests between one item of the thought-process and the next. All
the time this was happening he was aware that he was responding
slowly, but could not seem to muster any real concern. And yet at
no time did there appear to be any risk of his forgetting or misunderstanding the original question.

" Gauge reads twelve pounds."

Long pause.

" Thanks."

Bolus, Oram, and Bailey were still conferring together. All night
long they had been in close consultation, debating as hour followed
hour the changing circumstances and the changing actions that they
should take. The position could scarcely appear a very encouraging
one. True, they reckoned that the stern was out of the water, but
it had been light for some little while and still no one had located
them. Moreover, they could not be certain that the amount of
buoyancy they had achieved aft would be sufficient to withstand
the action of the tide in full flood.

Oram summed up things as he saw them. " I have heard that
a normal crew of a submarine can last for 48 hours with the air
available. But in this case we have two compartments flooded and
nearly a double crew. At a personal estimate I think about 24 hours
will be about the limit of activity. That will take us to approximately
3 p.m."

They all knew that they could not afford to wait any longer.
However quickly escapes could be made from the after escape
chamber—the only one at a reasonably shallow depth—the full
complement would barely have sufficient time to get out. This
supposed that no salvage vessel would turn up in time to carry out
the plan they had drafted earlier that night and that had been
written out by Roy Glenn.

So their considerations ran. " I feel in my own mind," continued
Oram, " that there might be a merchantman or fishing vessel standing
by on the surface, while we are needlessly delaying escape, because
we do not know that she is there."

The reasoning seemed undeniable. Oram offered to go up to the
surface with the plan strapped to one arm in a watertight cover, so
that, if he did not survive and was found, the message would still
be intact. Bolus and Bailey agreed.

They heaved themselves against the slope into the control-room. It seemed a good idea to have some one to accompany Captain Oram through the escape chamber and up to the surface, to double the chances of a message-carrier being found.

" Bert, pass the word for a volunteer to go up with Captain Oram," Bolus asked his First Lieutenant.

Slowly, with laboured breaths, the request was passed round. In the course of being relayed it was almost immediately abbreviated to " Skipper wants a volunteer." It was certainly in this form when Woods heard it. He was sitting resting on the deck at the for'ard end of the control-room.

" I'll go," he said.

Two seamen of *Thetis's* ship's company made the same reply, although none of them had any idea for what he was volunteering.

There was a pleased, tired grin on Sam Bolus's face as he turned to discuss the problems of selection with Oram. The senior officer's view was that he would prefer Woods to accompany him. The torpedo officer's greater knowledge of submarines in general, and particularly of that part of the *Thetis* to which the disaster had occurred, would be of more value in explaining the situation and helping the salvors, he felt.

So Woods was chosen and was told what his volunteering entailed. He joined the group in the centre of the control-room, and their conversation turned to technicalities.

The buzz about what was going to happen went round the boat. It was a good idea to send Oram, Arnold thought when he heard the news. The senior officer ought to be able to get things done in a hurry. And Woods seems in good shape, the Leading Stoker mused. No complaints !

" Come on, Arnold." He felt a tap on his shoulder and saw it was Roy Glenn. " You and me'll work the chamber for them. Let's get aft. They're coming now."

8

*8 A.M.–10 A.M.,
Friday, June 2*

Escape

INSIDE the engine-room of *Thetis* Frank Shaw was still busy with two or three other Cammell Laird fitters, continuing to pump out the after tanks. It was just after 8 A.M. He looked up slowly from the valve at which he had been heaving—not very vigorously by this time—between long, frequent, burning, unsatisfying breaths. Two people were pulling themselves along between the two Sulzer diesels, up the hill from for'ard to aft. They were the R.N. captain —Oram—and the young, curly-haired torpedo officer, who had made those two courageous attempts to get into the flooded compartments over twelve hours ago. Over twelve hours ago! It seemed an eternity.

Shaw had heard the buzz that Oram and one other were going to have a go at getting out to take a message up to the surface.

The right two people to go, too, his tired mind muttered silently to him. The youngster still looks pretty alert, but the old man, like a lot of the others here of his age, doesn't seem to be taking this bloody awful air any too well. Good luck to them.

The two officers struggled aft. Against the steep slope it was very hard going, and they valued the helping hands they got from the men lying quietly along the deck-plates almost as much as they did the whispered words of encouragement.

" Good luck, sir." . . . " Tell them not to flog all our farewell dance-tickets till we get up topside." . . . " Mind you tell the accounts department to watch our overtime." . . . " Good luck."

Through the motor-room progress was just as slow. By the time Oram and Woods had completed their few yards' obstacle course from the control-room to the after escape compartment and had recovered enough breath to start the next stage of the proceedings, they realized that they had taken between 15 and 20 minutes. And time was their unrelenting enemy. They must hurry, hurry, hurry ; even though they had no knowledge that any ship would be in sight once they got to the surface.

With the help of Glenn and Arnold they stripped off some of their outer clothing, rubbed a few handfuls of grease over exposed arms and shoulders, and put on their D.S.E.A. sets.

" Remember the long yarn we had with that D.S.E.A. Coxswain —Rowkins—when he came up to check the gear, sir ? " asked Arnold.

" Funny, I was thinking of that," grinned Woods. " Good idea as it happened."

Oram was still exchanging a few last words with Chapman, who had also climbed up aft from the control-room. " All right, sir. Those are the signals we'll stick to. Good luck." With the suspicion of a smile and a reassuring thumbs-up, *Thetis's* First Lieutenant watched the two men climb into the chamber. He nodded quietly to Glenn.

In went the D.S.E.A. mouthpieces, and, with the first rush of clean, pure oxygen to the lungs, Woods found his breathing quieten down from its turbulent end-of-a-strenuous-game-of-rugger searchings to a peaceful, relaxed cadence. The door was shut and they flooded up. The process started quite happily, but suddenly, when it reached a certain level, the water refused to rise any higher. Woods had no idea what was wrong and could not communicate with Oram, so he dispiritedly reversed the controls and the chamber began to drain down.

" Bert, what the hell's happened ? " he asked as soon as the water had drained low enough for the door to be opened.

" Don't know, old boy," came the reply. " Perhaps the top of the chamber's above the sea. Have another go."

Just as the door was shutting for the second time there came a sound that electrified the whole boat : a series of dull, subdued, *c-r-r-umps* that signified that charges had been dropped from a vessel on the surface. A croaking cheer from inside the boat squeezed its way between the heavy door and its seating as a wave from Chapman motioned them to carry on with the escape. Thank God, thought Woods, they'll surely all be got out now.

In *Thetis* the cheer was followed by a brief burst of excited conversation. Around the chamber this soon fell away again to silence as all eyes concentrated on Chapman, Glenn, and Arnold as they operated the escape. Suddenly a shaft of light struck down into the water inside the chamber and showed up through the scuttle.

" That's daylight. The hatch is open. They're out. Oh, well done." The news stimulated another throaty cheer from the men in the after ends, and for the second time within minutes a shiver of excited confidence ran through the boat.

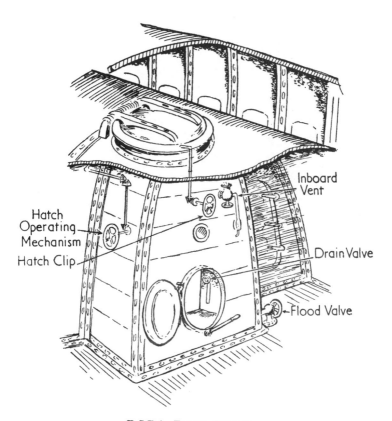

Hatch
Operating
Mechanism

Hatch Clip

Inboard
Vent

Drain Valve

Flood Valve

D.S.E.A. Escape Chamber

Inside the chamber the escape had gone quite smoothly at this attempt. Both Oram and Woods found great difficulty in concentrating on the correct drill. Must be the CO_2 poisoning, thought Oram. Makes one's mind sluggish. But as the chamber finished flooding they pushed up the top hatch, found that it was still, in fact, under water—although only about 20 feet down—and began to float clear. Oram got momentarily caught on the way out; but before any serious situation could develop Woods was by his side, freeing him. Seconds later they were both shooting upward.

Back in *Thetis* Chapman, Glenn, and Arnold were busy draining down the chamber. Soon the level of water was down almost to its normal low, and one of the men swung open the door. In their impatience they had not waited long enough. There was a sudden gushing, and a quantity of water slopped out around their feet. Normally, this would not have mattered; but the extreme angle of the boat meant that the coaming of the bulkhead door alongside the chamber was not high enough to contain all the water that had escaped. Within seconds the few gallons that there were had swirled into the motor-room and on to the main motors and the switchboard—to both of which items, had it not been for the steepness of the slope, water would only have access in cases of complete flooding.

Immediately there was the crackle of the sharp, dry flashes of a short-circuit, and a cloud of thick white, suffocating smoke welled up.

" It's an electrical fire," called Chapman. " Put on a gas-mask. If you can't find one put on an escape apparatus."

The group of men on the stokers' mess-deck around the escape chamber seized gas-masks or D.S.E.A. sets and within moments were breathing more freely.

" Shut the bulkhead door," Chapman then told Arnold. For a few minutes they sat until there were signs of the smoke subsiding. Then Arnold opened the door to the motor-room once again, and, on signals from Chapman, the gas-masks and the escape sets were removed. The change in the air was remarkable. Before the short-circuit Arnold had thought that he could scarcely imagine breathing conditions getting any more difficult than they already were, but the brief period of combustion had consumed a surprising amount of the remaining oxygen. Breaths, that had a few minutes previously been merely difficult, were now distinctly painful. And the extent to which one had to dig down to the bottom of one's lungs to rouse sufficient energy for even the slightest exertion had increased frighteningly.

Things don't look so good now, thought Arnold. I don't like to think how some of the older blokes, who looked rough enough when we left the control-room, are taking it now. And look at how many D.S.E.A. sets we've used—bearing in mind the 29 sets abandoned in the fore ends, and the five sets used in the attempts to get for'ard and shut the rear door, and the ones we've had on during the fire, there are not enough to go round anyway, in spite of the excess we carried.

He was stirred out of his dismal reverie by the voice of Lieutenant Chapman.

" You see . . . how easy . . . it is," gasped the First Lieutenant. " Two of them . . . straight up . . . no trouble." The looks on the faces around him reflected this confidence. The success of Oram's and Woods's escape had done more to increase hope than the sudden diminishing in the quality of the atmosphere had done to decrease it.

"I'm sending . . . four of you . . . this time." Chapman's thinking was obviously based upon the rapid worsening of breathing conditions, the conviction, which he may well have had, that the only hope for those aboard *Thetis* was in escape and not in rescue—in spite of the message that Oram had taken with him—and the awareness of how little time was left. He signed to two of *Thetis's* crew—Leading Stoker Kenny and Stoker Hole—and two of the Cammell Laird men, who were half sitting, half lying propped up around the chamber.

What Chapman did not know was that, not many months previously, Kenny had lost consciousness in the D.S.E.A. training tank at Fort Blockhouse, and had only been saved by the emergency quick-draining system. The regulations as they existed made ' passing the tank ' essential only at new-entrant stage. There was no mechanism for failing a submariner at any later point in his career or for recording any mishap on a man's papers. But the fact remained that had Chapman been aware that Kenny was in any way a doubtful quantity in a D.S.E.A. set he would not have used him on so vital an occasion.

The four men, looking, to Arnold, very much weaker than either Oram or Woods had done, pulled themselves gradually along to the chamber. The two Cammell Laird hands had the working of the D.S.E.A. gear briefly explained to them, and then they all climbed over the coaming and the door was shut. The chamber, designed for two, would scarcely let the last man squeeze in.

Arnold glanced at Lieutenant Chapman and received an answering nod. Another stoker, standing beside him, worked the hatch wheel and removed the safety clip, so as to leave the escape hatch free to open as soon as the pressure inside had equalized with that

T.A.R.—6

of the water above. Arnold operated the flood valves. As the water was rising a few new faces were appearing round the chamber. With the expectation of some speed-up in the process of escape Bolus had ordered some more people to make their way aft.

Chapman and Arnold peered through the glass scuttle as soon as the chamber was flooded. They were looking for the same sudden shaft of light that had appeared when Oram and Woods pushed open the escape hatch. The minutes passed without any sign. Five minutes. . . . "They must . . . be having . . . difficulty." . . . Ten minutes. . . . " Not easy . . . for four men . . . to get a good push . . . at the hatch." . . . Fifteen minutes. . . . Twenty minutes.

" Drain down," whispered a very worried-looking Chapman. Just as the water was about down to the level of the coaming he once again caught the eye of the attentive Arnold. Once again Chapman nodded an unspoken order, and the Leading Stoker pulled slowly at the door lever.

All eyes watched as the door swung gently open. Sure enough, the men had not got out. They were still . . .

" Christ, they're falling out. They're . . . dead ! "

Out of the chamber slumped a tangle of wringing wet bodies, all spattered with the accoutrements of escape—the rubber bags, straps, breathing tubes, and goggles of the D.S.E.A. sets. Arnold grabbed at them as they fell towards him. So did Frank Shaw, who, by this time, was standing alongside the chamber.

He found himself supporting a Cammell Laird man whom he knew well. The man was moving. " He's alive, this one," gasped Shaw, and pulled the mouthpiece of the escape apparatus out of his friend's mouth.

" Frank," he heard, " it was terrible. . . . We couldn't open the hatch. . . . It's jammed. . . . Oh, my God ! " A second later the head fell forward and the man had collapsed. Though still alive, he looked as if he would not last much longer. Shaw lowered him on to the sloping deck.

Chapman and Glenn had come to Arnold's assistance at the chamber door. All the other three men were already dead. Wearily the two officers and the stoker disentangled the three bodies and, with the help of some of the other occupants of the compartment, started hauling the sopping wet bundles further aft and down into the after machinery space, out of the way of any farther use of the chamber.

" Look at them," wheezed Glenn. " No mouthpieces in. This one's been ripped out . . . the elastic strap's broken. And foam round the mouth. None of them've got nose-clips on . . . not even that civvie . . . the one that's still alive."

" What went wrong, Roy ? " asked Chapman. " They didn't
seem nervous . . . and they were breathing from the sets all right
when they went in. Perhaps they were . . . too weak. . . . My fault."

" Stop worrying, Bert," replied the engineer. " Not your fault
. . . blame the bastards . . . who got us here."

There was a tenseness around the chamber as the three of them
climbed down. Every so often another piece of loose equipment
would shift as the angle of the boat—moved, presumably, more
by the tide than by her own exertions—increased. Sam Bolus had
pulled himself through the bulkhead door from the motor-room
by this time. The first thing that Shaw noticed about him, as he
looked up from the only thinly breathing body of the man he had
helped out of the chamber, was his encouraging, though undeniably
sad and weary, grin. The second thing he noticed was that Bolus
was standing more on the bulkhead than on the deck of the compartment. He's probably right, thought Shaw, the angle is over
45 degrees—well over—nearer 60, in fact.

" Carrying on in twos, sir," whispered Chapman.

Bolus inclined his head.

" Will you have a go, Arnold ? " asked Chapman.

Arnold hesitated the merest second. Having been at Blockhouse
at the time, he knew that Kenny had perhaps been somewhat
accident-prone, so he was not really deterred by what had happened.

" You bloody well go, Arnold," Glenn growled at him.

" O.K., sir. I'm on."

" Good man," he was told. " Tell them we'll be escaping at
regular intervals from the after escape chamber. Keep the rescue
vessels clear of the surfacing area."

Chapman looked at the group of Cammell Laird men. Which
should he take ? There was a pushing and shoving. " You go,
Frank," croaked out a hoarse voice. A fat little engine fitter, who
looked fit enough anyway, had come out to the front. It was the
man who had hauled out that only survivor of the chamber.

" Yes, you. Fix his set, Arnold."

The two men looked at each other. For a moment or two Shaw
was still undecided. He could not forget that impassioned " It was
terrible. . . . We couldn't open the hatch." But if he didn't go soon,
he told himself, he couldn't last much longer.

He had known Arnold previously, although he thought the big
stoker did not remember him. The submarine *Sealion* had been a
Cammell Laird boat, and Shaw could recollect seeing Arnold from
time to time during that building period as well as around *Thetis*
for the last several months.

I reckon he's a determined man, thought Shaw. He's one

who will sell his life dearly. I'll go. And he lifted his arms to have the straps of the D.S.E.A. set put round them.

Shaw was right. He had made no previous impression on Arnold, either during the *Sealion* days or in *Thetis*. All Arnold saw was a face which indicated reliability, and a shape which, though plump-looking, indicated toughness. In fact, he found that the little engine fitter's powerful shoulders, deep chest, and plentiful abdomen were such that the straps of the breathing apparatus would not fasten properly. " All right," he muttered, " I'll tie them in the middle of your back. They'll be O.K."

Arnold was the first into the chamber amid a small shower of water dripping down from the upper hatch. Try and see why the others couldn't work it, he had been told. But the light from his torch had almost run out, and his attempts to probe the recesses under the hatch showed him nothing. I don't know why they couldn't—but it doesn't matter, he thought. Impatiently, for a burning headache was nag-nag-nagging at his tired brows, he leant out and beckoned to Shaw.

" So long, sir," he murmured at Glenn. " Be seeing you blokes soon," he vouchsafed to the group of stokers and yardmen around the chamber. Bolus nodded at him, and for the last time he caught his First Lieutenant's eye. Chapman just looked at him, not moving a muscle. Arnold thought he was not going to speak. Then his lips formed an almost soundless greeting. " Good luck. Thanks."

Shaw forced himself to climb into the chamber. He felt terrible. The air was so thick that he could hardly speak, and he had a choking feeling round his throat. As he scrambled over the coaming he looked back into the compartment. Apart from Chapman, Glenn, and one of the stokers around the chamber, and the captain beside the bulkhead door, nearly every one was lying down. There must have been 16 to 18 of them all told. Two or three were wearing D.S.E.A. sets, presumably in expectation of an early opportunity of escape. All were showing signs of serious distress. Shaw glanced at his watch. It was almost 10 A.M. He snatched a last glimpse back into the compartment. His final impression, before he ducked his head in and the heavy door of the chamber banged shut behind him, was that the door by which the captain was standing—the one that had been closed during the short-circuit fire—was also shut once again. For a brief second he wondered why.

Then Arnold nudged him.

" Remember what I told you ? " the big stoker whispered. " You know how to get on oxygen ? "

" Yes, Mac."

" And don't do anything until I tell you . . . you'll be all right.

Just remember to open the exhaust cock on your set when you leave
the chamber. You go up first when I tell you . . . and open the
hatch. . . . Leave the rest to me."

" O.K., Mac . . . and thanks."

Shaw's confidence was growing with Arnold's instructions. The
big stoker looked almost frighteningly determined. I *must* make it,
Shaw told himself. If I don't, he'll not hesitate to go up over the
top of me.

It had been agreed that they would flood the chamber from inboard, so that they could regulate the speed of the water coming in.
As they were not very deep and there were consequently no pressure
worries, and as Shaw looked quite fit and in reasonable shape,
Arnold decided to let the water come in pretty fast. It was only
half-way up the side of the chamber when it stopped. Arnold
reached for the outboard vent to allow sea-water from outside to
enter and flood the remainder of the space and equalize the pressure.

He tugged at the vent valve, but it wouldn't budge. Another
heave, but still no effect. In desperation he threw the whole weight
of his tired body over against the valve handle, and suddenly it
shifted. A couple of twists, quite easy once the first turn had been
made, and the water gushed in from above them.

The level was rising again, quite quickly it seemed to Shaw. As
it advanced up his body he could not stop thinking about the three
dead men he had seen fall out of the chamber and about the " It
was terrible. . . . We couldn't open the hatch " of the man he had
held, almost dying, in his arms. As the water came up to his neck
he whipped in his mouthpiece and went over to oxygen. The water
came higher and higher, until it was over his eyes and he could not
see properly.

His mind was going fast. I wonder if the hatch is jammed ? . . .
we're trapped . . . no, we're not . . . but we must keep cool . . .
must wait till the pressure is the same as outside . . . thank God
Mac's here !

Then the stoker gripped his arm. In the dim light and through
the distortions of the water swirling round his face Shaw could see
that Arnold was pointing up at the hatch and making as if to push it.

Shaw nodded. As Arnold reached up and released the clip Shaw
put up one hand to push against the hatch. It did not move.
Instinctively he kept on pushing hard. Supposing . . . supposing
. . . but, before he had time to lose his head, he felt Arnold's hand
on his arm once again. A shaken head and a few signs told him
to wait. The water had to come up higher to equalize the pressure,
Arnold indicated.

A minute or two later Arnold motioned him to try again. He

pushed. For the merest fraction of a second there was no movement. Then—it moved. Within the smallest particle of conscious time it was wide open. There was light. And life. And Shaw felt himself shooting upward.

He was scarcely aware of a hand clutching at him as he left the chamber, but in fact Arnold had done him one more service. He had completely forgotten to open the exhaust cock on his breathing apparatus, although Arnold had explained to him, before they got into the chamber, that the purpose of doing this was to prevent the oxygen, that would be retained in the breathing bag if the cock were shut, from expanding under the sudden reduction in pressure during the ascent, and choking him. But as he soared upward the stoker managed to snatch at his set and flick the little valve open.

Up, then, went Shaw. He hit two wires after leaving the hatch, but they could not stop the speed of his ascent. In seconds he was on the surface. Suddenly he remembered Arnold. Where's Mac? his confused mind wondered. Then he realized he was almost alongside a rowing-boat. Somebody was shouting to him.

Arnold had not had a very pleasant time in the chamber. If Shaw had thought that the water was coming in quite fast, he had been most dissatisfied with its comparative slowness. Because we're so shallow, he told himself. He was keeping his eye on Shaw the whole time and felt decidedly in charge of the situation until the water came up high enough for him to go on oxygen. Then, immediately, he was violently sick inside the mouthpiece of the set. The impact of the warm, sweet oxygen on the sustenance-starved tissues of his body had caused instant nausea. And, as he had postponed going on oxygen until the water was up to his chin, there was now no opportunity to take his mouth out of the set, for the level was over his lips.

He wondered whether the set would seize up. What would he do if it did? And then he was distracted by the need to motion Shaw to make a first attempt at the hatch. With each breath he could feel the vomit around his mouth. As he breathed backward and forward he could hear the gurgling that it made as the contaminated oxygen found its way through to his lungs.

He stopped Shaw straining at the hatch. They would have to wait a little longer for the pressure to equalize. The water was very cold.

I hope I'll be able to stick it on the surface before they pick me up, his mind ran. I'm not a bad swimmer. Used to enjoy the water-polo for the flotilla. Should be all right.

Then things started happening, and in no time Shaw had gone. He watched until he could see the little fitter had cleared the jumping

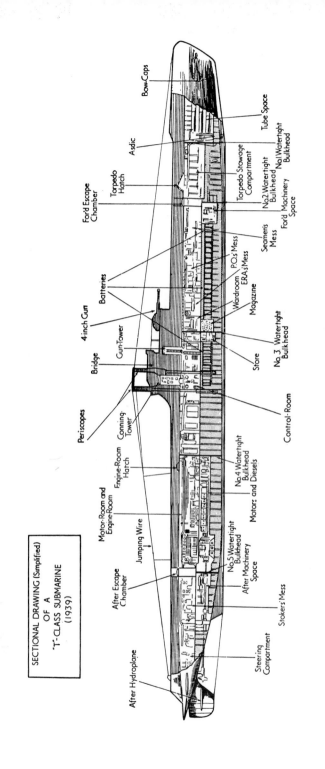

SECTIONAL DRAWING (Simplified)
OF A
"T"-CLASS SUBMARINE
(1939)

Periscopes

Bridge

4-inch Gun

Gun-Tower

Batteries

Ford Escape Chamber

Torpedo Hatch

Asdic

Bow-Caps

Tube Space

Torpedo Stowage Compartment

No.2 Watertight Bulkhead

No.1 Watertight Bulkhead

Ford Machinery Space

Seamen's Mess

P.O.s' Mess

ERA.s' Mess

Wardroom

Magazine

Store

No.3 Watertight Bulkhead

Control-Room

Conning-Tower

Engine-Room Hatch

Motor-Room and Engine-Room

Jumping Wire

After Escape Chamber

No.5 Watertight Bulkhead

After Machinery Space

Stokers' Mess

Steering Compartment

After Hydroplane

No.4 Watertight Bulkhead

Motors and Diesels

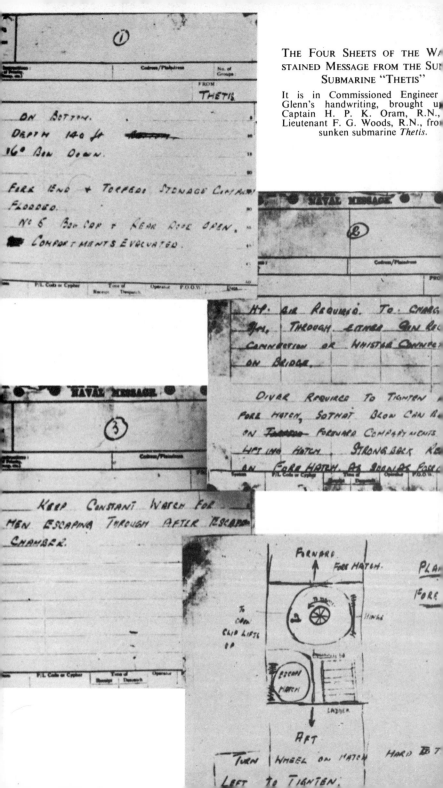

THE FOUR SHEETS OF THE WATER-
STAINED MESSAGE FROM THE SUNKEN
SUBMARINE "THETIS"

It is in Commissioned Engineer R. Glenn's handwriting, brought up by Captain H. P. K. Oram, R.N., and Lieutenant F. G. Woods, R.N., from the sunken submarine *Thetis*.

(1)

FROM THETIS

ON BOTTOM.
DEPTH 140 ft
36° BOW DOWN.

FORE END & TORPEDO STOWAGE COMPARTMENTS FLOODED.
No 6 BOW CAP & REAR DOOR OPEN.
COMPARTMENTS EVACUATED.

(2)

HP. AIR REQUIRED. TO CHARGE UP, THROUGH EITHER GUN RECUPERATOR CONNECTION OR WHISTLE CONNECTION ON BRIDGE.

DIVER REQUIRED TO TIGHTEN UP FORE HATCH, SO THAT BLOW CAN BE PUT ON FORWARD COMPARTMENTS.

LIFTING HATCH. STRONG BACK KEEP ON FORE HATCH AS SPRINGS FORCE

(3)

KEEP CONSTANT WATCH FOR MEN ESCAPING THROUGH AFTER ESCAPE CHAMBER.

FORWARD
FORE HATCH.
PLAN
FORE

TO OPEN CLIP LIFTS UP

HINGE

ESCAPE HATCH

LADDER

AFT

TURN WHEEL ON HATCH HARD TO THE LEFT TO TIGHTEN.

LAUNCHING OF "THETIS" AT THE CAMMELL
LAIRD YARD, BIRKENHEAD, ON JUNE 29, 1938

Fox Photos

(*Right*) THE MENU OF THE DINNER GIVEN FOR
THE LAUNCHING

MENU ::

Grape Fruit

Saumon Froid, Sauce Mayonnaise
Concombres

Suprême de Volaille, Neva

Jambon d'York
Salade Printanière
Petites Pommes au Beurre

Fraises en Timballe Romanoff
Délices des Dames

Café

Cammell Laird & Co. Ltd.,   29th June, 1938
Birkenhead.

Liverpool Bay, Friday, June 2, 1939

The stern of *Thetis* (circled) is sticking out of the water. The outer ring of vessels is made up of (le**ft**
right) two *Tribal*-class destroyers, H.M.S. *Brazen*, the tug *Grebecock*, and the salvage vessel *Vigile*

Keystone Press Agency

"Tribal"-class Destroyers of the 6th Destroyer Flotilla

In formation at full-speed *en route* for Liverpool Bay.

Fox Photos

A Flagged Buoy marks a Position in Liverpool Bay
Fox Photos

Wreck Master Brock at work on the Stern of "Thetis"
boat from the salvage vessel *Vigilant* lies alongside. The submarine's rudder and hydroplane can be clearly seen.
Courtesy of Kemsley Picture Service

CHIEF PETTY OFFICER "DICK" OLIVER, SENIOR DIVER OF THE NAVAL DEEP-DIVING VESS[EL]
H.M.S. "TEDWORTH" (not shown) PREPARES TO GO DOWN ON "THETIS"

Other naval divers are handling his lines. The heavy wires leading from the small salvage vessel a[re]
attached to the sunken submarine.

Courtesy of Kemsley Picture Service

A NAVAL WHALER, A SMALL MOTOR-BOAT, AND THE TUG "GREBECOCK" LYING CLOSE [TO]
THE STERN OF "THETIS"

Courtesy of "Liverpool Post"

wo NAVAL WHALERS AND A BOAT FROM ONE OF THE SALVAGE VESSELS ATTENDING ON
"THETIS"

Keystone Press Agency

(*Above*) A MEMORIAL CARD FOR "THETIS," PREPAR[ED]
IN BIRKENHEAD

The name of Leading Stoker Arnold appears (erroneousl[y]
of course) 4th from the top of the 2nd column.

(*Left*) LEADING STOKER ARNOLD SAFF AT HOME A F[EW]
DAYS AFTER HIS ESCAPE

(*Below*) CROWDS AT THE CAMMELL LAIRD OFFICES

Mr S. Woodward, secretary of the company, addresses relati[ons]
and friends.

Courtesy of Kemsley Picture Service

THE LATTER STAGES OF DIVING ON "THETIS" OFF THE COAST OF ANGLESEY

(Left to right) Commander S. Raw, R.N. (now Vice-Admiral Sir Sydney Raw and Flag Officer Su... marines 1950–51); Mr M. Smith (Salvage Officer); Mr W. Linton (civilian diver from H.M.S. *Tedwort...* and Petty Officer J. Dymond (also from H.M.S. *Tedworth*).

VIEW OF "THETIS" BEACHED AT MOELFRE BAY, ANGLESEY

Courtesy of Kemsley Picture Service

LEADING STOKER WALTER ARNOLD AND MR FRANK SHAW
On their way to attend Mr Justice Bucknill's Tribunal of Inquiry at the Law Courts, July 1939.

ANOTHER VIEW OF "THETIS" BEACHED AT MOELFRE BAY

THE MEMORIAL TO HIS MAJESTY'S SUBMARINE "THETIS" AT HOLYHEAD
Unveiled and dedicated November 7, 1947.
Photo: L. V. Burrows. Courtesy of Caernarvon Herald

H.M. S/M. "THUNDERBOLT"

the bridge are her First Lieutenant, Lieutenant J. S. Stevens, R.N., and, on his immediate left, her Coxswain, Chief Petty Officer C. S. Jones.

C.O.I. Crown copyright reserved

"THUNDERBOLT" RESCUES THE CREW OF S.S. "GUELMA"

One of the life-boats comes alongside.

(*Above*) "THUNDERBOLT'S"
SKULL-AND-CROSSBONES

Displayed by a group which includes Chief E.R.A. George Cu[...]
(extreme left) and Coxswain "Ch[...]
lie" Jones (extreme right). The [...]
displays seven successful torp[...]
attacks (two of them U-boats), [...]
successful gun actions, and [...]
'special service' operations.

C.O.I. Crown copyright reserv[...]

(*Left*) ANOTHER VIEW OF [...]
SAME JOLLY ROGER

The larger group includes L[...]
tenant R. L. Bird, R.N.R. (l[...]
Lieutenant B. J. Andrew, F[...]
(centre); and Lieutenant J. Ed[...]
R.N. (right).

Official Admiralty Photograp[...]

"Thunderbolt" returning from Patrol

"Thunderbolt's" Control-room

tenant-Commander C. B. Crouch, R.N., at the periscope. Lieutenant R. L. Bird, R.N.R., at the chart-table.

"Charlie" Jones

From a portrait by William Dring of Chief Petty Officer C. S. Jones, D.S.M. In the background depth-gauges, hydroplane controls, etc.

C.O.I. Crown copyright reserved

wires. Then he relaxed. For a brief moment before he heaved himself up through the hatchway he let his mind expand again.

I'll make it now. Whatever happens I'll see May again. Even if the set packs in, I shall cope. Thank God.

With one pull he came head and shoulders up through the rim of the hatchway. The angle had caused him to come through rather squeezed against one side, and one of his straps caught on the hatch clips. He kicked . . . once, twice . . . then he was clear. He could see a wire, then two. He banged into them fairly heavily with one shoulder, but they only jerked him a little. Then, up again. He could see the sun through the water.

A second later he had broken surface. He could feel the air on his face. That was what he must have been trying to imagine during those day-dreams back in the steering compartment. The feel of fresh air on his face. Christ, it was good.

" Here you are, mate," a voice called. He turned in the water. It was a boat.

9

7.54 A.M.–12.30 P.M.,
Friday, June 2

Hope

CARRY ON, please, Number One," Lieutenant-Commander Mills
called down from the bridge to the fo'c'sle of the destroyer *Brazen*.

Twelve underwater signal charges were hurled into the water
alongside *Thetis*, and the two whalers, which had been ready manned
in anticipation of this moment, were slipped from their falls.

Thetis was found. And with her tail being already out of the
water, the waiting world could readily expect—or so it seemed
aboard *Brazen*—that the rescue of her crew would be a reasonably
simple and speedy task. Turning to his signalman, Mills dictated
his second W/T message.

> To Rear-Admiral Submarines; Admiralty; C-.in-C. Plymouth.
> From *Brazen*.
> Nose of submarine appears to be stuck into bottom, tail projecting
> about 18 feet. Time of Despatch 0807.

Within seconds the surface of the water was broken by a splash,
wreathed in bubbles. Then by another. Two heads, each garbed
in Martian goggles and mouthpiece, bobbed weirdly about in the
waves.

" Look, sir ! Two of them are up ! " shouted the Officer of the
Watch. " They're being hauled into the whaler."

Mills felt a great weight off his mind. He had found *Thetis*;
he had signalled his presence to her; and within minutes the first
two men had gone out. His racing thoughts were divided between
the news he was eagerly awaiting to hear from the two men in the
whaler and the calculations he was making about how long it would
take for the whole complement to escape.

He clattered down the steel ladder from the bridge and was
leaning over the guard-rail as the two dripping, blanket-clad
individuals came on board.

" They're Captain Oram and Lieutenant Woods, sir, "he was
told. He gave them a glance and a word of welcome. Then he

was ushering them below, helping them find warm clothes and hot drinks, and hearing what they had to say.

" Every one is alive on board," Oram said. " They will be escaping at regular intervals of about 20 minutes. Don't try to go alongside, it would only endanger the attempts to get out. I'm confident the majority will be saved."

Thank God, breathed Mills to himself. And it was with comparative peace of mind that he watched Captain Oram go off to lie down on a bunk in one of *Brazen's* after cabins. Neither of them looked very good after their experience, he thought, but Oram— only naturally, for the older man—looked by far the worse.

But, in spite of the reassurance he had received, Mills decided not to cancel the instructions he had given for the destroyer's 150 feet of armoured air hose to be prepared—just in case. And as he dictated his next signal he was pondering in his mind, if it should later be advisable to go alongside, just how he would use his cable to support the submarine's stern.

> To Rear-Admiral Submarines; Admiralty; C.-in-C. Plymouth.
> From *Brazen*. Immediate.
> Captain Oram and Lieutenant Woods are in *Brazen*. All the rest of the crew are alive in submarine and endeavouring to escape by D.S.E.A. Time of Despatch 0826.

By this time the salvage vessel *Vigilant*, under the command of Captain H. V. Hart, had arrived. She immediately put one of her boats in the water. From this she had a light wire—designed ultimately to pull something heavier, such as a cable, and known as a ' messenger ' wire—connected to *Thetis's* stern. She watched the heads of Oram and Woods break surface and saw them being picked up by one of the destroyer's whalers. She waited a few minutes. No sign of further escapes. Perhaps there hadn't been sufficient time since the first one, but this was no occasion for exercising patience, so she had the boat's crew hammer in Morse code on the exposed plates of the submarine.

—·—· ——— ——· ——— ··— —

C–O–M–E   O–U–T

Once, twice, six times, eight times, ten times. Again and again the message was pounded, loud and resounding, against the steel hull. But, try as they might, the men in the rowing-boat could hear no sounds of any kind of reply.

At 8.55 A.M., nearly an hour after Oram and Woods had escaped and with no further signs of activity of any kind from *Thetis*,

Captain Hart sent a message by wireless to the Mersey Docks and
Harbour Board:

" Send burners and burning gear at once with tug."

No sooner had this been despatched than Lieutenant Coltart,
who had transferred to *Vigilant* from *Grebecock* during the night,
and Lieutenant-Commander Bittlestone, the Naval Liaison Officer
at Liverpool who had come out in *Vigilant*, went over by boat from
Vigilant to *Brazen*. Soon they returned with a copy of the duplicate
salvage plan which both Oram and Woods had brought to the
surface.

Immediately Captain Hart sent another message back to
Liverpool:

> Please send out with a tug with utmost dispatch, portable motor air
> compressor connexions for air pipe to compressor. Burners and
> burning gear Foreman Fitter and from Cammell Lairds 400 feet of
> air pipe for air compressor with suitable connexions to attach to the
> hose connexions on Gun Recuperator. Send Foreman Fitter Black,
> also send diver and tender from the Liverpool and Glasgow Salvage
> Association, but do not delay gear if diver and tender are not ready.

The minutes and hours were ticking mercilessly away. At
8 A.M., when Oram and Woods surfaced, those on board *Thetis*
had been in the same unreplenished air for 18 hours. If, as received
wide publicity at the time, the limit of endurance for a " T "-class
submarine was 36 hours, the fact of *Thetis* having double her
normal complement on board could only mean—especially as the
air supply of two compartments had been lost—that every second
of time was precious.

Unfortunately, Captain Oram was suffering badly from the
effects of carbon dioxide poisoning, and it was not until he had been
aboard *Brazen* for over an hour and a half that he recovered
sufficiently to despatch a signal based on the plan he had brought
up on his wrist.

It was at 9.43 A.M. that he informed C.-in-C. Plymouth of the
position inside the submarine when he escaped, asking for the
information to be relayed to Rear-Admiral Submarines and Cammell
Laird. " Air is urgently needed," a phrase in the message ran.
" Air in submarine is getting very foul," it concluded.

A quarter of an hour later it was ten o'clock: the middle of the
forenoon and little sign of progress. Worry and depression were
gnawing fiercely again in Mills's mind. He was tempted to break
the instructions he had had from Oram, but how could he know, he
felt, but that a whole new series of escapes would start the moment
he began shifting position. He would wait just a little longer.

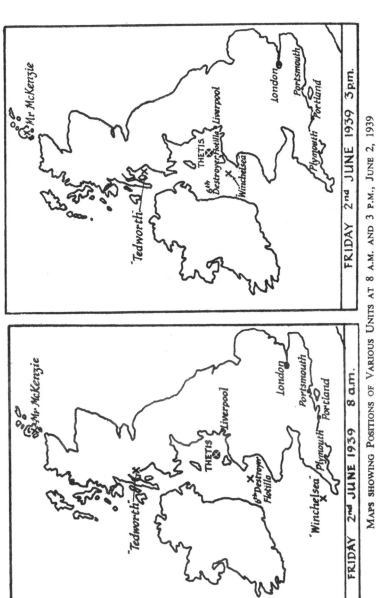

FRIDAY 2nd JUNE 1939 8 a.m.

FRIDAY 2nd JUNE 1939 3 p.m.

Maps showing Positions of Various Units at 8 a.m. and 3 p.m., June 2, 1939

It seemed as though his decision was the right one. Almost immediately there was a shout as scores of watching pairs of eyes caught sight of a splash, just about where the two officers had come up. It was another head. Just the one ? Then, after an appreciable pause, another came up a few yards away. The nearest boat was the one from *Vigilant*.

" They'll be starting now, I suppose," hazarded one of the destroyer's fo'c'sle party. " Must have been waiting to get something sorted out inside."

" Suppose so," replied his mate. " Wonder what those two bastards are thinking now ? "

Arnold could feel the fresh air on his face. Christ, it was good.

" Here you are, mate," a voice called. He turned in the water. It was a boat.

Seconds later he had been hauled over the gunwale.

" Put this round you." It was the same voice he had heard when his head broke surface. A grinning, leather-faced, stoop-shouldered little man was wrapping fold upon fold of two thick woollen blankets round him.

" We're from the *Vigilant*, that salvage vessel there," the little man continued. " Here, a minute," he went on as he reached forward and wiped a rough, dirty, brass-buttoned sleeve across Arnold's mouth. " Get some of that oil off you and then have a drag of this." He pushed a lighted cigarette between Arnold's lips.

The stoker dragged in hard and exhaled slowly. " Thanks, chum. Thanks. It's the sweetest smoke I've ever had."

By this time the boat's oars were biting into the water, and she was being heaved along to where one of *Brazen's* whalers was hurrying back from the destroyer, having just taken aboard Frank Shaw.

" We've got to transfer you over to them, mate," the little man confided. " Sorry we can't look after you ourselves. But see what you can do with this first." He produced a flask of brandy. Arnold took a long pull, then another. Immediately the warmth hit him. It was as though he was coming back to consciousness out of a daze. The warmth started in his stomach, but within moments it seemed to be all over his body. And as his senses reawakened he realized that he had the most terrible of all heads. He had known most sorts of hangovers. But this was different. And as *Vigilant's* boat swung carefully alongside the whaler he wondered whether he could even manage to step over from one to the other.

" Have another swig before you go, mate," his little benefactor's voice vibrated somewhere behind his ears.

" No thanks, chum," he managed to reply. " But, thanks for everything."

And, as the blue-uniformed, meticulously capped and chin-stayed Leading Seaman helped him ease down on the aftermost thwart, his whole inside revolted and he was sick—horribly, achingly, hideously, almost unendingly sick—all over the bottom-boards.

" Sorry to mess up your boat, chums," he murmured. " And what a bleeding waste of brandy."

Minutes later he was being helped over the side of *Brazen*. Captain Oram and a Lieutenant-Commander, who turned out to be the captain of the destroyer, were waiting for him.

" Well done," said Oram. " How are things in the boat ? "

" Three men drowned in the escape chamber just before Shaw and me," replied Arnold. " But Lieutenant Chapman told me to say that they would be escaping from the after chamber at regular intervals and to tell you to keep the rescue boats clear of the surfacing area."

" Thank you," commented Oram.

" About the ones that drowned, sir," continued Arnold. " They must have panicked when they couldn't open the hatch straight away."

" Good lad," intervened *Brazen's* captain. " You can tell us all the details when you get dry and warm again. These men here will look after you."

Arnold turned to the group of men standing quietly a few yards away. He found himself being patted encouragingly on the shoulder and taken for'ard to the seamen's bathroom. There seemed to be three of them looking after him. As his awareness of things slowly returned after the bout of sickness he felt them stripping him out of his wet and oily clothes.

Soon his naked body was being lowered into one of the Admiralty-issue round, shallow tin baths. Two of the mate-lots started pouring buckets of hot water over him, and the third was talking, although Arnold had no real idea what he was saying.

Then he was out of the bath and being rubbed with harsh, warm towels. Some one brought him a sweater and an overall, a pair of socks and canvas shoes. " Good of somebody," he murmured; for he knew that the clothes were a gift. (Even during the War the Navy never carried gear for survivors: but rescuing crews invariably gave away their own property rather than see a man in discomfort.)

He was taken into the adjoining seamen's mess-deck. " Have some hot soup, Scouse," he was urged. He smiled at his nickname. He wasn't aware of having said much, but his Liverpool accent must have come through, none the less.

"No, thanks. Don't feel like it. Don't think it would stay down. But I could do with a fag." He selected one from the half-dozen that were immediately pushed at him. Two full packets were slipped quietly into his overall pocket. He drew in the comforting smoke and sat relaxing. He was noticing with appreciation that while people were speaking to him the whole time no one was asking him any questions.

It was then that a young stoker—the others seemed to call him Charley—pushed his way in front of Arnold. He had a bottle in his hand, full of a scintillating, golden-brown, rich-looking liquid that needed no identifying: naval rum from Jamaica.

"Here you are. This is from the stokers. We're only sorry there's not more of your mates to share it yet."

Arnold took the bottle a trifle hesitantly and had a gentle swig. "Thanks, Charley," he smiled as he handed it back, "but I couldn't possibly drink any more." The young stoker took the bottle back, grinned, and disappeared.

Two minutes later he had returned. He was still holding the bottle of rum and offering it to Arnold. "You've got to take it," he said, "or else they'll knock my bloody block off."

"O.K., Charley," Arnold told him. "I'll have another try." This time he put the equivalent of two tots, or about quarter of a pint, down his throat before once again handing the bottle. This seemed to satisfy Charley's messmates, for the youngster did not this time reappear.

Bathed and refreshed, Arnold felt he should make his way up to the bridge. In theory there ought to be some more heads breaking surface in the deserted patch of water between the two vessels. At the top of the steel ladder he could see Oram, Woods, and Shaw standing in a group. As soon as they caught sight of him Woods shook his head slowly.

So no more had come out, thought Arnold. And no more will, he suddenly told himself. Whatever the theories might be, he knew that his premonition was right. And what he had seen in the last hours and minutes before he climbed into the escape chamber confirmed this ugly thought. He had been by far the fittest man there, he now realized. He remembered the conviction with which he had decided that Shaw was the only other person worth chancing an escape with. And over half the people he had left had then already reached such a soporific state that they would not even be able to make an attempt at escape, let alone hope to succeed. God, how awful!

He turned to an officer on *Brazen's* bridge and indicated the tail of the submarine.

" Unless air is got to them they won't be able to get out, sir, I'm certain," he said.

The officer nodded and turned quietly away to join a small conference that was going on at the other wing of the bridge. Arnold kept looking at *Thetis*. He had not realized the boat's extreme angle until he saw her this time. Surprisingly, it hadn't seemed so bad inside.

" Arnold." It was *Brazen's* coxswain at his elbow. " I think you should come down to my office and let me take your temperature. Ought just to have a look at you, you know."

This seems odd, thought Arnold. There was no sign of asking any of the others. Perhaps they've been done already. Perhaps the coxswain just takes his medical duties seriously. But as the door of the coxswain's office clicked unnecessarily shut he began to realize.

" Had to say something to get you below," the coxswain grinned. " My name's George Rose. Ex-submariner. Here, have a tot."

So the ritual continued. It was broken only when news came down that a seaplane had arrived with a doctor on board, and had landed near *Brazen*. Arnold rejoined the group on the bridge. The same whaler that had brought him aboard was ferrying the doctor across. Soon a gold-and-red striped, uniformed arm was saluting the captain of *Brazen* before turning to the four of them. He examined Shaw first, telling him to look up at the sun. Shaw did so, and Arnold noticed that he blinked rather a lot. The doctor sent him below.

It was Arnold's turn next. He was determined not to blink as he felt perfectly fit enough—even if the fitness were a species of Dutch (or Jamaican) courage—not to fall into the clutches of the Medical Branch. He succeeded in not blinking too. But he was still ordered below to the sickbay. Shaw wasn't there, he found, but, before he could ask anyone why, the doctor had followed him down, pushed a handful of pills at him, and injected him in the left arm.

" Just get your head down for a little while in that sickbay cot," he was told. " A short rest will make you feel fine."

Bloody nonsense, Arnold thought. There's nothing wrong with me. I'm not even tired.

And so thinking he lost consciousness.

Meanwhile, in *Vigilant*, Captain Hart and his assistants had been pondering the action they should take if the situation did not change soon. In addition to the messenger wire that they had fixed to *Thetis's* stern they had had a light line, weighted in the middle to keep it down, pulled under the for'ard end of the submarine. The purpose of this was to help a diver in locating the fore hatch and the gun recuperator valve as soon as the flood-tide slackened and allowed him to make a descent. But, as they all appreciated, the strength of the tide in that part of the Bay was such that Diver Frederick Orton would not be able to go down until immediately before High Water. And the limit of his time down would be only about half an hour.

Another of Captain Hart's senior men, Mr Charles Brock, the Wreck Master of the Mersey Docks and Harbour Board, was in one of *Vigilant's* boats. A few seconds before Shaw and Arnold had come up he had seen a very distinctive air bubble break surface close to the stern of the submarine. When first one head and then the other followed the bubble he not unnaturally concluded cause and effect.

It was not very long afterwards, only a little while after the two men had been taken one after the other aboard *Brazen*, that Brock saw another air bubble, unquestionably the same as the earlier one, come up in the identical position. And at the same time, seemingly synchronizing with the emergence of the bubble, he could hear a sound of hammering from where the submarine lay.

" There'll be two more up any second," he excitedly told the seamen in the boat, confident that his deduction was correct. But the seconds dragged on and no heads broke surface. Brock grew despondent.

Then, suddenly, some five or ten minutes after the first fruitless phenomenon of sight and sound, there came another burst of underwater hammering and another huge, identical bubble. Brock strained his eyes at the patch of water. For several seconds his wishful imagination played him false. There was an unusually large ripple, perhaps a backwash of the air bubble, which, for a fraction of a moment, he thought might be a head breaking surface. He saw an eddy and a shadow—or perhaps he thought he did. But before long he told himself the truth: what he had seen and heard was certainly not the forerunner of a *successful* escape, whatever else it might have been.

In Captain Hart's mind one series of thoughts, plans, and calculations jostled with another the whole time. There was the possibility of holding up the stern of the submarine, to make sure that it didn't slip back below the water with any change of the tide. The need for this was growing with the increasing depth of water coming in on the flood. Soon after Arnold and Shaw had come to the surface the angle of the submarine's stern had increased by about five degrees from what it had been when *Vigilant* arrived. But what was to be done ? Captain Oram's instructions had been quite categoric about the danger to people escaping if any heavy vessel approached too near the submarine. And, calculated Hart, neither a destroyer nor a small salvage vessel, nor even both combined, could possibly hold up the half of an ocean-going submarine.

The trouble was that he had not had a talk with Oram and therefore did not know the state of the trim in *Thetis*. Had he been able to do so he would have known how little weight there actually was in the ballast-free tail of the submarine, and his calculations might well have reached a different conclusion. Regrettably there was no fit senior submarine officer present to advise him.

It was at 10.40 A.M. that the Sixth Destroyer Flotilla, commanded by Captain R. S. G. Nicholson, in H.M.S. *Somali*, arrived from Portland. They had come at tremendous speed and looked a magnificent sight as they steamed in perfect formation from the south-west. Immediately Captain Hart went across to *Somali* to tell Captain Nicholson, now the senior officer present, what had happened so far and what had been done to prepare to put Oram's plan into operation. He needed, too, to make sure that the destroyer flotilla could muster 400 feet of hose suitable for pumping air into *Thetis* as soon as a connexion could be made.

Briefly the two captains weighed their own knowledge of submarines and found it very little. They could advance no reasons to fault the " keep away from the escape area until you can connect an air-pipe " instructions that Oram had brought with him.

This conclusion seemed all the more correct in the light of the impression that prevailed in both *Brazen* and *Vigilant* that Oram expected *all* the personnel of the submarine to escape successfully through the after chamber. That on the existing evidence such an expectation was completely ill-founded, nobody seemed to appreciate.

But the evidence was none the less there. Even on the most optimistic calculations of a rate of escape—and the number and frequency of escapes by that time in the forenoon could certainly not encourage optimism—the length of time that would be required for a further ninety-odd men to come out would be much, much more than the calculable CO_2-saturation of the boat would allow. And, as Arnold had known some time before his escape, the flooding of the for'ard compartment had meant that there were not sufficient D.S.E.A. sets to go round anyway.

The tragedy was that the decision to rely upon the guidance of the senior submarine officer present—namely, Oram—was taken without sufficient regard to that officer's possible physical and mental state following a most harrowing and exhausting experience. As the destroyer flotilla's Medical Officer was later to discover, Oram was—more than understandably—an ill man.

The lack of even one officer, in the vessels around *Thetis*, who was both experienced in submarines and completely fit and in full possession of his faculties, was being keenly felt. It was, one might have thought, a most obvious necessity. And yet, Captain I. A. P. Macintyre was still chugging slowly northward in the old and wheezy duty destroyer from Portsmouth. And Warrant Engineer Bob Ostler, whose intimate knowledge of the construction of an identical submarine would have been invaluable, was fretting and fuming 38 miles away at Birkenhead, trying in vain to get a hearing for his ideas for giving *Thetis* emergency two-way ventilation.

One of the things he had in mind was for the rescue vessels to drill a hole and push a tube into one of *Thetis's* aftermost tanks, and for the submarine to be held up by the destroyers with a supply of fresh air—and also egress for the foul air— being provided through the tube. As he argued each point with his engine-room artificers it became more and more clear to him that this idea would prove speedy, simple, and successful, if only he could get some one to listen to him.

The point of providing *two-way* ventilation was an important one. Not everybody, either inside or outside *Thetis* that fine Friday morning, appreciated that the air supply to the gun recuperator position, as proposed in Captain Oram's signal, was to be used solely for blowing the water out of the abandoned compartments. It was not intended to supply air for breathing. The reason for this was simple.

Carbon dioxide poisoning is related to the *amount* of CO_2 in the atmosphere and the *pressure* at which it is being breathed, rather than to the *proportion* of the atmosphere that it forms. If vast quantities of fresh air had been supplied to *Thetis* without there being any corresponding outlet, the absolute amount of CO_2 would naturally increase—as a direct function of people continuing to breathe—and the pressure at which breathing was taking place would be increased dramatically. The result would have been almost immediate asphyxiation. It was for this reason that Sam Bolus had not hours earlier released into the boat some of the remaining contents of his high-pressure air bottles.

Soon it was approaching High Water. Orton, *Vigilant's* diver, was already in one of the several boats laying off from *Thetis*, fully dressed except for his helmet. Shortly before 11.30 A.M. the last bolt was being screwed down and he was being helped on to the diving ladder. Slowly his heavy-booted feet clumped down step by step until he was floating in the water, waiting for his surplus air to be expelled.

There was still a certain amount of tide running as he pulled himself beneath the surface. He was using the fine galvanized wire of the indicator-buoy to guide him downward. Down he went until, through the greenness of the water, he could see the dark outline of the submarine's conning-tower. As he worked along hand over hand on the indicator-buoy wire he found that this was tangled round the bridge and the gun-platform in a number of great bights. Thinking that this must have considerably shortened its effective length, he set to work.

His first task was not, as might have been expected, to look for one of the H.P. air connexions that had been mentioned in Oram's message. Instead, he spent precious minutes, as he had been instructed, fixing guide lines for future descents. This excellent orthodox practice would have been more justifiable if life could have been expected to remain aboard *Thetis* by the next slack-water period.

In other words, there was really no future for which to prepare. Hope lay in the present—or not at all.

He then turned to the problem of connecting the air-pipe to one of the two vital connexions.

From the surface all that could be seen was the continuous, slow-moving stream of bubbles. Their regularity produced a metronomic, almost hypnotic, effect on those who stood or sat quietly watching. If one let one's mind relax one could dream sweet day-dreams of success and safety. It *must* come right, one could tell oneself.

But any illusions that there were in *Vigilant's* diving-boat were very soon shattered. In what seemed no time at all the half-hour time-limit had expired, slack water had ended and the ebb had started to run, and the diver's helmet was above the surface. Quickly he was pulled alongside the ladder. Less quickly he heaved himself up the rungs until he could get his arms and shoulders inside the boat and his helmet could be removed.

He had not succeeded. He was painfully disappointed. But there was nothing more he could do.

It was not, of course, his fault. His previous experience, as far as was known in *Vigilant*, had been limited to about 15 fathoms, or 90 feet. He was completely unfamiliar with the layout of any class of submarine, let alone of the first " T " to be built at Birkenhead. The frantic preparations of the previous night had not allowed opportunity for a quick inspection of either of the other two sister-submarines in the Cammell Laird yard, even if this had occurred to anyone.

But, for whatever reasons, an opportunity had been lost.   In the words of the Tribunal of Inquiry:

> The first High Water and diving time passed without anything effective having been done in execution of the plan for raising the ship, and the next opportunity for work by the diver would be about Low Water at 5.30 P.M.

And this really meant, as far as those in *Thetis* were concerned, that there would be no further opportunity.

At about the same time that Orton was first pulling himself down beneath the surface Lieutenant Woods came aboard *Somali* from *Brazen*, and reported to Captain Nicholson.   When he had been brought aboard *Brazen* after his escape Woods had appeared completely dazed, and seemed quite incapable of giving any assistance. He had been persuaded to rest, which he did for large parts of the forenoon.   But as his mind began to clear he realized that there was much he wanted to say.

" I'm very anxious about what's happened inside her, sir," he told Captain Nicholson.   " I think the situation is desperate, and I think it's pointless to expect any more escapes."

Nicholson thanked him and hurried across to *Vigilant* to consult with Captain Hart.   As they were talking, and torturing their minds to discover what course of action was the right one to pursue, there came the ' nil return ' from the diving-boat.

This was the deciding factor.   Belatedly perhaps—they had had strong advice to the contrary—but certainly quite wisely, they agreed to try to get the stern of the submarine high enough out of the water for a hole to be cut in her by which the whole complement could escape, or by which some one from outside could get in. So, in order to raise the stern, they gave orders for a $3\frac{1}{2}$-inch wire rope to be passed round it and made fast to the bows of *Vigilant*. All sorts of people immediately began to feel a sense of relief. The fact that some sort of positive action was at last being taken might still mean that Hope could stay and Despair be repelled.

But if Hope were to stay she demanded two things: speed of action, for Death, if not already present in *Thetis*, was not far away; and an absolute certainty that the stern would be held out of the water at whatever cost.

10

Despair

THE Metal Industries divers, under the leadership of Mr Thomas McKenzie, Chief Salvage Officer of Cox and Danks, Ltd, were busily employed beneath the waters of Scapa Flow, in the Orkney Isles. They were at work on the raising of the scuttled First World War German battle-cruiser *Derfflinger*, and the morning of June 2 found them at a depth of 138 feet.

It was 10 A.M. before McKenzie heard what had happened to *Thetis*. He immediately telegraphed to the Admiralty and to Cammell Laird, offering his services and those of his divers.

At 12.30 P.M. he received Cammell Laird's reply. " Thank you for your offer, but the ship has been located and all are reported safe."

Happy at the good news, he allowed the day's diving programme to continue uninterrupted.

While the telegraph lines between Scapa Flow and London, and between Scapa Flow and Birkenhead, had been buzzing, the divers and crew of the deep-diving vessel *Tedworth* had been fuming amid the frustration and delays of the Greenock coaling base. Not only were no attempts made to get them down to Liverpool Bay by road or air, but the coaling arrangements could scarcely have been worse.

Chief Petty Officer Dick Oliver, *Tedworth's* Chief Diver, was being continually assailed by members of his team. " Why the hell aren't there any special arrangements ? " he was asked. " Why do we have to wait for the ordinary day-to-day routine ? "

He tackled one of the foremen of the ' coalies ' about it. " Look," he was told. " Mind your own bloody business. The papers say that the submarine's got enough air for thirty-six hours, and nobody from the Admiralty's been hurrying us up, to the best of my knowledge. So what the hell are you yammering about ? "

Oliver returned to the diving flat. For the tenth time he and his divers sorted out the gear, hours in advance of the first opportunity they would have to use it. For the tenth time he checked through the list of divers and their attendants, and double-checked all the small items of organization, which he knew from experience could make the difference between success and failure.

He was particularly proud of his team, reckoning that the Royal Navy had never had a better crowd of deep divers than the men who had been on the point of completing their course at Inveraray. Even to go on the course was high recommendation. Each year the Admiralty selected 12 divers from the various units of the various fleets and took them to Scotland for a specialized deep-diving course. The aim was to produce men capable of going to, and working at, 50 fathoms (300 feet), a depth which was also the practical diving limit of the Navy's submarines. To reach this depth was no mean achievement for a diver. For a number of physiological reasons the large majority of qualified divers could go to 200 feet without any trouble; but the adding of the extra 100 feet was a task only for the man at the top of the profession.

Dick Oliver himself was especially qualified. Not only did he have all the possible deep-diving experience, but he had also dived on the sunken submarine *M 1*, which had been lost in collision with a merchantman 14 years previously. And he had trained in submarine salvage on the artificially scuttled *L 18*. In an extraordinarily esoteric field he was quite probably the most experienced man in the country. But long after Arnold and Shaw had escaped from *Thetis*, and at a time when the air inside the sunken submarine was calculably almost incapable of sustaining life, he was pacing the deck of a stranded coal-burner in the Clyde.

It was around noon before *Tedworth* had enough coal in her bunkers. As soon as the last of the 'coalies' could be ushered over her side her berthing hawsers were let go and she was headed for Liverpool. And as the unhappy Diver Frederick Orton was returning aboard *Vigilant* from the diving-boat, after his fruitless dip over *Thetis*, the diving team in *Tedworth* was watching the funnel and shouting blasphemous encouragement at the sweating stokers of the 'Black Squad.'

"Come on, m'lads," one of the divers called down, "see if you can make up some of the leeway that the lackadaisical bloody Admiralty has caused."

Back in the Cammell Laird yard another man was cursing the inflexibility of authority. Bob Ostler was still making efforts to 'sell' his emergency ventilation idea. He had first suggested it soon after the news that *Thetis* had been found had reached Birkenhead. Certainly the proposal could have been signalled to those in charge out in Liverpool Bay in plenty of time before the morning

High Water. The two senior naval officers said that they entirely agreed with him, and assured him that his suggestions would " be thought of and fully considered by the people on the spot." But this was not what Ostler wanted. He asked to be allowed to go out to Liverpool Bay and present his ideas at first hand. " That," he was told, " is neither desirable nor necessary."

After this last and obviously unalterable refusal he left his office and went out through the yard gates. He knew it was his duty to comfort the crowds of relatives he would find there.

The women were calm, but anxious. They turned to him, saying they wanted to be told the truth, but clutching at the hope that they wanted him to give them. " In my opinion a large number can be saved. I hope they will be. Everything possible is being done," he replied. But he knew this last to be untrue, and could only pray that his face would not disclose his heart.

At Submarine Headquarters at Gosport similar ideas were being put forward. Two Chief Petty Officer D.S.E.A. Coxswains—Harry Rowkins (who had supervised the final installation of the escape gear in *Thetis*) and George Howard—had volunteered to help. One of their ideas was to execute, in self-contained breathing apparatus, a scheme for supplying ventilation through one of the underwater guns. They also had plans, admittedly ones entailing great personal risk to themselves, to enter the submarine through the escape chamber.

The new " T "-class submarines were unusual in having as many as three underwater guns (or signal-flare ejectors). And two of the three were situated aft, in such a position that one of them would be not more than 15 or 20 feet below the surface at the angle at which *Thetis* was lying. This meant that a four-inch diameter orifice, capable of having caulked into it a pipe wide enough to provide two-way ventilation, was available at a depth shallow enough for a diver to attempt working outside the limits of dead slackwater.

The only problem lay in getting the minimum amount of co-operation necessary from inside the submarine. Two valve handles would need to be turned to open a sluice and the breach. And who could say but that, if the plan could be put into operation early enough, before conditions in *Thetis* became too bad, this co-operation could not be satisfactorily described from outside, and then satisfactorily obtained? So argued Rowkins and Howard.

The Senior Submarine Staff Officer heard their proposals. Immediately he arranged for them to be flown up to Liverpool Bay, where, within a short space of hours, they arrived, setting an example to their senior officer ineffectually chugging his way northward. Their services and their suggestions were placed before Captain Nicholson in *Somali*.

The underwater gun had already figured in the conversations aboard *Vigilant* and the destroyer, but, unfortunately, Captain Hart had been given to understand that the aperture was still a considerable distance beneath the surface, and the idea was condemned. Nor would Captain Nicholson agree to let Rowkins and Howard try to get into *Thetis* through the escape compartment. This he described as " a most hazardous proposal."

Was he right in stopping the two brave men? Had he considered the value of risking two lives, if by so doing he might have saved 90 or more? Rowkins and Howard argued their ideas impassionedly. They were, of course, arguing in a world which knew none of the present-day popularity of underwater swimming. Nor was there any general knowledge of a technique for getting into and out of a submarine, such as was later developed for the Navy's X-craft. But the actual entry that they proposed would have offered few obstacles to men as skilled and as resolute as they.

Once they could knock off the retaining clip on the outside of the escape hatch they would be free to enter and operate the chamber to their own ends. And if the men in the adjoining compartment in *Thetis* were still capable of realizing anything, they would quickly have appreciated that something was going on in the chamber to their advantage.

What in the heat of the moment Rowkins and Howard did not fully understand, as they cursed the barrier that Captain Nicholson had put in front of them, was that the destroyer officer had only his own opinion and, possibly, also that of Captain Oram on which to rely. Without experience of submarines he had no means of weighing Rowkins' and Howard's knowledge of the risks that they were prepared to accept, nor of judging the likely benefits that might accrue. Indeed, it would have been grossly unfair to Captain Nicholson to assume that he knew more than the Chief of Staff to Flag Officer Submarines, who had already clearly demonstrated that he could see none of the need for hurried action that the two Chief Petty Officers were so insistently urging.

But there was a good reason for refusing to allow Rowkins and Howard to attempt to enter *Thetis*. It was true, as they said, that any plan needed co-operation from inside the submarine and that their scheme was the best way of ensuring co-operation. But this presupposed that there was a plan for which they could be spokesmen. They knew that the effect on them of suddenly entering an atmosphere highly charged with CO_2 would have been extreme. It would not be long before they would lose consciousness, and they might well not last as long as many of those inside *Thetis*, who had been brought gradually to the high level of CO_2 concentration. It was therefore essential that all the necessary outside arrangements should be ready before any attempt to enter the submarine was made. But whether these outside arrangements encompassed holding *Thetis* up or providing her with ventilation or cutting a hole for her complement to escape—or any combination of the three—all that Rowkins and Howard could see spelled lethargy, foolish optimism, and delay.

It was only the coldest of comfort for them to learn later of another Chief Petty Officer, whose offers of help had been much less courteously and much more foolishly refused. At the same time as they were putting their ideas to the Senior Submarine Staff Officer at Gosport, Frank Jenner, one of the senior divers from the Naval Diving School at Portsmouth, was also applying for permission to be flown up to *Thetis*.

" No," he was told. " You know that I have to keep you here for an emergency."

Back in *Vigilant* the two ends of the 3½-inch wire hawser had been made fast. The wire led from the salvage vessel's bows, round the stern of the submarine, and back again. The time was ten past one in the afternoon, 48 minutes short of the time that would mark *Thetis*'s complete 24 hours submerged.

" Heave in handsomely," came the command to the man on *Vigilant*'s for'ard winch. With a click, the heavy clutch was engaged, and, with a grunt, the winch-drums started taking the strain. And as the steam wheezed its way into the winch's power-unit, and as the spindle slowly chugged its way round, the free end of the wire began moving almost imperceptibly inboard.

Vigilant's bo's'n was standing with one foot on the taut wire, ready to judge from his years of experience if an undue lack of resilience in the feel of the wire should betoken any likelihood of its parting.

" I think her stern is just beginning to move," he called to the men in his fo'c'sle party. But almost immediately he was wanted aft, to secure the lines from two of the tugs that had not long arrived on the scene. Within minutes they were towing *Vigilant* astern, and the combined efforts of the three vessels were soon to be seen on *Thetis*.

By 1.30 P.M. she was noticeably higher out of the water. The whole of her propellers were well clear, and a sizeable piece of her after hull had been exposed.

" 'Vast heaving," the fo'c'sle party were ordered. " 'Vast towing," was shouted to the tugs.

These manœuvres had been surrounded by a circle of expectant ships. *Brazen* was actually making arrangements to leave Liverpool Bay and resume her journey back to Devonport, having been informed by Captain Nicholson that her services were now no longer required. And the whole flotilla of new, shining, sleek, swift *Tribal*-class destroyers seemed to have come in closer to the tragedy. How much more able than *Vigilant*, it seemed to a few of the people present, would a couple of these steel warhorses have been, to guarantee the safety above water of the stern of *Thetis*.

Wreck Master Brock, who had earlier watched the meaningless bubbles and heard the unexplained hammerings from inside *Thetis*, was back in one of *Vigilant's* boats again, to carry out the next stage of the plan.

" Easy oars," the boat's coxswain called. " Watch your blades starboard side," he continued as the boat scraped gently along the submarine's stern plates. " There you are, Mr Brock, she's all yours."

Brock managed to find both handhold and foothold, and pulled himself up on to the wet, sloping, slippery hull. Somebody passed up to him his bag of tools. Kneeling precariously, he started work. His immediate target was one of the manholes near the stern. He had been told that it was fitted, first with an outer cover plate, and then with an inner cover. With a quick look down at the boat, some 14 or 15 feet beneath him, he levered his heavy screwdriver against the four screws of the outer plate. They offered little real resistance. Thank goodness *Thetis* was a new submarine, he thought. At least, the supposedly movable parts hadn't had time to go solid. But it was still a slow job.

" I'm starting on the inner cover," he shouted down to the boat. This time he selected a spanner and fitted it around the bolt-head. Slowly he applied the force of his arm and shoulder. The first bolt moved slightly. He pushed harder, and it moved still more. Then, just as the bolt started shifting freely, he stopped suddenly. He thought he heard a hissing of air. Another slight turn. The hissing increased. And then, a fraction of a turn later, as the lifting of the bolt allowed the two surfaces of metal to come clearly apart, it became a distinct jet—of air under pressure. To make sure that it was not a momentary phenomenon Brock turned two or three more of the bolts. As the freeing of one after another opened up a gap along a sizeable section of the perimeter of the manhole the pressure produced a snarling, frightening surge of air from inside the submarine.

Brock had not been prepared for this. Was it a good thing to let the pressure escape? Would he be ruining some internal plan for building up buoyancy?

Rapidly he swung his spanners back on to the bolts he had freed. In a matter of seconds the inner cover was tight again, and the frightening noise had stopped. He shouted down to the boat what he had done.

He hung to his precarious perch as his information was relayed back to *Vigilant* and while those on board the salvage vessel pondered what should be done. There was distinct movement to be combated. It was the same sort of feeling that one got in a ship at anchor, before the changing tide caused her head to swing. He clung a little tighter, and listened in vain for sounds from inside *Thetis*. His progress up the slippery tail and his heavy-handed swinging at the manhole bolts must have been clearly audible on the other side of the pressure-hull. And yet, no sound in reply.

But that did not mean that all hope was gone, he told himself. And, in the wave of confidence that came over him, he was relieved when the message came back from *Vigilant*, " Carry on." He had been clinging to the submarine by this time for the best part of an hour. Once again he began unscrewing the bolts.

One by one the group of ships had started shuffling round, to come head on to the newly running ebb-tide. As far as *Thetis* was concerned, any movement in her was apparent only to Brock. There seemed to be no visible change in her position or stability from where her would-be salvors watched on *Vigilant's* bridge. Not until 2.40 P.M.

Then, quite quickly for so awkwardly poised a vessel, she pivoted round on her stem. Within a few moments her stern was pointing to the west, with the result that the west-running ebb was pushing hard against her, acting to force her back beneath the surface.

When she first swung Brock clung tight.

" Come down, Mr Brock," shouted the coxswain.

He hesitated, but the instructions were repeated from *Vigilant* and, as the submarine swivelled still farther, he quickly tightened up the bolts once again and scrambled down the greasy, grey plates, back into the fitfully bobbing boat. Somehow the coxswain had managed to keep close enough in to pick up his passenger without getting caught up in the dangerously uncertain gyrations of *Thetis's* stern.

Subdued, they pulled back to *Vigilant*. Temporarily, at least— but perhaps permanently, they realized—another chance had gone.

Before they were alongside *Vigilant* a fast, hard-chine, three-seater motor-boat (known to the initiated as a ' skimming dish ') had bounced over the surface of the water. With a flurry of spray it had shuddered and stopped by the salvage vessel's ladder, and Captain Nicholson had jumped out and bounded aboard.

"The position is desperate," he told Captain Hart. "Something more must be done—and at once."

"I'm sorry, but I'm afraid the only course to take is to hold her stern in position until Low Water, and then to heave her up sufficiently to cut a hole in the stern."

"But Low Water is the best part of three hours away and the position is desperate. I suggest that *Vigilant*, with the tugs to help her, should try to tow her stern higher out of the water, at once, so that we can cut a hole large enough for the men in her to get out without any loss of time."

But Captain Hart could not agree. "I think that any towing might cause her to cant round again. We might do serious damage to her."

"But think of the critical state of the men inside her," Nicholson riposted. "With them in mind we must take any risk—even a risk involving them."

This argument eventually prevailed. The two men eyed each other, nodded, and returned without further loss of time to their respective posts in the next stage of the enterprise.

Once they had decided on action, things moved fast. *Vigilant* steamed in close to *Thetis*, taking in the slack on the 3½-inch wire, and preparing to heave in once again at the submarine's stern. Minutes later *Somali* had berthed alongside *Vigilant*, in order to use her electric drill for cutting a hole in the submarine's stern. But as she did so the group of ships was joined by the tug *Crosby*, bringing the oxy-acetylene cutting gear that Captain Hart had signalled for five and a half hours previously. Quickly *Crosby* and *Somali* changed places. And once more the winch on *Vigilant's* fo'c'sle began heaving in, and the two tugs astern *Vigilant* began towing the salvage vessel. Slowly the stern of the submarine increased its angle and came farther and farther out of the water. Captain Nicholson's plan was working.

A quiet, almost cheerful, perhaps congratulatory murmur of conversation ran round the decks of the assembled ships as, inch by inch, more and more of *Thetis's* plates showed above the surface. Then, quite without warning, in less time than it took any of the watching men to draw breath, the stern suddenly started to cant over.

"'Vast heaving," was called on the instant. But, in the few seconds before the brake could bite and the steam be shut off from the winch, the angle of *Thetis's* stern had fallen through several degrees.

Her stability had gone. What Captain Hart feared had in fact taken place. Dismayed comments ran amok. " She's going." . . . " No, we'll hold her." . . . " What's going to happen ? " . . . " Can we do it ? " And doubtless there was a certain element present who wondered why the stricken submarine could not have been held up by two vessels (even two spanking new destroyers), lashed one on either side, instead of being pulled about by a wire.

Thetis was canting farther and farther over. The strain on the 3½-inch steel-wire rope, the same size hawser that the submarine would have used as one of its several berthing springs, any time it made fast alongside a mooring-place, was tremendous. The strain on the hearts and minds of the men who were endeavouring to secure the welfare of the men aboard her was scarcely less great.

For seconds *Thetis* seemed to stop moving. The singing of the tautened wire intensified. Then . . . *cccrrrack!* With a thunderous pistol-shot, that nearly split the ear-drums of the whole of the terror-struck assembly, the wire parted. As it snapped the two free ends, either side of the break, whip-lashed up into the air and flailed back across *Vigilant's* decks.

Momentarily, there were sighs of relief as it was realized that no one had been in the way—no injuries, no mutilations, no fatalities. But in the same moment all eyes refocused on *Thetis*.

Free from the wire that had first pulled her off her balance and then sought to sustain her, the submarine slid quietly and gracefully —barely leaving a ripple to mark her disappearance—beneath the surface. It was ten past three.

" She's gone ! " And so she had. With the going of the substance those up top were doubtless glad to clutch at what shadow remained. So it must have provided some grain of diminution of the tragedy that had occurred when it was realized that—for the time being— her stern had subsided, not right down to the sea-bed, but only a matter of feet below the surface. Speedily *Vigilant* got another wire made fast to her as her shape still peered hauntingly up from just underneath the little wave-tops.

It was not long then before she slid down farther and could be seen no more.

Hope had demanded an absolute certainty that *Thetis's* stern would be held out of the water at whatever cost. The stern had disappeared. At a little after three o'clock in the afternoon Despair reigned unrelieved.

11

Death of a Submarine

SO LONG, sir," Arnold had murmured at Glenn as he leaned out of the chamber and beckoned to Shaw. " Be seeing you blokes soon," he had vouchsafed to the group of stokers and yardmen around the chamber. Bolus had nodded at him, and for the last time he had caught his First Lieutenant's eye. Chapman just looked at him, not moving a muscle. Arnold thought he was not going to speak. Then his lips formed an almost soundless greeting. " Good luck. Thanks."

They all watched quietly as Shaw followed Arnold through the door of the chamber. Then it was banged shut. There was a brief pause—presumably Arnold was giving Shaw a last-minute briefing, they reckoned—and then they could see the duplicated controls working inside the compartment. Arnold had commenced the flooding.

The compartment was in complete silence. Minds were remembering what had happened to the four unfortunates who had preceded Arnold and Shaw in the chamber. But surely it would be all right this time ? The waiting was eerie. After what seemed an age Chapman looked over towards Glenn. The engineer grinned quietly. " Don't worry, Bert." His throaty voice broke the silence. " Arnold'll make it."

The seconds dragged on. Every action of Arnold's on the duplicated controls within the chamber was immediately visible in both the compartments. But while some of the men were noting the progress others were quietly dropping off to sleep. In the time it took Arnold to prepare the escape and flood up the chamber a number of his well-wishers became no longer actively interested in his and Shaw's success.

Then, as if to confirm Glenn's confidence, quite suddenly, as though at the turn of a switch, the same shaft of light that they had seen when Oram and Woods had got out shone down through the water in the chamber, and lit up the circle of grey in the scuttle.

" The hatch is open. Thank God ! "

Instead of the cheer that had marked Oram's and Woods's success, the realization of this escape brought forth nothing more than a relieved murmur of congratulation and—in the case, at least, of the fitter men around the chamber—of hope. A fair amount of time had elapsed since the earlier escape, and conditions had got very much worse. Active rejoicing would have needed more energy than most of them could have found.

The carbon dioxide concentration was increasing every minute. It was, in fact, way above the normally accepted fatal density. Only the slow acclimatization of the long day and night hours had managed to provide a sort of immunity. But the time at which the atmosphere in *Thetis* would no longer sustain life could not be long away.

Bolus, Chapman, and Glenn looked at the men around them. They had to decide who should make the next attempt to escape. By a process of natural selection the men in the steering compartment tended to be those who were least badly affected by the quality of the air. Although, as Bolus realized, there were a number of submariners who were deliberately remaining for'ard to give others in the boat a better chance of getting out. He could name several of his Chiefs and Petty Officers, and some of the ' passenger ' officers, in this category.

Of the men in the steering compartment, however, and setting themselves aside, the three officers could see at least a dozen who still seemed in a fit state to escape. At least a dozen who were withstanding the searing headaches of the carbon dioxide. At least a dozen—in spite of the fact that at the end of a full breath-in one felt as short of wind as if one's lungs were empty, so thin of oxygen was the air—who looked as if they could muster the necessary exertion to operate the chamber. If only the angle on the wretched boat weren't so steep they might have expected more people to cope. But the long pull ' uphill ' was frighteningly tiring. And the angle still seemed to be increasing.

" Screw down the hatch, son," Glenn croaked at the submariner who had taken Arnold's place beside the chamber. " We'll want it shut for the next pair."

" Aye, aye, sir."

The touch of formality had a heartening effect, and as one man screwed down on the hatch-closing gear, another pulled himself over to operate the drain valves and empty the chamber as soon as the hatch was shut.

In between panting breaths the man Glenn had addressed kept revolving the operating wheel, and the external gearing was slowly forcing the hatch back on its seating. Soon it was shut, and the water was draining down. In a matter of minutes the chamber would be ready again.

Taking a breath and a rest after he had reported the hatch shut, the man at the operating wheel reached up for it once more. He was carrying out the remainder of the drill. The remote control gear that was used to close the hatch could not be used to open it. On the contrary, the gearing that had been wound across the top of the hatch to close it from inside the submarine would prevent the hatch being opened again until it was completely unwound. For this purpose the operating wheel had to be turned back, through a number of revolutions, to its opposite limit—to the ' hatch spindle free to revolve ' position. Then, and only then, the hatch could be opened from the inside. This was the drill that the man at the operating wheel was all set to complete.

He took a breath. He reached up for the wheel. He turned it back. But only for one revolution ! The drill was not complete.

What happened will never be known. Perhaps there was some distraction. Perhaps it was at that moment that Chapman announced the names of the next pair to get out. Perhaps all that occurred was that one man's tired, starved, denuded mental processes at last stopped working properly. But whatever the reason, the hatch-closing gear was still to a very large extent foul of the hatch. And nobody knew.

By this time the chamber was drained down and the door had been re-opened. Two more men were struggling aft to take their places under the escape hatch. Bolus had called up from the engine-room *Thetis's* young navigating officer, Lieutenant W. A. W. Poland. It was essential at this stage that the success of Arnold and Shaw should be capitalized. What was wanted was another first-time escape with no fuss and no nonsense. That would put heart into those who were to follow. And Poland looked just the man to lead such an attempt. To accompany him Chapman had pointed to one of the Cammell Laird men from the group in which Shaw had been standing. The principle of one submariner and one civilian was being preserved.

From inside the steering compartment the attempt followed, to start with, exactly the same pattern as its predecessor. The door was shut . . . then a pause . . . then the flood valve was opened. Two or three minutes later they knew that the vent valve was being worked. That meant that the water was almost up to the hatch. They would be out soon.

For Poland and his companion things went quite satisfactorily to start with. The water came up, not too slowly. The D.S.E.A. sets presented no problems. The vent valve seemed to let out the last of the air.

Poland swung on the hatch clip. The lever moved at the first attempt. The locking mechanism was free. All that was needed was one good push, and the hatch would be open. And then the two of them would be on their way up to the surface—to freedom.

He squared his shoulders and pushed. The hatch lifted and then stuck. As it did so a huge bubble of air—all that had been trapped above the inboard vent and below the rim of the hatch—squeezed its way out and sped upward.

The hatch had lifted four inches. Poland kept pushing. But without success. He reached down for the heavy spanner that he knew was lying at the bottom of the chamber and found the watchful hand of his companion already passing it up to him. With what movement he could manage in the restricted space of the chamber, and cushioned as he was by the pressure of the water, he swung at the underside of the hatch. One, two, three. Then three more heavy blows. But the hatch still refused to move. Sucking deeply from the corners of his breathing bag, he pulled himself up closer and bang-bang-banged again. To no avail.

Exhausted both in body and mind, he let the spanner float down to the bottom of the chamber. He pulled down the hatch and heaved the clip across. They were shut in again. Quickly he signalled for the chamber to be drained down. Soon the two of them would be back in the safety—ironical thought—of the steering compartment.

Inside *Thetis*, as the water started draining down, people realized that the attempt had not succeeded. And in a boat on the surface of Liverpool Bay Wreck Master Brock had been first excited by the air bubble and the hammering and then dejected because no escapes resulted.

And it was while the water was still draining down that Lieutenant Poland collapsed—and died. Either his violent exertions in trying to open the hatch had used up the last of the oxygen in his exhausted escape apparatus, or—and this is much more likely—the rapid coursing of the riotous oxygen through his blood vessels, inflicted on a constitution that had been terribly weakened by continuous exposure to bad air, had proved more than he could stand. If he was not quite dead when the men in the steering compartment pulled him out of the chamber, then he died very soon afterwards.

They dragged his body farther aft and down into the machinery space. Sadly and quietly Bolus conferred with his First Lieutenant and his engineer. They decided to continue with their attempts.

The Cammell Laird man who had been in the chamber with

Poland was sitting, haggard and demoralized, propped against one of the benches of the stokers' mess. He had not bothered to take off his empty escape apparatus. Slowly he wheezed out what little he knew.

Bolus wasted no time. If he were to re-establish morale he must have another escape as soon as possible. Anyway, the air in the boat would soon be so bad that no one would be able to arouse even the energy to climb into the chamber. As he looked around him—from his vantage-point at the bulkhead door he could see into both the steering compartment and the engine-room—fully half of the men in the boat were already wearing escape sets ready for use. Quickly he and Chapmen picked on two men, one submariner and one civilian. These two, in turn, pulled themselves, and were pushed and pulled along by the men near them, up to the side of the chamber.

" Look," they were told, " the hatch appears to have stuck . . . probably got jammed by the angle . . . but, don't worry . . . Lieutenant Poland will probably have loosened it . . . but, for God's sake . . . don't bang at it too long . . . shut it, and we'll drain down . . . if it doesn't open . . . almost straight away."

Slowly the items of the previous attempt were repeated. The chamber started flooding. The hatch clip came off and the bubble of air surged up to the surface. The hatch stuck barely four inches off its seating. And, in spite of another bout of furious banging and hammering, it refused to move any higher. Once again the hatch was shut and the chamber began draining. This time the two men had stopped struggling with the hatch before it was too late. Dejected, but nevertheless alive, they were helped back into the steering compartment.

The hatch had won. It seemed that it was stuck beyond relieving. Minds must have sagged beneath the pressure of yet another imposition of a baleful Fate. Certainly none of the minds in the steering compartment thought to check with the hatch-closing gear for the source of the trouble. Thinking processes were far too dulled to be analysing cause and effect.

The atmosphere was one of resignation. Either one was so dazed, already so half-asleep as a result of the lack of oxygen in one's body, that one quite happily resigned the responsibility for thinking and worrying to other people in the boat. Or, if one still accepted some responsibility for thinking, one reasoned that all that could humanly be done from inside *Thetis* had already been done. It was ' their ' move up top, now. And, surely, if no one came up soon, ' they ' would appreciate that some action was needed from ' them.'

The boat was getting quite cold. The batteries were no longer discharging heavily; no machinery was running; there was scarcely any oxygen in the air to generate heat. With the cessation of activity the coldness of the deep water in which the bows of *Thetis* lay wedged was permeating up through the boat.

Bolus passed the word for'ard for people to move together as much as possible. The few people who were still right down in the control-room and in the for'ard accommodation spaces were told to come up into the engine-room. " Daddy " Jackson was among them, and it spoke much for his determination that in spite of his age and size he was able to manœuvre himself successfully against the slope.

" All moved aft, sir," Chapman was able to whisper, soon. " About thirty-odd in the steering compartment and almost seventy in the engine-room."

" Thanks, Bert." Bolus paused. " Closed up together, they ought to keep a bit warmer."

Then his eye caught sight of a young stoker at the after end of the engine-room. He was shivering and looking extremely cold and weary. He seemed to be short of warm clothing.

Bolus took off his uniform jacket. " Here," he said, " take this. Put it on. I'm warm enough anyway."

The boy hesitated.

" Go on," Bolus urged him. " It's not every day you get the chance to be a Lieutenant-Commander."

And as Bolus quietly heaved himself back around the bulkhead into the steering compartment and propped himself up with a shirt-sleeved arm, a light ripple of laughter undulated around the engine-room. And the young stoker hoped nobody saw that he had to wipe something that almost felt like a tear from his cheek. Warmer or not, a lot of the ninety-odd men were certainly a morsel happier.

The minutes dragged into hours. Nobody moved. Scarcely anybody talked. Quite a few slept, and it seemed kinder not to wake them and not to inquire too closely into the nature of their sleep. And if any of those awake had dreaded the waiting, they found it—if they even bothered their minds sufficiently to consider it—distinctly bearable. Perhaps the pages of a mental scrap-book turned gently before them: wife, children, home, fiancée, a beer at the local, and that day when old Joe next to you had . . .

Or perhaps the very inactivity was solace enough in itself. They were almost, had they thought, the latter-day Lotus-eaters. For they too were saying:

Let us alone. What pleasure can we have
To war with evil ? Is there any peace
In ever climbing up the climbing wave ?
All things have rest, and ripen toward the grave
In silence; ripen, fall and cease:
Give us long rest or death, dark death, or dreamful ease.

How sweet it were, hearing the downward stream,
With half-shut eyes ever to seem
Falling asleep in a half-dream ! . . .

Surely, surely, slumber is more sweet than toil, the shore
Than labour in the deep mid-ocean, wind and wave and oar;
Oh rest ye, brother mariners, we will not wander more.

And when Mr Brock started scrambling over the tail of *Thetis* above their heads, and then began banging at the manhole covers above ' Z ' tank, it is doubtful if the noises meant—for most of the men, certainly—anything more than a background lullaby for their rest, their day-dreams, and their slumber.

The metallic cradle-song continued, then stopped, then started again. They had by this time set on one side any concept of time. The mists were forming—slowly, surely, but sweetly.

Then, as if a giant hand had seized the submarine and twisted it round, there came the first of the huge jerks that caused Mr Brock to be recalled. The twistings and turnings of *Thetis* stirred some of the men out of their reverie. A fleeting recognition of the urgency of their situation, and of the apparent need for them to save themselves if they were to be saved at all, spurred some of the stouter hearts to action.

" We'll have another go."

" Have to tell them . . . that there's not long now."

" Perhaps that jerk . . . will have shifted . . . the hatch."

So two more men entered the chamber. At the flood valve control in the steering compartment Roy Glenn sat leaning against the bulkhead. The door was shut and the flooding system was opened to the sea. Up came the water inside the chamber. And those in the steering compartment who were still watching the proceedings just sat and waited.

Then it happened. Perhaps the two men trying to escape had got as far as trying the hatch. Perhaps they had not. Certainly nobody had turned off the flood valve and the chamber was still open to sea-pressure. But whatever the state of things inside the narrow confines of the escape contraption, whatever tragedy had occurred or had even appeared to occur to the two men struggling in their dungeon of loneliness, one of them opened the for'ard door of the chamber—into the engine-room.

For the second time in two days *Thetis* found herself in a submarine's state of ultimate catastrophe: two adjacent apertures were open simultaneously, and the awe and majesty of the sea could find nothing to gainsay it admittance.

First, it had been the two doors of No. 5 torpedo tube. Now, it was the flood valve and the engine-room door of the escape compartment.

The water poured in. At a depth of 25 feet the flood valve was admitting the sea to the chamber, and thence to the rest of the boat, at a rate of three-quarters of a ton a minute. Together with the water came the bodies of the two men. One of them caught the latch of the opened door with some of the loose clothing round his waist. He hung there, suspended amid the torrent of water, with no one to help him.

The operating of the chamber had been controlled from the steering compartment. The men in the engine-room were, for the most part, scarcely aware of what was happening. And the door between the engine-room and the steering compartment was closed. No chance shout was able to penetrate the ventilation flaps in the bulkhead and warn Roy Glenn—still sitting with one hand on the compartment flood valve control—the moment the chamber door suddenly opened. Isolated in the security and ignorance of the after escape chamber position, he did not know that a few quick turns of the valve handle might have saved their lives at that instant —or, more correctly, might have prolonged for a little while longer the half-life that remained.

Nor did he ever know what had happened. Within seconds— a bare minute or so at the most—he and all the other occupants of His Majesty's Submarine *Thetis* succumbed to the abrupt rise in the concentration of carbon dioxide that the rapid increase of pressure instantaneously caused. Long, long before sufficient water had entered to bring about the struggle and fight against drowning, the merciful gas had quietly and quickly taken them all away—many of them in their sleep—into the downward stream of death.

For a brief eternity some of them watched with silent fascination as the water kept pouring in. Nothing represented any kind of mental effort. And then things quite peacefully stopped.

Their being had ripened, fallen, and ceased.

It was three o'clock on a Friday afternoon. The men in *Thetis* had died, but the death of the submarine still continued.

For a while the additional weight of water, finding its way for'ard into the deeper compartments, acted to keep her upright. Then, with the loss of buoyancy caused by the unremitting filling of the boat, the thin hawser between the submarine and the surface parted under the strain. The stern zig-zagged slowly down, and, as the water kept pouring in, creating aft, around where Roy Glenn and the others sat in the steering compartment, a sort of reverential air-lock, *Thetis* slid gradually through the dark, quiet waters that had overcome her, until she came to rest in the mud of Liverpool Bay.

At three o'clock that Friday afternoon the destroyer *Winchelsea*, with Captain I. A. F. Macintyre aboard, was passing the west coat of Caernarvonshire and approaching the Isle of Anglesey.

At the same time the diving vessel *Tedworth* was steaming down the Firth of Clyde, with the Isle of Arran to starboard and the Ayrshire coast to port.

And at the same hour Mr Thomas McKenzie, at his Scapa Flow headquarters, received a telegram from the Admiralty. It read:

> Grateful for your assistance, request you start immediately to submarine.

Together with this telegram he received another message, from the King's Harbour Master at Scapa Flow:

> *Thetis* position is desperate. There is aeroplane waiting at Longhope to take you and 3 or 4 divers to Liverpool changing at Inverness to be at Speke Aerodrome at 5 P.M.

He immediately called his divers up from the 140 feet of water in which they were working.

Macintyre, *Tedworth*, and McKenzie had, that afternoon, one thing in common. For entirely different reasons, and in entirely different circumstances, each one of them was tragically and undeniably too late.

12

2 A.M., Friday, June 2, to
4.10 P.M., Saturday, June 3

" The Admiralty regrets . . ."

DURING the morning and early afternoon of Friday, June 2, there had been mounting activity at the Cammell Laird yard. Some of it was fruitless. Chief Petty Officer Telegraphist " Egg " Barter's attempts to get out to the scene of the disaster were one example. Having quite accidentally decided not to go out in *Thetis* as a passenger, the previous morning, he felt an almost proprietorial obligation to be out in the middle of Liverpool Bay. He felt he should be doing whatever he could to help those of his mess-mates and the Cammell Laird and Admiralty men who were trapped beneath the sea.

He made his formal application to join one of the several vessels making the trip out from Birkenhead to the senior naval officer present in Cammell Laird.

" There are a number of us submarine Chiefs and Petty Officers, sir. We've got detailed experience of two absolutely identical boats being built here. May we go out to *Thetis*—just in case we can be of any help at all ? "

" No, thank you, Chief," came the reply. " The best brains are already out there."

" But they are all General Service [*i.e.*, non-submarine] brains, sir."

" I said ' No, thank you, Chief.' That's all."

Dispiritedly Barter made his way through the yard towards the gates where he knew the crowds of relatives to be waiting. The atmosphere among some of the yardmen was far from pleasant. " What are the Navy doing ? " he was asked. Sadly he turned away controversy with a quiet answer.

Among the relatives Mrs Bolus was still continuing her magnificent work. By some touch of irony she had been spending the previous evening at the cinema, before *Thetis* had been posted as overdue, and she had seen a newsreel version of the salving of the U.S. submarine *Squalus*. Back again with many of the women she had comforted and then driven home during the early hours of the morning, she was still seeking to allay anxiety while disguising her own. Rumour was running rife. Looking in many ways like the crowds that gather at the pit-head after a mining disaster, the *Thetis* next-of-kin differed in one important respect. They were so far away from the scene, in terms of both time and distance, that hours could elapse between one message and the next. There was little organized news; not through any fault of Cammell Laird but rather because there was no news in Birkenhead to give. Those in charge in Liverpool Bay were obviously far too preoccupied with the problems on the spot to worry about sending back wireless news bulletins. And, unfortunately, it was taking a tug anything between three and five and a half hours to make the journey from *Thetis* to the yard.

Also among the relatives during most of the morning and afternoon was Petty Officer Jack Webster, the Torpedo Gunner's Mate of *Trident*. He was continually trying to counteract some of the worst of the rumours, and occasionally succeeded in persuading some of the tearful wives to let him drive them home for a meal and a rest.

Like Barter, he had been trying to ' sell ' the services of his opposite numbers and himself. Knowing of Barter's lack of success, he had tried the direct approach—by telephone, straight to the Admiralty in London. Inevitably he failed too.

As he gathered together his umpteenth carload he could not restrain a dry, sympathetic, admiring smile, seeing two of the women he had taken home not half an hour previously. They had barely had time to set foot inside the door before feeling compelled to make their way back as near as possible to where their menfolk lay.

It was shortly after 10 A.M. when Mr R. S. Johnson, the Managing Director of Cammell Laird, arrived in Birkenhead. With several of his colleagues, he had been aboard the liner *Mauretania*, carrying out trials in the Firth of Clyde. As soon as he heard the news of *Thetis* the previous night he left the ship for Glasgow, whence he came down by road to Liverpool. He had not been able to leave Glasgow until 2 A.M., but he had arrived at Birkenhead eight hours later.

His journey of 213 miles had not been very much shorter than the 234 miles from Gosport that would have confronted Captain Macintyre, had he decided to come by road. At the same rate of progress an 11 P.M. departure from Submarine Headquarters would have meant an 8 A.M. arrival at Birkenhead. In other words, there could have been a senior submarine officer at the scene of the disaster from almost immediately after *Thetis* was first found.

Soon after Mr Johnson arrived he left again by sea to join the ships clustered together around the protruding stern of *Thetis*.

During the afternoon three more submariners arrived in Birkenhead. Chief Petty Officer " Charlie " Felcey, the newly appointed coxswain of *Trident*, was in charge of a draft of two stokers due to join *Thetis*. Had they travelled north two days earlier they would all three probably have been in *Thetis*, for Felcey was certain that he would have been required to join his captain, first lieutenant, and engineer officer, in a ' makee learn ' trip. As his departure, and therefore that of the two stokers, had been delayed by a purely fortuitous senior officer's inspection of the submarine in which he had previously been serving, all three of them were feeling extraordinarily fortunate—and exceedingly sad.

They dropped their baggage at the station and went direct to the Cammell Laird yard. By this time the main gates had been opened to the crowds of next-of-kin, and it was difficult to push a way through the throng that surrounded the submarine offices. Inside, Felcey found two junior sub-lieutenants, both of whom were wearing civilian clothes. Not unnaturally the crowd appeared to treat him, in his Chief Petty Officer's uniform, as much more of a symbol of authority.

There were mothers, wives, sweethearts—and reporters. All were asking for news, news, news. No matter how bad, they said, they wanted to know. But, as Felcey learned from the small amount of information available inside the office, there was nothing to tell them. As far as the relatives were concerned, they took his unsubstantial consolations very well indeed. Not so two of the several reporters.

" News is being deliberately withheld from us," one of them protested.

" We have a right to know," joined in the other.

An offensive note in their voices riled Felcey. He thought of the dangerous predicament of the men submerged in Liverpool Bay. He looked at the quietly whispering crowd of sorrowing women.

" Come here on one side," he told the two newspapermen. " I've got something to tell you, after all."

Expectantly they hurried to the side of the crowd. " What is it ? " they asked.

" Go to b——y," said Felcey. " That's my message to you. And remember, any one of these women here has a thousand times more right to any news that's going than any one of you. Now leave me alone." He stalked off.

Fifty-odd miles away from this scene of heightening emotions, at Llandudno, the town's motor-lifeboat had set out at 1 P.M. on the Friday afternoon for where *Thetis* lay surrounded by her circle of attendant ships. With the lifeboat went Dr A. Maddock-Jones, a local doctor, carrying medical equipment. The sea across the Bay was moderately choppy, and it was not until after 3 P.M. that Dr Jones was put aboard the destroyer *Somali*—only a few minutes, in fact, after *Thetis's* stern had slipped beneath the surface. From the destroyer the doctor was then transferred to *Vigilant*, where three of the four survivors—the other being Arnold—had by this time been taken. They had, of course, all been treated by the destroyer flotilla's medical officer, and Dr Jones wondered why he—in addition, as he discovered, to another civilian doctor, who had been flown out from Anglesey—had been called from his surgery. He gathered that the intention was to have as much medical assistance as possible available to deal with the mass escape from the submarine that was hoped for, even if not fully anticipated. Gladly he sorted out his equipment and settled patiently to wait, sending a message back to Llandudno with the returning lifeboat that he might be away some little time.

At exactly 5.20 P.M. there came the long-awaited arrival of H.M.S. *Winchelsea* and Captain Macintyre to a scene that no longer was distinguished by the stern of *Thetis* sticking out of the water and offering, at least, some visual encouragement for hope.

Twenty-six and a half hours had elapsed since *Thetis* had first disappeared. That this would be the approximate interval when *Winchelsea* arrived must have been implicit in the navigational calculations made before she left Portsmouth. But the delay was still accepted. Even the interception of *Brazen's* signal announcing the finding of *Thetis*—a signal which allowed the depth of water and the tidal difficulties to be seen by reference to a chart—did not seem to have suggested that altering course to the nearest harbour and commandeering an alternative means of transport would still have improved the time element.

Discussions between the four senior officers—Macintyre, Oram, Nicholson, and Hart—were immediately started. While they were still continuing a 'camel' arrived under tow from Liverpool. ('Camels' are familiar pieces of salvage-lifting equipment. Usually employed in pairs, they are large steel chambers or pontoons. They are placed alongside the vessel to be salved, flooded to a depth of several feet, secured closely, and then brought up to the surface again by having the water pumped out of their tanks, thus lifting the wrecked vessel with them.) Immediately the wire leading from *Thetis*, just below the surface, was transferred to the camel.

Rowkins and Howard, the two D.S.E.A. instructors who had wanted to try to get into *Thetis*, were standing alongside a coil of rope on *Vigilant's* deck. They were very worried. They had been told that every one was confident that the stern of the submarine would appear at slack-water, and that something would be done then. What that something was going to be, no one really seemed to know. It seemed to them that there was some unwillingness to take responsibility. Certainly there was as far as the suggestions they were making were concerned.

But as they looked across the surface of the water the tide was already slack and there was no sign of *Thetis* emerging. No matter what the risk of getting rebuffed, they must try again. They picked on one of the officers of *Vigilant*.

" I reckon that a diver could very easily reach and unscrew the top fitting of the bifocal periscope," Rowkins began. " An air-pipe could be fitted to the top with an adaptor, and air could be passed down into the boat that way. The pressure would probably blow out the lenses and the desiccator fittings, so the air would have no trouble getting in."

" It wouldn't work," came the reply. " The periscope would not take the pressure."

" I suppose every time a submarine dives the captain unships the periscopes and shoves them in his bunk," retorted Rowkins.

" I don't know about that," he was told, " but it's a bloody silly idea."

" I suppose he might have been right without knowing it," Rowkins reflected with Howard, later. " We'd have had to fix some exhaust outlet, otherwise we'd just have pushed up the CO_2 content." They returned to their impotent watching and waiting.

Whether or not it was because of the changing tide—now starting to flood—or whether the juggling with the wire did something to disturb *Thetis*, it was not long after this that one of the seamen for'ard in *Vigilant* noticed some signs of movement from where the submarine lay. Simultaneously the hawser from the camel tautened and the submarine's indicator-buoy started to dance about at the end of its wire.

" She's moving. Look at the wires."

But before anyone could do anything the indicator-buoy broke adrift from its wire, leaving only the wire from the camel to mark *Thetis's* position.

The movements under the water intensified. Suddenly there was a violent twisting and turning beneath the surface. The single, thin wire cut backward and forward through the water. The dark shape that was *Thetis* vibrated and quivered for every one to see.

Then, all at once, the wire went limp, the struggling stopped, and the dark shape disappeared. *Thetis* had gone. There was now no wire attached to her. Her exact position was not known. Things could scarcely have appeared more desperate, although, in fact, the time for desperation had passed.

The evening hours ticked slowly away. For a while there was complete inaction. Then, at 8.30 P.M., the *Salvor*, a salvage vessel from the Liverpool and Glasgow Salvage Association, arrived. The first task was to find *Thetis*. Wires were rigged between *Salvor* and *Vigilant*, and the two vessels swept backward and forward across the area of water. Disappointingly they had no immediate success.

While they were still sweeping one of the *Tribals*—H.M.S. *Matabele*—came steaming back into the circle of ships, after having been sent to the Princes Landing Stage at Liverpool. Aboard her were Mr Thomas McKenzie and the divers from Scapa Flow. They had had a remarkable·journey.

As soon as he received the Admiralty message at 3 P.M. McKenzie called his divers to the surface. They went by motor-boat to Lyness, in the Orkneys, removing their diving dresses on the way; and then by car to Longhope airfield. From there seven of them— McKenzie, an assistant salvage officer, three divers, and two attendants—left by plane for Inverness. The take-off had been quite a problem. Owing to the nature of the Longhope runway it was not normally considered safe to embark more than four passengers. But they made it with the seven of them, even though they had to leave all the diving gear behind.

At Inverness they changed into a faster plane and were flown to Speke airport, just outside Liverpool. Cars were waiting to rush them to the landing stage, and the destroyer had wasted no time in getting them out into the Bay.

A conference was convened in *Somali*. Nothing could be done by the divers until *Thetis* was found again, but McKenzie suggested that as soon as she was the most important thing was for a diver to go down at once, to see if there was still any sign of life. Meanwhile the two salvage vessels continued their sweeping.

Just before midnight the destroyer *Eskimo* was detached from the ring of ships to make the return trip to and from Liverpool. One of the people she took ashore was Lieutenant Woods, who appeared still to· be suffering badly from shock. He was taken straight to hospital.

A few minutes after *Eskimo* had left there were shouts of excitement from both *Vigilant* and *Salvor*. Their sweep wire had caught an obstruction. *Thetis* had been found again. With *Salvor's* equipment the position was immediately buoyed, so that, even if the sweep wire slipped, the location of the submarine would not again be in doubt. What sort of an opportunity did this represent for the divers from Scapa Flow?

While the vessels were manœuvring in the darkness and the divers contemplating their chances the crowds around the Cammell Laird headquarters had scarcely lessened. At midnight there were some 2000 of them, only a few of whom could have been kith and kin of the men in *Thetis*. In spite of the tragedy that pervaded the whole of their thinking there was still marked evidence of hope for a successful outcome. Much of this—certainly in so far as it had reached the reporters in the crowd—appeared to depend on the magical figure of 36 hours' supply of air. It was, perhaps, as well that a more accurate calculation had not been transmitted to the sorrowing congregation of people.

So the date changed to Saturday, June 3. High Water had been more or less at midnight, but it was not until almost an hour afterwards, at 12.55 A.M., that the senior of the three Metal Industries divers entered the water above *Thetis*. Sinclair McKenzie, no relation to his chief, had borrowed some equipment from *Salvor*. Speedily he swung down the shot rope, and within seconds all that could be seen of him in the beam of the destroyers' searchlights was the steady stream of exhaust bubbles.

A little over quarter of an hour later he was back. Because he had not been able to go down at dead slack-water, the tide had proved too strong for him.

" What happened, Mac ? " he was asked.

" Well, I hammered on the hull, like you said. I *thought* I heard a faint tapping in reply, so I hammered back. No luck. The sound had seemed to come from the far end of the submarine, and, with the tide pulling at me, I couldn't get over there. Certainly it wasn't regular Morse code."

" What about the after escape hatch ? "

" I never got near the hatch. I couldn't hang on any longer. So I couldn't say whether it was damaged. The vessel's lying right down on her keel, on a firm, hard shingle bed. But she's got a list of about 30 degrees."

As they listened to McKenzie's report the men in charge realized that this meant that until the next slack-water—the 6 A.M. low tide —they were condemned to wait, completely powerless. For nearly five hours the only defence they could offer against the laws of Nature and the tearings at their heart-strings was to be an unconfident show of patience.

It was still in the very early hours that Chief Petty Officer Dick

Oliver, in *Tedworth*, woke to find the quartermaster shaking his hammock. Together with all the other divers, he had ' slung ' in the diving flat rather than in his mess, in order to be ready for action in a matter of minutes.

Throwing off his blankets, he was out and on to the deck before the astonished quartermaster realized he was even awake.

" Shake the others, son," he ordered.

Hastily he climbed into his trousers. He felt a queer excitement. Here was the chance he had been waiting for ever since Thursday evening. How long ago that sounded !

The whole of his team were still asleep. That wretched boy hadn't called them. He was on the point of shouting when the quartermaster, from the other side of the hammock, found his voice again.

" They want to borrow some of your gear, Chief. Hoses."

" Like hell they want to borrow our hoses. Who the bloody hell is going to use them ? "

" They are wanted over in *Vigilant*, Chief. Some divers from Scapa Flow. I was told to shake you by the Officer of the Watch."

Oliver handed over the gear. He should have been fighting mad, he felt. There could have been no greater insult. Here he was, leading the best qualified team of deep divers in the country. He himself had more submarine-salvage experience than probably any man diving. And all they wanted him for was storeman of a supply department. Hadn't the Navy any more faith than that in its own trained men ?

Despondently he stood around. He couldn't be bothered to turn in again, although it was only 3 A.M., so he lashed up his hammock and idly went to wash and shave. Then he went up top to see what the weather had in store.

The cool breeze and the stillness before dawn heartened him a little, and it was not long before he was ' selling ' to all and sundry the importance of having Royal Navy divers down on *Thetis* at the earliest opportunity.

" Doesn't matter what you call it. Say we're only going down to help the ' experts,' if you like. But for goodness' sake get us there, sir," he said.

Some time before Low Water two more camels arrived from Liverpool. And, as 6 A.M. approached, the other two Metal Industries divers, Taylor and Thomson, prepared to go down. At first the position about *Tedworth's* divers was not resolved, but in the end, not very long before diving time, it was decided that they could in fact go down too, and overlap with the two civilians.

By the time this news came through Dick Oliver was completely dressed. Soon he was swinging himself off the foot of the diving ladder. A bare minute later he was on the deck of the sunken submarine.

Thetis was lying slightly over on her port side. Visibility at 140 feet was poor and, even at slack-water, there was a fair amount of movement. It was quite a tiring business to pull oneself for'ard or aft. The sweep wire that had located the submarine must have drifted away, for there was no sign of it. He did, however, find a paltry 2½-inch wire rope connected to the guard-rail of the bridge. Whether the wire would have parted before the guard-rail pulled away, once any weight were applied, he found it difficult to guess.

In disgust he walked clumsily for'ard. He reached the bows and called for a heavy wire rope to be slid down to him. Carefully he made this fast to the shackle of *Thetis's* anchor cable. His job finished, he turned to leave. Then, almost as an afterthought, he took off his light distance line and secured it to the anchor shackle as well, to act as a guide line for future descents. As he started on his way up he caught sight of one of the Metal Industries men knocking on the hull beside the conning-tower.

Immediately he reached the surface he was replaced by Petty Officer Jack Dymond, who found the gun recuperator connexion within five minutes of having left the surface, and then went for'ard again to check and double-check the connexion at the bows. Soon he too was able to return to the surface and report that *Thetis* was finally and firmly attached to a stout wire of reasonable proportions.

The other two divers, Taylor and Thomson, had knocked all along parts of the hull, but had heard no reply. They, also, had made a wire fast to *Thetis*, they reported. But they admitted that it was only of light weight.

By 7 A.M. the tide was running strongly, and diving was suspended until midday. As the hours wore on the only activity was sweeping with another wire, to endeavour to get something lodged under the after end of *Thetis*. The question of whether there was any hope of life aboard the sunken submarine at this late hour was by this time not being asked, even by the most sanguine or least knowing of the men who clustered around the guard-rails of the encircling ships. Slowly a new question started the rounds. " When will somebody announce that it's all over ? " people were wondering. " How much longer can we keep up this farce ? "

Well before noon both teams of divers were ready to go below again. But, at the last moment, they were told to postpone diving operations as far as the midday slack-water period was concerned. The sweep wire was said to be satisfactorily under *Thetis's* stern. Together with Dick Oliver's wire from the bow, it was shackled on to one single camel out of the three that were available. An orthodox salvage lift was tried. Perhaps not surprisingly, it failed.

During the day the Commander-in-Chief, Plymouth, Admiral Sir Martin Dunbar-Nasmith, V.C., K.C.B., himself a distinguished submariner of the First World War, had arrived on the scene. Signals passed between him and the Admiralty, in London. Then, at 4.10 P.M. on the afternoon of Saturday, June 3, some 25 hours after the last man alive in *Thetis* had perished and 13 hours after a normal crew's air would have been exhausted, a statement was issued from Whitehall:

> The Admiralty regrets that hope of saving lives in the *Thetis* must be abandoned.

13 *June 1939*

Aftermath

AT LAST, officially, it was all over. But, for many people, work on *Thetis* was just beginning. On the night of the final announcement from Admiralty a conference was held on board the destroyer *Somali*. It was conducted by Rear-Admiral B. A. Fraser—later Admiral of the Fleet Lord Fraser of North Cape—in his capacity as Third Sea Lord. Among those present were Admiral Dunbar-Nasmith, Rear-Admiral B. C. Watson (Flag Officer Submarines), Mr R. S. Johnson, of Cammell Laird, and the commanding officers of all the destroyers.

It was 3 A.M. the following morning—Sunday—before discussions broke up. During that day the various senior officers began returning to their headquarters. Admiral Dunbar-Nasmith set off for Plymouth in the flying-boat that had brought him north. Before he left he had a few words with Captain Hart. " In my opinion, everything possible has been done in the circumstances," he said.

Signals and messages started flying. An Admiralty statement issued at 11.15 A.M. on the Sunday morning read:

> Salvage work on H.M.S. *Thetis* is proceeding, but it may be some little time before the vessel can be brought to the surface. Messrs. Cammell Laird and Co. will be responsible for the work from now onwards, but H.M.S. *Tedworth* . . . will remain on the spot to render any assistance or advice required by the firm. A full inquiry is being held as soon as possible.

The First Lord of the Admiralty received an expression of sympathy from Their Majesties King George VI and Queen Elizabeth, thousands of miles away on their tour of Canada. The King himself received a telegram from the German Chancellor, Herr Hitler, conveying his own and the German nation's sympathy over the disaster. The French Ministry of Marine described its " fraternal anxiety " and " affectionate compassion."

On the Monday it was announced that the eight *Tribal* destroyers would be leaving within 24 hours to resume their normal programme. It was on the Monday, too, that Lord Stanhope, the First Lord of the Admiralty, returned to London.

He had been away from his seat of power in Whitehall since May 26, on a visit to the Home Fleet and to various naval establishments, in the Admiralty yacht *Enchantress*. When the accident to *Thetis* was first reported he was at Plymouth, where he conferred with Admiral Dunbar-Nasmith. He did not, however, cancel his arrangements in favour either of returning to the Admiralty or of going to Liverpool in person.

In the words of a naval spokesman:

"The First Lord has remained in close consultation with the responsible Commander-in-Chief, and all the information coming to the Admiralty was sent to him at Plymouth."

But his absence was not everywhere seen in this light. It could be argued that the First Lord could play his part equally well at Plymouth as in London. In retrospect, however, it would seem likely that, at best, the continuance of his programme must have deprived the Commander-in-Chief, at Plymouth, of the fullest possible opportunity for shouldering the burden that was partly his, and might well have detained him in Plymouth after he could, with value, have first flown to Liverpool Bay. This was only one of the long series of queries and criticisms that were to be debated throughout Britain in the days that followed.

To Plymouth at the same week-end came a slightly less senior—although, in the circumstances, possibly at least as well known—naval personality. Leading Stoker "Mac" Arnold was landed at Devonport from the destroyer *Brazen*.

As soon as the *Tribal* destroyers had arrived in Liverpool Bay on the Friday morning Lieutenant-Commander Mills was relieved by Captain Nicholson and told to proceed back to Plymouth. Before he left he transferred to *Vigilant* Captain Oram, Lieutenant Woods, and Frank Shaw. The afternoon tide was turning as he swung away from his position in the circle of vessels around *Thetis*. As he was conning his ship round to a westerly course he suddenly saw the stern of the submarine swivel round at a steep angle. Mills's heart sank. He realized that the situation inside must be getting pretty grim. But what more could have been done, he asked himself. And, as the destroyer slowly gathered speed, he kept recalling the firm instructions he had had to keep away from *Thetis*, as the men would quite certainly be coming out at regular intervals.

Holyhead was abeam before the effects of the injection wore off and Arnold came to. The moment he woke he felt the vibration of the main engines running. He was up on deck in a flash. Quickly he found that he was the only one of the four survivors still on board. And the only rating, too, he thought to himself. He felt furious about what had happened and expressed himself forcibly to that effect to any one who would give him an ear. " It's not only the hint of snobbery," he explained. " I'm just as anxious and interested as the officers are about the safety of all the rest of the blokes inside *Thetis*."

He had already sent two radio-telegrams to his wife via the destroyer's wireless office. This meant that by the afternoon of the Friday Mrs Arnold had received four communications relating to the disaster that had befallen *Thetis*. At 11.46 P.M. on the Thursday she had heard from Gosport. " Submarine *Thetis* has failed to return to surface after diving trial off Liverpool to-day Thursday. Leading Stoker Arnold is believed to be on board." Just after noon on the Friday she had another telegram from Gosport. " Leading Stoker Arnold has escaped safely." Then, during the afternoon, she received the two radio-telegrams. The first one read " Am alive and kicking, Mac." It was followed by " Am oke, will see you soon. Mac."

It was 4 P.M. on the Saturday before *Brazen* arrived at Devonport. She was met by an ambulance, equipped with doctor, and—ironically, thought Arnold—baggage party. He was taken straight off to the sickbay at the Naval Barracks, for a quick inspection before being transferred to the Naval Hospital at Stonehouse. There he was immediately isolated in a private ward, where—so it seemed to him—he was put on show to the entire medical profession of Plymouth.

The next morning—it was Sunday—an excited Wardmaster dashed in and told him to straighten his bed: the Surgeon Rear-Admiral was coming. In due course the great man appeared, and there ensued a conversation which Arnold still remembers with pleasure.

" Morning ! How are you ? "

" All right, sir, thank you. My back's a bit painful, but not too bad."

" Well, I really came to tell you not to talk to anyone about what happened in *Thetis* until you get permission from Admiralty. Understand ? "

" Yes, sir. And, sir . . . ? "

" What is it ? "

" May I have afternoon leave ? "

" Don't be stupid. Of course you can't. Anyway, you've only got a borrowed overall suit."

The great man made for the door. He was half-way through it before he spoke again.

" But I'll send you a crate of beer straight away. Can you drink ' Hammerton's Nut Brown ' ? "

Not unnaturally, Arnold thought he could.

During the afternoon his parents came to visit him, having travelled over from Portsmouth. Fearful of disguised newspaper reporters, the hospital authorities would not admit them until they had been recognized by Arnold through the window of his ward.

The next morning he was taken to the Naval Barracks to be kitted out afresh. Later in the day the Commander-in-Chief's car called for him at the Naval Hospital and took him to Admiralty House in Plymouth for an interview with Admiral Dunbar-Nasmith, who was by this time back from Liverpool Bay.

From Plymouth he was sent by train to London, *en route* for the Admiralty. As the car which had been sent to meet him swung down towards Whitehall they found the whole of the street swarming with crowds of people around the front entrance to the Admiralty. They were plainly clamouring for an inquiry. Quietly and tactfully Arnold was admitted via a doorway at the back of the building.

He was hurried into a large office and introduced to Rear-Admiral Bruce Fraser, Mr Geoffrey Shakespeare (the Parliamentary Secretary to the Admiralty), and several others. For a few moments he was overawed. Then he found himself being charmed by the tact and kindness that Bruce Fraser was soon to display during the long years of the War that was to make him famous throughout the world, and—probably, who knows, of greater importance to him— loved and respected throughout the Royal Navy. Arnold was led to a table covered with large blueprints of the plans of the " T " class of submarine. Soon he was engrossed in the detail of the boat he had come to know so well. For an hour or more their questions and his answers continued. Then it was all over, and he was told he could go home on leave. But again he was cautioned not to talk to the Press. No public discussion may precede the official inquiry, he was told.

So it was that at 2 A.M. on Tuesday, June 6, he arrived home at Tranmere, Birkenhead. At 5 A.M., the same morning, the reporters started banging on his front door. At a later stage in his experience of the Press Arnold was often to tell himself that " they've got a job to do, and most of them do it without making a nuisance of themselves." But after barely one hour in bed on his first day home he felt neither tolerance nor understanding. Nor, in what he said, did he express either quality.

It cannot be said that the Press in general endeared itself to the Submarine Service over its handling of the *Thetis* disaster. As the shadows of the Saturday that carried the " hope must be abandoned " statement darkened into Sunday the wardroom and messes of the Submarine Headquarters at Gosport were the scene of much adverse comment. What the submariners did not realize was the extent to which much of the inaccurate reporting was due to the lack of satisfactory information available.

Much of the anguish that was caused among the public at large, and especially among the relatives of the men in *Thetis*, stemmed from inaccurate estimates of the endurance in hours that the complement of the submarine could expect. The initial Admiralty statement had given details of her tonnage, length, armament, and —inevitably—endurance. " *Thetis* can stay underwater for 36 hours," the wording ran. And from this phrasing sprung the calculations behind nearly every newspaper headline.

The statement was far from precise. It should have indicated clearly—or had even the Admiralty not realized ?—that 36 hours was the endurance of the submarine's batteries and air with her normal crew on board. Admittedly if careful thought had been given to the statement the real truth of the position should have become evident. The endurance of the air supply was obviously directly related to the number of people on board. Admiralty did not know at the time of the first statement how many people were, in fact, down in *Thetis*. Therefore the endurance quoted could not have been in respect of the dive that had actually taken place. And, once it became known that the submarine had double her normal complement, it would have been a not too difficult guess that 18 hours was more like the real figure.

None of these calculations was the business or the responsibility of anyone other than Admiralty. It was completely understandable that the submariners at Gosport should fret at long, optimistic, hope-building articles based on a fallacious time-limit. But the figure of 36 hours received the widest possible publicity; Admiralty could not have been unaware of the currency it was getting; and one word of correction from Whitehall would have been instantly heeded.

At the same time it was unfortunate in the extreme that no leading article could have accurately calculated the real time-limit for rescue operations. The sense of urgency that could have been created might possibly have got something done before it was too late. As it was, the " safe until the early hours of Saturday " reports only helped to build up a false sense of security; and newspaper editors up and down the country must have kicked themselves, later, for missing the scoop of the decade.

The actual target for newspaper criticism seemed to be Cammell Laird rather than the Admiralty. At Birkenhead, on the Saturday, a considerable amount of complaint was being voiced by the Press. Already many paragraphs had appeared in print on the subject. But with more and more reporters arriving, things became even worse. Nearly 100 journalists, representing all the great newspapers and news agencies of the country, as well as several from American and French agencies, met with blank refusals or negative statements in answer to their inquiries.

At first it had been impossible for them to see anyone in authority. They had been brusquely dealt with. Many of them had been ordered off the premises. Some had even been driven into clashing with naval personnel, like Charlie Felcey, who were not allowed by the Naval Discipline Act to communicate information anyway.

Eventually a letter of protest was drafted, and later in the day Mr Johnson agreed to see a deputation. Having just returned to Birkenhead, after taking an active part in the operations in Liverpool Bay, he was able to give an authentic report of what had been happening. He also promised better co-operation in the future.

But by this time the damage had largely been done. It had been impossible, for instance, to get any accurate information as to the numbers on board. Estimates varied between 100 quoted by one newspaper on the morning of June 2 and the 78 sponsored by two others.

Minor inaccuracies were legion. One correspondent wrote of chlorine gas poisoning, on the basis of a Cammell Laird official's supposition that sea water must have got to the batteries and on an incorrect diagnosis of the condition of Frank Shaw after he was landed at Liverpool. There were widespread references to carbon monoxide, as opposed to carbon dioxide, poisoning. Another report mentioned divers being able, in the conditions that existed, to stay underwater for two hours at least. But the known tidal conditions of the part of the Bay in which *Thetis* was sunk were bound to restrict diving to a maximum of between 30 and 60 minutes at any one period of slack-water.

Perhaps the reporting that was the most injurious to the relatives and friends of the men in *Thetis* was all the jubilation, the " thank God they're safe " editorials, that appeared immediately after the submarine's stern was found early on the Friday morning. Once again, to a very large extent, the blame for these reports must lie other than with the Press, for they only seemed to reflect the attitude of mind of many of the people in authority.

Nevertheless some of the Friday-evening ' copy ' made sad

reading afterwards. " The first happy tidings of the *Thetis* " . . .
" joyous scenes . . . laughing and smiling faces . . . sobbing with
joy " . . . " wonderful news . . . all happy to-day." By the time
these words were being read all the 99 men remaining in *Thetis*
were dead.

Once the final Admiralty announcement had been made, the
papers' treatment of the *Thetis* story changed from report to
comment. Unfortunately, not all of the comment was well-
informed, either. In at least one instance it produced the age-old
canard under the headline " Submarines should be abolished."
To add point to its plea for the abolition of the submarine, this
article stated that the vessel's usefulness had passed, quoting the
Parliamentary Secretary to the Admiralty to the effect that " the
submarine is no longer a menace to us in a war. Wherever they
are our ships will hunt them down and kill them." The years of
war that were to follow so closely upon this appreciation of one
sphere of potential naval development did not go very far to substantiate this hypothesis. In 1942, according to Sir Winston
Churchill, the German wolf-packs nearly brought us to a halt. And
it was the activities of our own submarines in the Mediterranean—
the relaunched and renamed *Thetis* among them—that cut off
the supplies to Rommel and his Afrika Korps, and paved the way
for the conquest of North Africa and Italy.

At the end of the same article, as if finally to convince readers
that the submarine was the most inhuman of all war machines,
these words appeared—" The submarine commander cannot be
chivalrous. He can seldom spare lives, and never rescue them."
Ironically, the very submarine that had provided the reason for the
article in question was also to provide one of the many examples
of rescue-by-submarine that were to disprove completely the last
three words of the condemnation. In so doing they almost certainly restored to the bereaved next-of-kin of the men in *Thetis*
the consolation of knowing that their men had died for a worth-
while cause.

The ill-informed newspaper reporting, the unwarranted optimism
of the men on the spot in Liverpool Bay, and the apparent lack of
sufficient concern at top level in the Navy, were all fostering a
growing feeling of resentment among the officers and ratings at
Fort Blockhouse. Emotions ran high enough for a bunch of
ratings, during the early hours of one morning, to paint in large
letters across the parade ground a message of complaint against
one aspect of the *Thetis* disaster. While the next forenoon saw the
message erased, it was significant that the Admiralty thought fit—
perhaps, of course, by coincidence—to take the very action that the

message had demanded. Surprisingly no whisper of this ever seemed to reach the Press.

Chief Petty Officer Charlie Felcey was still in the Submarine Offices in the Cammell Laird yard when the " hope abandoned " signal came through from Admiralty. It was the Saturday evening. Most of the relatives were already in the yard, many of them packed nside the offices alongside the naval personnel.

It seemed a bad idea to tell them all immediately, before having made some sort of arrangements to cope with the effect the news might have. Felcey sent out for plentiful supplies of coffee and had it generously laced with brandy on the way in. At the same time some one had telephoned the local hospital, and a car came over with a doctor and two nurses.

Eventually, the contents of the telegram were disclosed. Naturally, there were one or two cases of hysteria, but the medical attention soon took care of them. For the most part the women reacted quietly to the news that many of them must have known in their hearts long hours beforehand.

The days that followed saw the naval personnel at Birkenhead busily employed in collecting the dead men's effects. Much of the gear would be ultimately auctioned in Fort Blockhouse at fantastically high prices, as part of the Submarine Service's tribute to its fellows. Felcey went with one of the lorries on this task. He soon found that the work was taking far longer than planned. The same wives who had waited at the Submarine Offices in silence and gone home after the final announcement with only a nod, a smile of thanks, and a downcast head, were now anxious to talk—particularly with anyone who had known their husband as a messmate.

One of Felcey's first calls was on the wife of one of *Thetis's* petty officers. The two men had been together in the submarine *Rover*, and, when this came out in conversation, the poor young wife made Felcey stay and see her baby daughter, look through photographs of *Rover*, in China, recount some of the times he and her husband had spent together, and hear some of the tales that she most wanted to tell. It was a pathetic business. And similar scenes were recurring over the whole of the Liverpool-and-Birkenhead area.

Elsewhere the normal aftermath of a national tragedy was proceeding. Tuesday, June 6, found the Admiralty answering questions about the pensions that would be payable: from £180 a year, for the wife of a Commander, to 10s. 6d. a week, for the widow of a seaman.

The following day was the occasion of the Memorial Service at Sea. The cortège was led from the Mersey, over the 38 miles that *Thetis* had covered on her last voyage, by the minesweeper H.M.S.

Hebe. Most of the relatives and those intimately concerned with the lost submarine were standing on the open deck. Before she reached the last resting-place of *Thetis*, *Hebe* had been joined by a congregation of salvage vessels, lifeboats, and miscellaneous light craft.

The service was conducted from the minesweeper's quarterdeck by the Rev. G. H. Crouch, Royal Navy, the Submarine Service's Chaplain at Fort Blockhouse. Long before the notes of the first hymn, " Eternal Father, strong to save," had died away, there was scarcely a dry eye aboard. Later, after the wreaths had floated down upon the water, the prayer of the Royal Navy was read. Its phrases—" the Fleet in which we serve . . . the dangers of the sea . . . upon their lawful occasions . . . may return in safety to enjoy the blessings of the land "—had a strengthening effect. For, after the Church pendant had been hauled down from the yardarm, the volleys fired and the Last Post and Reveille sounded, the sternness of the voices singing the National Anthem carried more of challenge than of sorrow.

In London on Thursday, June 8, the Archbishop of Canterbury officiated at a *Thetis* Memorial Service in St Martin-in-the-Fields. Admiral the Hon. Sir Reginald Plunkett-Ernle-Erle-Drax represented the King. Simultaneously the Duke of Gloucester was deputizing at the Trooping the Colour ceremony, at Horse Guards' Parade.

The Lord Mayor of London, Sir Frank Bowater, presided over a meeting of the *Thetis* Appeal Fund. Within less than two days of the final Admiralty announcement it stood at £115,000. The Fund was notified that the Navy had decided to have three classes of dependents: officers, chiefs and petty officers, and ratings. It was agreed to divide up the civilian casualties in a similar way.

A few days later a rather dispirited Arnold travelled down to his parents' home at Portsmouth, to attend the Naval Inquiry being held in Fort Blockhouse. He felt he was being regarded as neither dead nor alive. First of all he had to be smuggled between his home and the Cammell Laird yard, in order to avoid the reporters while on his way to the Memorial Service at Sea. Then he found his name among the list of dead, in the programme.

He was acutely aware the whole time of a feeling of intense loneliness. While he had shipmates enough, elsewhere in the Sub-marine Service, he could not rid himself of the conviction that all his friends, all the people he now wanted to talk to, all the men he ever wished to serve with, were lost in *Thetis*. He was the only survivor among 48 ratings, but—as if to aggravate things—it seemed that, in the eyes of the powers-that-be, he was as lost as if he had never got out of the escape compartment.

Instructions were being sent to him regularly to assist in all sorts of inquiries, but he found it almost impossible to find any naval authority prepared to pay him. Eventually, he persuaded Fort Blockhouse that he ought to be on somebody's books. And he wrote to his wife, " I've managed to squeeze a couple of ' casual ' payments out of them, but never more than £2. And it really was squeezing ! ! "

The weeks that followed were, for Arnold and his wife, among the worst they had ever spent. It continued to be impossible for him to get other than occasional ' casual ' payments ; and a Leading Stoker's pay, in the late 1930's, had not been very conducive towards saving. The result was that they had to have recourse to desultory borrowing to keep him in cigarettes—he had virtually chain-smoked ever since the cigarette he got from *Vigilant's* boat's crew—and the family out of debt. Often and often he told himself that, while he might well be a public hero, as far as the Navy was concerned he simply did not exist.

Eventually he was called to Fort Blockhouse and sent from there to the Treasury Solicitor's office, in London. There he met Captain Oram leaving as he entered. After he had given a signed statement, in preparation for the official Tribunal of Inquiry, he returned to Portsmouth, only to find another instruction to travel. This time he had to go to the works of Messrs Siebe Gorman—the submarine and safety engineers and the designers and manufacturers of the Davis Submarine Escape Apparatus—at Surbiton, in Surrey. " I had to see Sir Robert Davis," he recalled later, " and was most touched by the appreciation he showed of all that had happened to me."

After this pleasant incident he was told to wait—for the beginning of the Tribunal and until the time when he would be required for the later stages of the salvage operations. He was to have many trying days ahead.

14

June 3, 1939, to
August 24, 1939

Salvage

FOR four days after the Admiralty announcement that salvage work was proceeding, the craft anchored above *Thetis* struggled against every sort of misfortune. The wind had got up unpleasantly from the north-west and conditions quickly deteriorated. But, in spite of the cold and the rough seas, *Tedworth's* divers kept working every minute of every slack-water period. The necessary wires were secured to *Thetis* and connected to the 'camels.' Then, at Low Water, late on the night of Wednesday, June 7, an attempt was made to tighten up, prior to lifting. But the strain that the long, heavy swell was imposing on 'camels,' hawsers, and salvage vessels alike proved too much. An after lifting wire parted and the remaining wires had to be slipped.

Additional lifting power and stronger wires were obviously required before any further move could be made. Accordingly, all craft engaged—*Tedworth, Vigilant, Salvor*, the tugs, and the 'camels'—were withdrawn to Liverpool on the following morning.

Meanwhile there was much speculation about whether *Thetis* should be lifted at all. A paragraph in the *Liverpool Echo* ran:

> It is understood that most of the relatives who attended the memorial services regarded them as the funeral services of their loved ones. For the vessel to be raised and the bodies of the heroic men exhumed from the tomb in which they have now rested for a week would, it is thought, only serve to reopen the wounds already deep in the hearts of those left behind, and create further sorrow without any compensations.

But the authorities continued to believe that the future interests of the Submarine Service were compensation enough, and the work was ordered to go on.

Heavy-eyed after a sleepless week at the scene of the disaster, Captain H. V. Hart disembarked from *Vigilant*. As soon as he arrived back in Liverpool a conference was held between Cammell

Laird, the Mersey Docks and Harbour Board, and the Liverpool and Glasgow Salvage Association. Obviously the raising of *Thetis* was going to be a far larger enterprise than most people had ever thought. *Vigilant's* terms of reference did not normally extend to deep-sea work, nor was her equipment designed accordingly. Moreover, her prolonged absence would be prejudicial to possible future salvage commitments within the Port area. So it was decided that the sole responsibility for, and control of, salvage operations on *Thetis*, as from June 9, 1939, should be entrusted to the Liverpool and Glasgow Salvage Association. It was agreed, however, that the assistance of *Tedworth* and her divers should continue to be supplied. A great partnership had been founded.

The work was under the overall direction of the L. and G.'s General Manager in Liverpool, Mr G. R. Critchley. He was represented at the scene of operations by his various salvage officers, and also conferred regularly with the commanding officer of *Tedworth*, Lieutenant-Commander W. J. Stride. Within a few days of the new chain of responsibility having been determined a complete survey of the conditions was made.

Thetis was sunk in a depth of 150 feet at Low Water springs. The tidal range was as high as 22 feet, so that diving could often be taking place in up to 172 feet. At times there was no slack-water period at all, and, at best, absolute slack-water did not exceed 30 minutes. The tidal movement at the surface reached a speed of 4 knots.

The position was exposed to wind and sea from all quarters—although the worst conditions could be expected with westerly winds—and the weather conditions were subject to very rapid change. All this meant that the lifting 'camels,' which had earlier been used in the emergency that existed while life was still thought to remain in *Thetis*, were quite unsuitable for a major salvage operation. In even moderately bad weather they could become completely unmanageable, and they afforded no protection for working parties, who might have to operate from their top surfaces. An alternative lifting medium would have to be sought.

But, while the problem that this posed was still besetting Mr Critchley and his advisers, diving operations over *Thetis* had been resumed. *Tedworth*, together with the L. and G. salvage steamer *Ranger*, had returned to the scene. The divers had begun the initial preparations: surveying the submarine in detail, ascertaining the nature of the sea-bed where she was lying (blue clay, with a high mound on the port side for'ard, and a hole about eight feet deep on the starboard side), attaching marker-buoys, and clearing away all the wire debris.

It was during this stage of the work that the first of several congratulatory signals about the performance of the *Tedworth* divers was originated. Sent by the L. and G. salvage officer on the spot, it read, " The *Tedworth* divers and their organization are of very great value, and the control of this unit is the admiration of every one." As Mr Critchley was to comment later, " The admiration deepened as the work proceeded, and these divers responded without hesitation to every requirement, often under conditions which would have justified some demur." They were the only divers employed.

Their great advantage was that they were a well-trained team. Diving victories were won on the diving ' flat,' that piece of deck where the attendants—all divers themselves—operated the pumps, the controls, the life-lines, and the telephones that kept the men down below working safely and efficiently. The diving flat was a place where a man's life could be stifled out in a split second by one false move on the part of an attendant not trained to act before asking. It was a world of its own; a world in which the clank of heavy, polished helmets being jostled together, the metallic scraping of the diving ladder heaving against its rail with each successive wave, the padding to and fro of white-sweatered, canvas-shod figures, provided an aural background for a visual pattern of order and neatness. And against this setting, whenever the deep-diving team went into action, was performed a series of manœuvres every bit as well-drilled as a complex, full-scale ballet. It was, in fact, the very correctness of the drill that was a diver's guarantee that his safety was assured at all times as far as the men ' up top ' were concerned.

Nevertheless, the weather conditions over *Thetis* were often such that it required an intrepid man to face the ordeal of climbing out of the diving port—a square hole in *Tedworth's* hull at one side of the diving flat—and into the waters of Liverpool Bay. First he would have to contend with the rolling and jinking of *Tedworth*, riding out the wind, as he vented his suit and lost sufficient buoyancy to submerge. Then, 150 feet later, as he sought the hull of *Thetis* he would be constantly jerked to and fro as the slack on his lines was savagely taken up and suddenly let go again. And all the time there would be the pressure, around 70 lb. per square inch, or five times the normal pressure of the atmosphere, to keep him aware of the short life he would have if he made a single mistake. Finally, when the time came for him to return to the surface, he would have to face the bruising buffeting of the sea and, like as not, be slapped hard against the hull of *Tedworth* before he could be hauled aboard.

Hurriedly he would be divested of helmet, boots, and weights, and then literally thrust into the recompression chamber. There he would be given—but this time in air instead of water—the pressure equivalent to that at which he had been working. Eventually, after a long, slow decompression, he would come out and be finished for the day—finished, of course, except for the part he would still have to play in the teamwork of the diving flat. " Hardships ? " he would say, if you asked him, with a twinkle in his eye. " Hardships ? You don't know what hardships are."

As the days passed the Liverpool and Glasgow Salvage Association were making good progress in their preparations for lifting *Thetis*. They had decided that the only lifting medium likely to succeed would be a merchant ship of approximately the same length as the submarine. She would need to be moored directly above *Thetis* and eight nine-inch wire slings would have to be used to connect the two craft together.

The vessel that was required had also to show specific character- istics in terms of design, internal structure, and buoyancy, as well as proving sleeping and feeding accommodation for a salvage party of some 50 men over and above her own crew. It was intended that the whole unit would be self-contained.

A widespread search was started throughout the whole country. It was not very long before a suitable candidate was found. She was the *Zelo*. Her length was 308 feet (*Thetis* was 275); her deadweight carrying capacity was 3350 tons (*Thetis's* submerged weight was said to be about 1000); she afforded the necessary accommodation. She was lying at Cardiff under Admiralty charter. Within hours the charter contract was revoked and she was placed at the disposal of *Thetis*.

In the frantic re-equipping that then took place at Birkenhead special arrangements were made for her to carry the huge wires and the tremendous weight that they would have to bear. Giant lifting beams were rigged athwartships across the deck at the points where it was planned the eight wires would be slung. Each beam was constructed of four one-foot-square pitch-pine logs lashed together. The beams overhung the deck by three feet each side, and these overhangs were built still larger into huge bobbins with beech and greenheart timber segments, into which the wires could bite. In addition, vast quantities of logs of even larger dimensions were used inside *Zelo* to strengthen the supports of her upper deck. In the last stages of the preparations she looked like a cross between a Christmas-tree and a woodyard.

She was ready to sail from Cammell Laird's basin on June 28; but, inevitably as it seemed, in anything to do with *Thetis's* salvage, the weather took a hand. For two days more she was held at

Birkenhead by a southerly gale; and conditions were still unsettled when she arrived out over *Thetis*. Five more days elapsed before the whole of the complicated arrangement of main and supplementary moorings could be laid to the six anchors involved.

On the night of July 5 and the morning of the 6th *Tedworth's* divers started going down to reeve medium-weight wires under the submarine's bow and immediately for'ard of her keel. These were the wires that would ultimately pull the huge nine-inch hawsers into position.

The divers operated in pairs. They had, at most, half an hour in which to work at any one time. Their link with their comrades ' up top ' and with each other was the traditionally temperamental diver's telephone. But here again Dick Oliver's careful supervision had worked wonders, for the telephones in the helmets performed perfectly throughout the whole of the time in Liverpool Bay.

A telephone log kept all the details of all the dives for later reference, if necessary, by the salvage officer. This log showed it as being 2027 (8.27 P.M.) on the evening of the 5th, when Diver " Soapy " Watson left the surface. In a minute or so his voice crackled over the headphones:

    " On the submarine."

    " I am still having a look round."

    " Don't hold me too tight."

    " I am ready for the next diver."

So the next diver, Dick Oliver himself, slipped quickly and quietly into the water, taking the reeving wire with him. Before he was half-way down to the bottom his voice came through:

    " Haul the wire up a bit."

    " Keep the wire up a bit, I'm having ear trouble."

    " O.K., it's cleared now."

At this stage Watson's circuit resumed activity. The two telephone records intermarry:

" I can see the other diver."

" Ease the wire slowly and tell Dick to mind his footing."

" He's O.K."

    And from Oliver:

    " On the submarine."

    " I can see Soapy."

    " On the hydroplanes."

    " Going down."

The two men had now to undertake the arduous business of pulling themselves under the hull of the submarine and into the mud, through which they had to pull and push the heavy, awkward reeving wire.

" Going down."

" More air."

" Am on the bottom. Ask Dick to shine his torch."

> " I am right under the sub., but can't see anything at all."

> " I can't see the other diver."

> " I am at the end of my line, but can't see the wire."

" Take up slack both sides."

" Hold on."

> " Haul up wire . . . hold on."

> " Don't ease away."

> " I can see Soapy."

> " I think I can manage it. Ease the wire."

> " Haul up."

" Am coming up the sub. Haul up."

" Take up slack of gear."

" Leaving bottom."

> " Am ready to come up."

That was how two men placed one of the first wires under *Thetis*. But their work was not long to remain untouched by Fate. In the early hours of the morning of Friday, July 7, a full gale from the south-west struck the small assembly of ships. Soon *Zelo's* starboard moorings dragged, and she swung broadside on to the sea, carrying away two heavy bollards, and fracturing other parts of her superstructure. Sadly she slipped the remainder of her moorings and returned to the Cammell Laird yard for repairs. The sea was leaving no doubt of her unwillingness to yield up *Thetis's* dead.

It was intended—ultimately, after *Thetis* was lifted—to carry her slung beneath *Zelo* to a point on the east coast of Anglesey. But large-scale charts of the area showed considerable unevenness of the underwater contours, and a number of wrecks were known to exist, more or less in her path. The naval survey ship, H.M.S. *Gleaner*, was therefore despatched to Liverpool Bay to plot a safe course for the salvors. This she did, but, in addition to supplying a charted ' corridor ' through which *Thetis* could safely be carried, she also revealed the somewhat disturbing information that the tidal currents along the sea-bed often ran in directions as much as 60 degrees different from those of the currents on the surface. Apparently there were plenty of difficulties ahead !

The weather continued unbelievably bad. While *Zelo* was being repaired the salvage ship *Ranger* set about laying a new series of 10 moorings, to take the place of the original six. From July 8-11 the gales and high winds were unabated. Shortly before midnight on the 11th *Zelo* sailed again. But wind and swell still made mooring impossible. By the 14th she had to take shelter in Moelfre Bay, near Llanallgo, in Anglesey. Finally, the weather moderated during the night of the 15th, and on Sunday, July 16, she was at last able to moor. Diving immediately recommenced.

But the sub-surface currents that *Gleaner* had reported soon began to cause trouble. Two of the divers passed a reeving wire through a gap between the pressure hull and a guard bar at the for'ard end of the keel. Then, during the tide that ran for six hours before the next slack-water, the port leg of the wire was swept right under the bow and out on the starboard side, where it jammed around the guard bar. It took one more complete dive to get them back to where they had started.

The divers had their personal troubles too. Just after half-past nine one morning Petty Officer Harknett slid out of the diving port. As he still hung on to the ladder, floating head and shoulders out of the water, he reported a leak at the back of his heavy corselet.

> " It's all right . . . I'll manage . . . it probably won't get any worse."

The story was recorded in his telephone log. He left the surface at 0944 and soon found his hands being cut by the rough serrations of the wire down which he was sliding.

> " Plenty of snags on the wire."

> " Tide very strong."

> " On the sub."

> " Tide is strong . . . pay out on line and gear . . . I'm by the foremost stanchion."

> " Over the port side now . . . tide is very strong."

> " Take up slack of rope . . . hold on . . . all right, take up slack of gear."

> " Pull me up. Sorry, it is the only way."

> " Water coming in helmet."

> " Hurry up, please. Water coming in helmet."

> " All right, now. That's better."

> " Still breathing."

He surfaced at 1017. It had been an exciting 33 minutes. Incidents such as these interspersed the whole of the diving, but by the afternoon of the 20th six of the eight lifting wires had been placed in position.

The divers' responsibility was very great. Not only did they have to work the reeving wires under the hull, they also had the task of checking the positions of the huge slings. These had to be exactly in position, to within a foot, or they were useless. If they were not just right they would either part or slip when the weight came on.

T.A.R.—10

As far as the Liverpool and Glasgow salvage officers were concerned, they accepted the divers without question as their eyes down on *Thetis*. Oliver took part in all the conferences that were held. " Even if we weren't worth spending the tax-payer's money on flying us down to *Thetis*," he told himself, " we're worth more than money to the salvors—and they're the first to admit it ! '"

The following day the stern of the submarine was lifted slightly to allow one of the last two wires to be rove right under the keel. In no time the eighth wire was in place, and everything was ready for the grand denouement—the lifting of *Thetis*. That same day H.M.S. *Trident*, *Thetis's* sister-ship and the second of the Birkenhead boats, carried out her preliminary trimming trials in the Cammell Laird basin. It was announced that she would subsequently be undertaking a one-day surface test in Liverpool Bay, before going north to Scotland for her diving trials. She had, of course, a completely new complement of officers—her original captain, first lieutenant, and engineer were inside the cold steel hull on which Oliver and his men were working.

The wires leading up from *Thetis* were hove taut round the bobbins projecting from *Zelo's* upper deck and pinned in position at dead Low Water. Weather conditions were, for once, ideal. As the tide rose the wires would take the strain, and by High Water the submarine would be clear of the sea-bed by however many feet the tide had risen. Meanwhile *Zelo* would have moved forward along the course that *Gleaner* had provided until *Thetis* grounded in shallower water. The first lift would be over, and the same process would be repeated at the next low tide.

But that was not how it happened. The lift started according to plan, but—perhaps because *Thetis* was not evenly flooded throughout her length—the wires and the beams lifting her bows soon came under greater stress than the others. The gigantic wooden beams began to twist. The action of the lifting wires compressed the groups of logs together, and soon they were spitting out the timber fibres from their centres. The tackles holding the ends of the wires carried away, and each time the tide made the submarine surge for'ard, so the wires rendered round the splintering bobbins, and allowed the bows to go jerking back on to the bottom. With the angle on *Thetis's* keel the wires started slipping, and there was no question but to call off the lift. A signal was sent to the headquarters in Liverpool : " Regret to report there has been no victory."

Zelo returned to Birkenhead. A conference was called by the Controller of the Navy at which it was agreed to replace the timber beams by steel girders capable of withstanding the concentrated loading. It was the Cammell Laird view that the salvage should be abandoned. Mr R. S. Johnson held that " the *Thetis* should lie where it is and the bodies be left in peace." But, once the decision was taken to go ahead again, Cammell Laird co-operated to the full in the modifications to *Zelo*, members of their staff agreeing to suspend their holiday leave during a vital week in early August. With continuous day-and-night work *Zelo* was able to sail on the morning of August 24.

Tedworth had been operating over the wreck during her absence. The previous evening, as part of a final survey before any further attempt at lifting was made, two divers were ordered down to examine *Thetis's* stern and propeller shafts. One of them was Petty Officer Henry Otho Perdue.

15

August 23, 1939, to
November 18, 1939

The Hundredth Man

THE helmet disappeared beneath the surface in the middle of a swirl of bubbles. The attendant at the after diving position, on the quarter-deck, started paying out the lines. " Diver's left the surface," he reported to the man keeping the log. The time was 6.33 P.M.

A few minutes later Perdue's voice was coming over the telephone set. " Send the other diver down now. The visibility's not good. I am by the draught numbers on the port side. Where are they on the sub ? "

It looked an innocent enough query, written in the telephone record. Bad visibility was nothing uncommon 160 feet down in Liverpool Bay. And as Petty Officer Dick Harknett, the other diver, saw the dirty blue-and-white of the swell, splashing against the front glass of his helmet, give way to the murky green of the deeper water, he had no reason to suppose that he was going to be an unwitting witness of tragedy.

For a little more than half an hour the two men worked carefully and slowly. In the difficult conditions they had to make doubly sure that they did not get foul of each other's gear. Then, with the tide having well and truly turned, and the tugging at their weighted bodies having become, finally, more than they could any longer resist, they each announced their intention to come up.

Harknett was the first off the bottom by a few seconds. " Leaving the sub," he reported over his telephone. Almost immediately Perdue's telephone sprang into activity. " Hold on," he called. " Lower me down a bit. I'm caught up on a grapnel." From where Harknett hung on the guide rope he could see that Perdue's heavy boots were barely four or five feet off the sea-bed. Quickly he telephoned that he wanted to be lowered, so that he could give his ' oppo ' a hand. For what must have been five long minutes the two of them struggled to free the prongs of the grapnel from Perdue's gear. Quite suddenly it came loose.

148

" I'm coming up now," Perdue reported to the surface. " Everything's O.K. I'm leaving the bottom."

By *Tedworth's* diving ladder Petty Officer Jack Dymond was pulling on a pair of thigh-length wading-boots. It was as well to be ready, he thought, just in case either of the divers needed helping up. The first helmet to break the surface was Perdue's. " Doc Perdue's up," called Dymond. " Time seven-fifteen." A second later he saw the helmet tilt over on one side and the legs and heavily shod feet come floating up. Perdue's air-intake had got out of control and his diving-dress had blown up into a horizontal balloon.

It was a common enough occurrence—a product of slightly too rapid an ascent—and it was simply remedied. Dymond swung his legs on to the ladder and climbed down. Grabbing Perdue's gear, he pulled the diver in towards him until he could open the necessary cock and vent the suit. As the air gushed out Perdue's feet responded to the call of gravity and, vertical once again, he was able to climb up the ladder himself.

Dymond's spanner spun the front glass round in its screw-in fitting in the helmet. The moment it came out Perdue spoke.

" Jack, I've got a ' bend.' It's a bad one. And I've got pins and needles all over."

" Call the doctor," Dymond shouted over his shoulder to one of the other divers. Immediately he began taking off Perdue's helmet, then his weights, then his boots.

Surgeon-Lieutenant P. K. Fraser, *Tedworth's* medical officer, was down within seconds. He took a quick look at Perdue. The diver was suffering from ' respiratory embarrassment.' He would have gone into the recompression chamber anyway, but this time he needed special treatment. Dymond would have to join him there.

So he started walking for'ard, along to the ' flat ' where the chamber stood. The longish walk for'ard was the one thing that made the after diving position unpopular. Out of its natural habitat a diver's suit and equipment did not make the ideal walking uniform. Perdue particularly had always hated the trek—" the old death walk," he had many a time called it.

This time he needed all Dymond's assistance to reach the chamber and to climb into it. Almost immediately he lost consciousness. Dymond started on the artificial-respiration and massage techniques, which he had learnt for just such an occasion. But Perdue remained unconscious.

As the pressure in the chamber increased his breathing improved. But he still stayed ' out.' Dymond tried sal volatile. But with no success. After a little while those outside the chamber lowered the pressure slightly. Perdue straight away showed signs of the same respiratory embarrassment, but this time it was more acute.

At 8.15 P.M., exactly an hour after his helmet had broken surface, Surgeon-Lieutenant Fraser climbed into the chamber beside him. He looked gravely ill. Dymond cut the diving-dress away and the doctor listened. Ten minutes later Perdue's heart stopped beating. Between them the doctor and the diver continued artificial respiration for 40 weary, hopeless minutes. But to no avail. Perdue was dead.

The inquest took place at Bootle, three days later. The routine information was exchanged: Perdue had been diving for about eight years, he had been medically examined regularly and found fit, his equipment had been tested before and after the dive and found to be in perfect order.

Then came the surprising piece of evidence. The post-mortem examination had shown that Perdue was suffering from disease of the lungs, " with firm adhesions over the upper part of both lungs which, at the back, were adhering to the chest wall. Both lungs were congested and the upper part was scarred. Through the upper lobe on both sides was an area of patches of a tubercular character. Twenty per cent. of the total lung was affected." This state was such that it was not discoverable by ordinary examination. Regular X-ray examination might well have indicated something, but— incredibly, 19 years later—X-ray examination of deep-divers' lungs was not a naval practice.

The cause of death was recorded as " asphyxia due to insufficient reoxygenation associated with the process of decompression after diving. This was made possible on account of the diseased condition of the lung." In reply to a juryman's question it was said that it was highly improbable that the condition of Perdue's lungs was due to his occupation. A verdict of Misadventure was returned.

Thetis had claimed her hundredth victim. Petty Officer Henry Otho Perdue had joined the 99 men in the sunken vessel, with the submariners among whom, at least, he had so very much in common. The atmosphere in *Tedworth* was one of sadness, a sadness which never completely departed during the remainder of her sojourn in Liverpool Bay.

It was on the day of the inquest—the 26th—that *Zelo* resumed her moorings over *Thetis*. The divers set to work once again securing all the lifting wires in position. They had persistent trouble with the wires getting foul through the action of the strong sub-surface currents, but by the very early hours of Monday morning, August 28, their work was finished.

Low Water was at 6.30 A.M., and aboard *Zelo* the huge nine-inch slings were hauled into position with the ship's derricks—they were far too heavy to be manœuvred by hand—and pinned round the new steel girders. The lift was on.

It worked without any snags. The morning tide raised *Thetis* gently off the bottom, and *Zelo* moved off on the first leg of the journey inshore.

It was a slow process. A low speed of movement through the water was dictated by the consideration that, if *Thetis* hit an ir-regularity of the bottom while travelling at anything more than minimum speed, the lifting wires might well part. In fact the second lift, during the early evening of the same day, provided just such a situation. *Thetis* was off the bottom and *Zelo* was moving inshore again. Suddenly the submarine wedged herself hard against a sand-bank. For three hours she stuck there, until the tide had ' made ' sufficiently for her keel to scrape over the top. It was an anxious time for *Zelo*. She was swung broadside on to a strong tide. Fortunately, the tugs that were manœuvring her managed to hold on satisfactorily, and the obstacle was safely cleared.

Progress on a series of lifts of this kind was rather a gamble. The distance covered depended on whether the bottom shelved steeply or gradually, and on whether there were any uneven contours to be negotiated. And every time that *Thetis* grounded the lifting slings had to be hove taut at the next Low Water and re-pinned around the girders.

Nine lifts were made in seven days. By the afternoon of the sixth day, Saturday, September 2, they had reached a depth of only six fathoms (36 feet) at Low Water. The final stage of the salvage was approaching.

Then, the next day, all ships of the Royal Navy received a signal from Admiralty. It read:

Commence hostilities against Germany.

War had been declared. Aboard *Tedworth* and *Zelo* the prospects for the future were the sole topic of conversation. But no one in either of the two ships gave even the slightest thought to the possibility of the wrecked submarine, slung beneath the surface, becoming, before many months were passed, one of the most successful units of the Royal Navy's submarine striking forces in the Mediterranean.

The ninth and final lift was completed that same fateful Sunday. As if in memory of all the bad weather that had earlier beset the salvage of *Thetis*, and perhaps also to mark the solemnity of the day, a squall sprung up just before the morning slack-water. Quickly the tugs came alongside *Zelo* and stopped her drifting away from her position directly over *Thetis*.

At twenty to three in the afternoon the submarine grounded gently on the edge of a sandbank. She had reached the farthest point inshore to which *Zelo* could transport her. The merchantman cast off the eight nine-inch slings, moved a short distance away, and dropped anchor. And, when the next Low Water came, *Thetis's* conning-tower could be seen lying just a few feet below the surface. It was over 12 weeks since she had last been visible from above water.

Tedworth, *Zelo*, and their accompanying vessels had successfully completed the major part of a quite remarkable enterprise. The method they had adopted was entirely new, and the results they had achieved were without parallel in the history of salvage in this country at that date. It was at this peak of success that *Tedworth* departed to her war station. Two of her divers remained with the Liverpool and Glasgow team to lead the Association's own two divers, Whitchurch and Hendrickson, in the work that was still to be done. They were Petty Officer Jack Dymond and Mr W. Linton, the latter being a civilian shipwright diver from Portsmouth Dockyard, who had been attending *Tedworth's* deep-diving course together with the naval divers.

What the salvage team proposed to do was to have the divers fit steel ' strongbacks ' to all the hatches except the one leading to the engine-room. The latter was to be removed and replaced with a plate, which had been specially constructed to carry a number of intake and outlet valves and pipes. Through this special construction air would be forced into *Thetis*, the water would be dispersed, and, eventually, the submarine would regain her natural buoyancy and float on the surface once again. The plan seemed perfectly straightforward on paper, but several more weeks were to pass before the salvage of *Thetis* was completed.

After three days' preliminary work the divers were able to go down and tackle the engine-room hatch. By this time the salvage ship *Ranger* had been joined by Commander Sydney Raw—now Vice-Admiral Sir Sydney Raw, K.B.E., C.B., and Flag Officer Submarines, 1950–51—and Leading Stoker Arnold.

Arnold had been almost continuously left alone—ignored, he sometimes felt—ever since the first part of the Tribunal of Inquiry concluded its hearing of evidence in July. Officially, he was on indefinite leave, awaiting any calls that should be made on him during the final stages of the salvage. He had reported periodically to the Submarine Offices at the Cammell Laird yard—ostensibly to see if there were any instructions for him, but really to endeavour to keep even in remote touch with what was happening to ' his ' boat. Two days before the outbreak of war he was told by the new First Lieutenant of *Trident* to take the night train to Holyhead and report to the Holyhead Police. He was to be shuttled between *Ranger* and the shore, as and when his services in identifying the occupants of *Thetis* were required. Some little time later he was joined by two leading seamen, ex-members of the crew of *Thetis*, who had been away on courses when the submarine sank, two representatives of Cammell Laird, and a member of the Admiralty overseeing staff at Birkenhead.

For two and a half hours on the morning of September 7 the divers were working without interruption, unscrewing the bolts that were holding down the engine-room hatch. When they came up they reported that everything was ready to lift clear. An additional small red flag was run up to half-mast on *Ranger*'s halyards, to emphasize the ' keep clear ' signal that she was already wearing. The whole of the crew packed around the salvage vessel's guard-rails in tense expectation. Commander Raw had joined a group of men in a small motor-launch, lying only a few yards away from where the divers had been working.

Down again went the divers. The sea was calm, undisturbed except for the streams of exhaust bubbles from the two helmets. Within a minute or two of the divers having gone down there was a slight commotion on the surface of the water. The hatch was off. Almost immediately, a dark object shot up from the shadowy outline of *Thetis*. It was the body of a man, barefooted, and wearing blue naval uniform. As soon as the motor launch could pick it up it was placed on a stretcher and hoisted by derrick on to the deck of *Ranger*. Later, the body was sewn up in green canvas and taken ashore to the mortuary of the hospital at Holyhead.

This first man out of *Thetis* after Arnold was Petty Officer Mitchell, the Torpedo Gunner's Mate, who had behaved so valiantly in the first hours of the submarine's suffering. He was, so the official report ran, " in a good state of preservation." Certainly Arnold had no difficulty in identifying a man whom he remembered with such affection and respect.

The work on the engine-room hatch continued for two more days. The original hatch-cover was hauled aboard *Ranger*. Then, as a temporary measure until the special plate could be fitted, the two Liverpool and Glasgow divers went down with some small-mesh wire-netting, to cover the open hatchway and prevent any of the bodies drifting away unbeknown to the men on the surface. Commander Raw meanwhile made the necessary arrangements for inquests to take place whenever further bodies should be removed from the submarine.

On September 10 the weather broke. The beach towards which *Thetis* had been carried by her salvors had been specially chosen as being sheltered from the westerly winds that were known to prevail. Now, in a complete change from what the local residents along the coastline had known for many a year, the wind started blowing strongly from the north-east. In no time there was a heavy swell, and the next day the seas were really rough, and all work had to be abandoned.

It was with no great disfavour that the salvage team viewed its enforced stay of three days in Holyhead, although its feelings might well have been different if the future performance of the weather had been known. In fact, *Thetis* was to lie on the beach at Moelfre Bay during 68 days, and on only 21 of them was work possible—on some of these, too, only for a few hours during the whole day. By and large, the wind kept in its unaccustomed quarter the whole time.

In order to open some of the bulkhead doors in *Thetis*, to permit the free flow of compressed air and the free drainage of water throughout the boat once the ' blowing ' stage of the proceedings was reached, and in order to shut off valves which would otherwise allow the compressed air to exhaust from the submarine, the divers had to get for'ard to the control-room. This meant negotiating the engine-room. It meant, too, removing all of the bodies that were congregated in the engine-room. The divers worked unflinchingly at the worst kind of task that their profession affords. No consideration of speeding the work of salving was allowed to interfere with the instruction that the removal of the bodies should be made with the greatest possible decorum. Frequently the log-book carried references such as " Message from divers— ' Stopping work. Tide too strong to deal with bodies.' " Inevitably, and together with the unexpectedly bad weather conditions, this meant that the necessary evacuation was not completed until September 30, some weeks behind schedule.

The sad business of identification went hand in hand with the removal of bodies to the surface. Tattoo marks, signet rings, laundry marks, operation scars—all were listed in the grisly records. The body of Stoker William Orrock, aged 22, of Glasgow, was found wearing his Captain's monkey-jacket. Funerals were arranged. Most of the victims were buried at Holyhead, but the last proud remains of Guy Howard Bolus, Lieutenant-Commander, Royal Navy, commanding officer of His Majesty's Submarine *Thetis*, were committed to the sea off the Anglesey coast, from the deck of a Holyhead pilot boat. He rested in the waters where his submarine had died.

Finally, the engine-room was clear. The divers were able to make their way for'ard to the control-room, although they had continually to make sure that their air-lines did not foul on any of the fittings as they heaved them along at right-angles to their path to the surface. Once they got to the control-room the men 'up top' noticed a sudden change. Instead of continuing to come up through the engine-room hatchway the divers' exhaust bubbles were reaching the surface direct from where they were working. There was obviously a leak somewhere in the control-room or in its fittings. The conning-tower was suspected, but wrongly—as it turned out. Eventually, the leakage was traced to the for'ard periscope which had, it appeared, been damaged during the later stages of the lifting operations. This meant a few more days' delay, while a plug was prepared and fitted into the periscope tube.

This stage of a salvage operation was inevitably a business of patching, testing, finding more leaks, patching again, and so on. After the periscope leak was plugged it was found that air was escaping through one of the main engine exhaust pipes. When this was remedied the divers discovered that some of the air injection valves, that had been fitted to the after external main ballast tanks, were buried in the mud, so that the connexions to the compressed air lines could not be secured.

This constituted a serious setback. One of the divers started work with a deck hose, to try to blow the mud away from the buried fittings, but *Thetis's* stern was so deeply wedged that he found he had no hope of succeeding. The next day compressed air was admitted to the main body of the submarine, bringing her to a state of just negative buoyancy, in the hope that the mud would be scoured from under her by the action of the tide. But she sank back just as deeply in the mud as ever before.

From this it was apparent to the salvage officers that there was a substantial weight of water remaining in the after crew space, where the divers had not penetrated and where lay 33 of the 35 men who had still to be removed from *Thetis* (the other two were half concealed in corners of the engine-room). To cope with this a hole was drilled in the pressure-hull beneath the deck-level of the crew space, and a large part of the excess water was driven out by compressed air. This lifted the stern sufficiently out of the mud for the main air-line fittings to be secured. Everything was finally ready for the ultimate salving.

On the afternoon of Monday, October 23, *Thetis* was given the full supply of compressed air. It was piped in through her engine-room hatch, through connexions to the external main ballast tanks, and through the torpedo hatch to the two fated for'ard

compartments.   At 2 P.M. her stern broke surface.   Half an hour
later her bows followed.   *Thetis* was afloat again.

She was an unhappy sight.   She had a slight list to port, her
periscope standards were bent or broken, her guard-rail stanchions
along the casing were twisted, and a mass of tangled wires decorated
her conning-tower structure.   Yet her salvors had brought her to
the surface intact and without any damage of significance.   Slowly
and carefully the tugs edged her towards the beach.   She was
grounded at high tide.   Thereafter she was ready for the further
evacuation of bodies, and—after certain deodorizing—for inspection
on behalf of the Tribunal of Inquiry.

With the draining away of the water and the exposure of the
remaining bodies to the rapidly deteriorating effects of the air,
the clearing of the after crew space was an unpleasant task.   Men
from a mine rescue squad, whose experience lay in this sad direction,
were supplied from a colliery at Cannock, in Staffordshire, to work
under Mr C. H. Burwood, of the staff of Siebe, Gorman and Co.
First, they rigged up baths for their own decontamination, benches
for laying out their breathing and other apparatus, racks on which
to hang their special-duty clothing, duck-boards, storage facilities,
and heating and lighting, all in two disused stables, not far from
the beach.   The weather then imposed further delays, and Mr
Burwood took the opportunity to recruit a number of the naval
ratings present—among them Leading Stoker Arnold—to add to
his team.   Briefly he had one of the colliery men instruct them in
the use of the "Proto" gear, which Arnold and his fellow-sub-
mariners found not unlike a D.S.E.A. set.

It was the 11th of November before all the preparations could
be completed and the sad work of evacuation finally commenced.
The whole of the mine rescue team went down into the after crew
space and worked for some 85 minutes during the afternoon.
Everywhere was covered with a greasy film of oil and water.   They
brought out seven bodies, each of which had been wrapped,
hoisted, and lowered in specially prepared sheets.   Conditions, the
team decided, were so bad that they could not face another attempt
that day.   Accordingly, six of the naval ratings took their places.
An hour later they had recovered a further nine.

The next day, Sunday, they operated in shifts during the whole of
the morning, being washed, disinfected, and re-clothed, and drinking
gallons of hot coffee in between spells.   There were 19 bodies still to
recover.   The first 14 of these were extricated without too much
difficulty, but the last five were the men who had died during two of
the unsuccessful attempts in the chamber, and who had been put
down the hatch from the crew space to the after machinery com-

partment. They were packed tight in a confined area that was awkward to approach.

This was rescue work at its most gruesome and the colliery team were not acquainted with the nooks and crannies of a submarine. Deck plates had to be removed, and it took a final 70 minutes struggling before the last five bodies could be recovered.

Once the last body had been removed and the 99 men in *Thetis* had joined Petty Officer Perdue in the rites of the burial service, the submarine was given an intensive survey. There were representatives from the Admiralty (including Chief Petty Officer Harry Rowkins, the D.S.E.A. instructor who had twice previously been concerned with *Thetis*), from Cammell Laird, and, in the person of a marine surveyor, from the Amalgamated Engineering Union (including Frank Shaw, there had been twelve A.E.U. men in the boat). The evidence they were able to assemble was kept secret until the Tribunal of Inquiry recommenced its sittings.

After their inspection *Thetis* was dry-docked at Holyhead. The physical soundness of her hull structure having been confirmed, she re-entered the water and was taken, still under the care of the Liverpool and Glasgow Salvage Association, back to Birkenhead. On November 18, 1939, Job No. 1027 returned to the place of her birth.

16

*July 1939, to
April 1940*

Tribunal

To the Right Honourable NEVILLE CHAMBERLAIN, His Majesty's
Prime Minister. I, ALFRED TOWNSEND BUCKNILL, Knight, one
of His Majesty's Judges of the High Court of Justice, having
been duly appointed . . . to be a Tribunal . . . make the following
Report in accordance with my duty under the said appointment.

THE Tribunal appointed to inquire into the loss of His Majesty's
Submarine *Thetis* opened its sittings in the Divorce and Admiralty
Division of the Law Courts on Monday, July 3, 1939. On the
bench with Mr Justice Bucknill, assisting him and acting as
Assessors, were Captain G. C. P. Menzies, R.N., a senior submarine
officer, Captain A. H. Ryley, an Elder Brother of Trinity House,
and Professor T. B. Abell, Professor of Naval Architecture in
Liverpool University. The Attorney-General, the Rt Hon. Sir
Donald Somervell, C.B.E., K.C., M.P. (now Lord Somervell),
appeared as senior counsel on behalf of the Government and
headed a total of 16 barristers, six of them ' silks.'

The first part of the hearing lasted for nearly the whole of the
month. Then the Tribunal adjourned until *Thetis* could be salved
and new and, presumably, corroborative evidence made available.
It resumed and concluded in December; and the resultant White
Paper was presented to Parliament by the Prime Minister in the
dark, cheerless days of the following April.

All in all, 49 witnesses appeared before the Tribunal and gave
evidence in front of the five-feet-long white scale-model of the
fated submarine. But the dramatic moments came almost entirely
from the four men who had escaped from *Thetis*: from the quietly
spoken, almost middle-aged, thin-faced Captain Oram; from the
curly-headed, unbelievably youthful, but none the less authorita-
tively voiced, Lieutenant Woods; from the tall, broad-chested,
square-jawed, commanding personality of Leading Stoker Arnold;
from the tough, stocky, laconic composure of Frank Shaw.

The two officers appeared throughout the Inquiry in formal,

dark civilian clothes, arriving with bowler hat and umbrella of meticulous similarity. Arnold, in contrast, provided a visual reminder of the sea, in his horizontally-creased bell-bottoms, his square blue collar, and his gold ' tiddley ' badges.

The formality of the Law, as it elicited the long, detailed, sad story, never forgot that it was participating in a Tribunal of Inquiry and not in a Trial. But the fact that the findings of the Tribunal would quite probably become the basis of a number of civil actions for damages was never far from people's minds. Nor, for all the people who had been concerned in the tragedy of *Thetis*, did this awareness diminish during the months in which the White Paper was awaited.

When it appeared Mr Justice Bucknill's Report spoke of " the many mischances which almost conspired to lose the *Thetis* in a sea of trouble ". In this he echoed a well-known maxim of the late Admiral Sir Max Horton, probably the greatest-ever British submariner, and Flag Officer Submarines at the time the Tribunal Report was published. As he was wont frequently to repeat, Admiral Horton held that any submarine can expect to survive a single, isolated accident or mistake, but that no submarine can expect to be proof against a simultaneous combination of more than one mishap. In the case of *Thetis* the simultaneous misadventures were manifold.

The Tribunal reported that at least six factors acting in sequence produced the full extent of the disaster. First and second came the complete blocking of the vital test cock with bitumastic enamel and the opening of the rear door while the bow-cap was open to the sea. Third and fourth came the failure aboard *Thetis* to shut the first water-tight door and the subsequent failure to expel the water from the two flooded compartments. Fifth came the failure of those outside *Thetis* to render effective assistance. And finally came the failure of those aboard *Thetis*, other than the four survivors, to escape by D.S.E.A.

The blocking of the test cock was obviously one of the reasons why Woods had not realized that No. 5 tube was open to the sea. The responsibilities in this matter were diverse. The work of applying the bitumastic was done by sub-contractors, Wailes Dove Bitumastic, Ltd, and completed on Monday, May 15. Cammell Laird stipulated that this work was to be to the entire satisfaction and approval of the appropriate Admiralty overseer. But the enameller did not take sufficient care to see that the test-cock hole was kept clear of bitumastic. And the Admiralty overseer—whose first experience it was of examining bitumastic work in torpedo tubes, but who, nevertheless, admitted that he was aware of both test-cock hole and rimer—failed to notice the blockage, and did not use the rimer. Nor was the rimer ever used by Lieutenant Woods. Two links in the chain of circumstances had already been forged.

There was a violent conflict of evidence between the Admiralty overseer—a Mr Edward Grundy—and the Cammell Laird charge-hand painter, Mr W. G. Taylor. The latter stated that Mr Grundy examined the tubes in his presence, after they had been enamelled. Mr Grundy, however, affirmed that he had given them an interim examination before the bitumastic and enamel had been applied, and that he had been waiting to be called to inspect the rear doors. According to Mr Grundy, this examination took place on Tuesday, May 16, but Mr Taylor put it one day later. In either case the Wailes Dove evidence would support the contention that the enamelling had been completed and the damage done in time for the Overseer to see. On this point Mr Justice Bucknill in fact reported that he believed the evidence of Mr Taylor. But, whatever the explanation, the inspection on which the enameller could perhaps have been expected to rely—certainly it would appear to diminish his responsibility—never took place in any effective form.

It was against this background that the rear door of No. 5 tube was opened. "The opening of the rear door," ran the Report, " was harmless with the bow-cap shut. With the bow-cap open it was suicidal. The act was the immediate cause of the disaster." Obviously the key questions that this part of the Inquiry had to answer, if it could, all centred round the bow-cap. Why was it opened ? When was it opened ? By whom was it opened ?

Perhaps the essential question was the one that asked " When ? "; for it was from this that the Inquiry's possible answers to the other two questions seemed to stem. The bow-cap was demonstrably opened, either before *Thetis* sailed from the Cammell Laird yard for her day's diving trial, or else at some time after this and before Woods and Hambrook opened the rear door. The Tribunal found on the evidence that was presented to it that the bow-cap had not been opened until " not many minutes before the accident, but there is no reliable evidence establishing the time more precisely than that." On the inevitability of this finding, and on the complete disregarding of the possibility that the bow-cap was open before *Thetis* sailed, it seems more than reasonable to demur. And yet, it is on this very point that the whole authority of the Tribunal hangs.

The relevant section of the Report reads:

There was evidence that if the bow-cap had been open for a considerable time while Lieutenant Woods and those under him were in charge of the tube compartment, they would probably have noticed it for certain technical reasons.

The principal evidence to support this seems to have been an assertion by Commander R. M. Edwards, the then Submarine Assistant to the Director of Naval Equipment, that this was his opinion. Yet there would appear to be *no* technical reasons to suggest that either the people for'ard or those in charge of the boat from the control-room would have realized that a tube was flooded during the passage from Birkenhead to the diving area.

Presumably if a flooded tube were going to be apparent it could be expected that its effect would be felt on the handling of the boat. But, as far as can be discovered, no trials have ever been undertaken to substantiate this. Certainly they had not been undertaken in either of the two " T "-class submarines in commission by the time the Tribunal sat. Nor would the war-time experience of a number of coxswains—the people whose hands and minds would be most directly aware of any such possibility—support the theory that this relatively small amount of weight on one side of the boat, rather than on the other, would be apparent even in a boat which they knew intimately. How much less likely was it that in *Thetis* anyone would be aware of anything slightly amiss—even if she did yaw a little or carry a degree or two of port helm?

For *Thetis* was a brand-new boat; her coxswain had never handled her at sea before, with the exception of the occasion on which her steering was connected up incorrectly; she had twice her normal complement on board, representing excess weight unevenly distributed, far in excess of the contents of one torpedo tube, even allowing for the effect of this being at the farthest point for'ard of the turning centre; and she was, anyway, so badly trimmed for'ard, as her initial attempts at diving were to prove, as far to outweigh any other consideration.

In terms of the sort of calculation that a submarine's First Lieutenant would have made, had he been trimming *Thetis*, two full torpedo tubes would have added approximately two tons' weight. But the effect of this upon the steering would be partly disguised by—in addition to all the extra complement—the huge boxes, each containing 28 sets of D.S.E.A. and weighing half a ton. One of them was in the fore ends, giving an additional unpredictable bias for'ard.

The Tribunal appeared to reinforce its conviction that the bow-cap was not opened until the last minute with the evidence that Woods gave about his reading of the indicators. Evidence given to the Inquiry stated that the mechanical indicators to the torpedo tube bow-caps were numbered 1, 2, 3, 4, 6, 5—with a reversal of the positions of the last two vital dials. Yet, in its assessment of the causes of the disaster, the Report accepted Woods's statement that he saw the mechanical indicator of No. 5 tube at ' Shut ' without suggesting that any doubt existed in the minds of the Tribunal as a result of this numbering. Nor, moreover, did the varying locations of the ' Shut ' positions on the mechanical indicators—on No. 5 indicator the pointer would be to the right of a vertical line while in the ' Shut ' position, and on No. 6 indicator it would be to the right while in the ' Open ' position—appear to have caused Woods's conviction on this point to have been qualified by the Tribunal. Yet there must be quite an element of possibility, at least, that, in the rather unusual state of the indicators, Woods's reading was less than accurate. In other words, not only was the mechanical indicator of No. 5 tube at ' Open ' when *Thetis* was salved, it was at ' Open ' for the whole of the passage out from Birkenhead.

From one's opinion about when the bow-cap was opened stem one's answers to Why ? and Who ? In the Tribunal's reconstruction of what probably happened their reasoning that the bow-cap was opened only a short while before the mishap led them to discuss, as a strong possibility, the likelihood that Leading Seaman Hambrook—who had been in charge of the bow-cap levers at the time of the incident—was, in fact, responsible for opening the bow-cap through some kind of error. As it would appear that the Tribunal's conclusions about when the bow-cap was opened were not *necessarily* correct, the amount of probability that the Report attached to Hambrook's being responsible might well not be justified. If this contention is reasonable it would seem exceedingly unfortunate that the widowed mother of Leading Seaman Hambrook should have been subjected—as she later was—to the three-fold anxieties of a High Court action for damages, an Appeal, and, finally, a hearing before the House of Lords, all arising out of the findings of the Tribunal in respect of her son.

Moreover, it would be nothing less than ridiculous to assume that an experienced torpedo operator had opened No. 5 bow-cap intentionally, through some misunderstanding. For if he had he would not have participated so willingly immediately afterwards in opening all the rear doors.

Imagine what would have had to happen. Hambrook had been working shoulder to shoulder with Woods. After knowing that telemotor power had been requested on the rams of the bow-caps, he would have gone for'ard to the control levers—to Woods's knowledge and probably to other people's too—knocked No. 5

open, and then returned it to ' Neutral.' For the next seven or eight seconds the noise of the ram operating the bow-cap, and the sound of the water rushing into the tubes, and the air bubbling strenuously out would have been quite audible to the fore ends crew. Then Hambrook would have returned to the rear doors and, under Woods's direction, opened No. 5.

It scarcely makes sense. Nor did any part of Woods's testimony to the Tribunal indicate that it had happened. And although there is ample evidence that telemotor power for'ard was requested by Woods in the control-room, there is no proof that this power had in fact been put on by the time of the accident. The only evidence is negative. Arnold was certain he had not heard the series of sounds that were associated with telemotor power being used and the reservoir subsequently being replenished. He was not bound to have heard them from his diving position, but it was quite likely that he would.

An explanation that would appear to accord with almost all the items of evidence, including the draughts taken before *Thetis* left the yard in the forenoon and the obviously incorrectly calculated trim for'ard, would be that No. 5 tube was flooded before *Thetis* left the basin at Birkenhead—presumably by Cammell Laird staff, at the instigation of one or more of the Admiralty overseers. Presumably, too, once the tube had been flooded the bow-cap operating-lever had been returned to the ' Neutral ' position without having previously been taken through ' Shut,' with the result that the bow-cap had remained open. Here, incidentally, would have been vindication indeed of the Submarine Service's insistence on keeping levers at ' Shut,' rather than ' Neutral,' whatever the theoretical arguments to the contrary.

That this in fact occurred would appear to be the most likely explanation, although the solution of this particular part of the *Thetis* mystery can probably never be more than a matter of opinion. But at least the air of inevitability that attached itself to the alternative explanation of the open bow-cap was surely by no means justified.

There was one other coincidental unfortunate circumstance that contributed to the disaster. Petty Officer Mitchell, the Torpedo Gunner's Mate, and the most experienced man in the boat with torpedoes and tubes, was on the for'ard telephone. He was not in the tube space in direct charge of the working of the tubes. In the circumstances as he first understood them Woods could not be faulted for putting so senior a man on a telephone position, for important messages could be expected to be passed and there was no knowledge, intention, expectation, or likelihood at the time of diving that anything appertaining to the torpedo tubes would be operated. But the fact remains that had Mitchell later been transferred to the Tube Space he would have gone about things differently from Woods.

During the years of peace-time competition between different boats in the same flotilla Torpedo Gunner's Mates had learnt not just the safe way of operating torpedo tubes, but the safe way of operating torpedo tubes in a hurry—which is to say, the safest of safe ways.

It was a common peace-time exercise for six torpedoes to be fired, for the tubes to be reloaded, and for the six reloads to be fired. The accuracy of the operation was a measure of the efficiency of the commanding officer. The speed at which it was executed—it would take some 18 to 21 minutes all told—reflected upon the abilities of the T.G.M. To inspect by the mechanical indicators, to look at the ' tell-tales ' on the bow-cap telemotor rams, to test each tube by the test cock, to check the positions of the operating levers: all this would have lost valuable seconds. Instead they used the drains.

For generations—that is, for the two generations of the Submarine Service—T.G.M.'s had used the drains. There could be no better method. The gushing of the sea-water gave all the required information. A continual rush of water would mean that the bow-cap was still open; the gradual dying of the volume of water would be indicative of the proper emptying of the tube. But when, due to the circumstances in *Thetis*, a young officer—still, in relation to his T.G.M., learning his trade—was able to take practical charge of, rather than merely to exercise authority over, a complex and dangerous piece of mechanism, this meant that the man who would have safeguarded the submarine had to be content with making two courageous but unsuccessful attempts in the hours that followed to fight the strength and majesty of the sea.

The Tribunal had referred to certain undisclosed " technical reasons," which would have caused the men for'ard to notice that the bow-cap was open. It might with advantage have concluded the relevant sentence somewhat differently from the way it did. It could well have said, adding the words in italics to what in fact appeared, ". . . they would probably have noticed it for certain technical reasons, *had the requisite tests been correctly and completely carried out*." For, unfortunately, and for various reasons, the vital tests never were completed. But Woods's conviction about the state of the mechanical indicators seemed to be fully acceptable to the Tribunal, even though he gave evidence to the effect that soon after the initial disaster he realized that No. 5 bow-cap must have been open. Might this realization on his part not have betokened an appreciation in *Thetis* that he could not trust the attenuated set of tests that he had undertaken? And might this appreciation at that time not have been worth more than his certainty during the Tribunal proceedings, on which so much was apparently based?

In dealing with the two factors that led up to the initial flooding it is surprising that the Report of the Tribunal did not remark upon the general subject of *Thetis's* trim, perhaps even listing it as the first of the several " factors acting in sequence to produce the full extent of the disaster." For it would appear that the lightness of the submarine could not, even through the most rosy-coloured spectacles, be described merely as " being on the safe side."

Obviously, errors in calculation had been made—it is impossible to estimate accurately just how light *Thetis* was, but it may have been as much as 10 tons, and she may have been short of sufficient basic pig-iron ballast along her keel—without which the disaster would almost certainly never have occurred. The existence of these errors is all the more inexplicable in the light of the successful trims achieved by the two earlier Vickers-built " T "-class submarines and by *Thetis* herself during her trim-dive in the yard. And had there been the requisite degree of certitude about the condition of Nos. 5 and 6 torpedo tubes the disaster would again have been avoided.

On factors three and four—the failure to close the for'ard water-tight door and the subsequent failure to expel the water from the two flooded compartments—the Report had little to say beyond recounting the facts and pointing to the gallantry of Chapman, Woods, Mitchell, and Smithers in being prepared to operate for'ard of the escape chamber in the full knowledge that failure to return would mean certain death. It would appear that the Tribunal accepted that on neither of these counts could things have turned out much differently in the circumstances that prevailed. And one of the circumstances that did prevail was that the for'ard watertight doors were fitted with eighteen turn-buckles instead of single quick-acting levers, in spite of Submarine Service requests to the contrary, based on the " buoyant with one compartment flooded but not with more than one " argument.

It would also appear that the Tribunal was perhaps a little less than fair in the wording of its reference to the three men who found they could not stick the conditions in the chamber. " Probably Chapman, Mitchell, and Smithers failed to use their sets correctly or to relieve the pressure on their ears . . . by the recognized methods," ran the comment. It might have been more just to refer to the fact that no D.S.E.A. training at depths greater than 15 feet was either prescribed or offered by the Admiralty in the years before the War—and it took a great deal of fighting on the part of a section of the Submarine Service for training at depths down to 100 feet to be introduced as late as 1954. So that, at the depth at which *Thetis* lay, authority had no reason or justification for expecting any submariner to be able to operate a breathing apparatus, other than for the urgent, brief purposes of escape, if at all. Here again it could appear that the Report had leant towards the criticism, however mild, of individual members of *Thetis's* crew and away from any possible criticism of the Admiralty or her contractors.

Some of the trouble that the three men experienced might well have been oxygen poisoning and not difficulty with their breathing sets or pressure on the ears. But nothing had been promulgated in the Submarine Service at that date about the symptoms and effects of oxygen poisoning. Had knowledge of it been more widespread, some one might have thought of sounding the bulkhead between the fore ends and the mess-decks to discover the height of the water, and thereby to find the size of the air-pocket that would be bound to exist for'ard. It could just conceivably have been possible for a determined man, operating from this air-pocket, to have dispensed with the dangers of oxygen under pressure while in the fore ends, and to have closed the door into the tube space properly. He would not have managed to shut the open tube by this means, but as *Thetis's* buoyancy would have lifted her off the bottom with only one compartment flooded, this would not have mattered.

The Report devoted a considerable amount of space to factor number five—the failure of those outside *Thetis* to render effective assistance. Such criticism as was either made or implied under this heading fell into three categories: that dealing with *Grebecock* in general and Lieutenant Coltart in particular; that concerned with the delay that there was in organizing a search for *Thetis*; and that referring to certain apparent lack of activity on the surface, once *Thetis* had been located—largely as a result of the expectation that escapes by D.S.E.A. would continue to take place—and particularly to the failure to hold up the stern of *Thetis* by lashing it to the bows of one or more of the attendant vessels, whatever the damage to a few bow-plates.

The criticism in respect of *Grebecock* would once again seem to have stressed the individual rather than the responsible authority. If the part played by the tug after the sudden disappearance of *Thetis* was less than might have been desired, this was surely a

The beached Thetis on the small Traeth Bychan, Moelfre, Anglesey. The configuration of her torpedo tubes is quite clear.

A Mine Rescue Team, having the unenviable job of recovering the bodies from Thetis, being briefed by Navy personnel on the layout of the submarine.

When all had looked bright!. The crew of Thetis marching along Conway Street in Birkenhead. The entrance to Birkenhead Park and the Queens Hotel are in the background. Stoker Walter Arnold is in the back row on the right hand side of the picture.

Thetis leaving the River Mersey in 1939

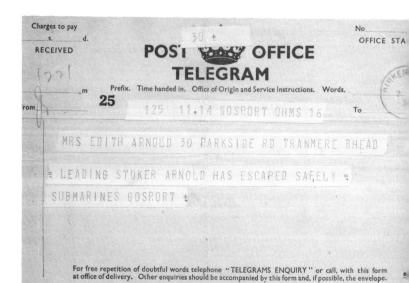

POST OFFICE TELEGRAM

No. OFFICE STAMP 3048

Charges to pay d. RECEIVED

Prefix. Time handed in. Office of Origin and Service Instructions. Words.

33   8 833 10.40 PORTSMOUTH OHMS 33

LIVERPOOL : m

To 1 JUN 39

MRS EDITH ARNOLD 30 PARKSIDE RD TRANMERE BIRKENHEAD

SUBMARINE THETIS HAS FAILED TO RETURN TO SURFACE AFTER

DIVING TRIAL OFF LIVERPOOL TODAY THURSDAY LDG STO

ARNOLD IS BELIEVED TO BE ONBOARD

SUBMARINES GOSPORT +

doubtful words telephone "TELEGRAMS ENQUIRY" or call, with this form at office of delivery. Other enquiries should be accompanied by this form and, if possible, the envelope.

The cold, clipped language of some of the telegrams that flashed between the Admiralty, the Merseyside home of Walter Arnold and Submarine HQ at Fort Blockhouse.

POST OFFICE TELEGRAM

Charges to pay s. d. RECEIVED

No. OFFICE STA

Prefix. Time handed in. Office of Origin and Service Instructions. Words.

25   125 11.14 GOSPORT OHMS 16

To

MRS EDITH ARNOLD 30 PARKSIDE RD TRANMERE BHEAD

= LEADING STOKER ARNOLD HAS ESCAPED SAFELY =

SUBMARINES GOSPORT +

For free repetition of doubtful words telephone "TELEGRAMS ENQUIRY" or call, with this form at office of delivery. Other enquiries should be accompanied by this form and, if possible, the envelope.

POST ✠ OFFICE
TELEGRAM

Prefix. Time handed in. Office of Origin and Service Instructions. Words.

98

198 W 1011 2 WARSHIP BRAZEN

SEAFORTHRADIO 11

To

MRS ARNOLD 30 PARKSIDE ROAD TRANMERE BIRKENHEAD =

AM ALIVE AND KICKING +

30 +

In 1939 the telegram represented the fastest method of delivering a written message. Charges would be made by the letter, hence the short, sharp messages.

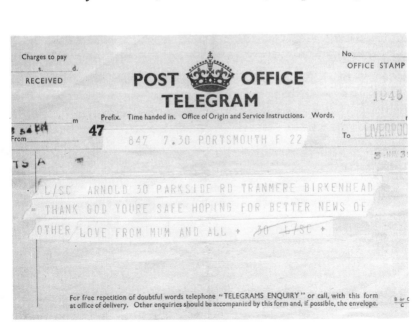

POST ✠ OFFICE
TELEGRAM

1946

Prefix. Time handed in. Office of Origin and Service Instructions. Words.

47

847 7.30 PORTSMOUTH F 22

To LIVERPOO

From

L/SC ARNOLD 30 PARKSIDE RD TRANMERE BIRKENHEAD
= THANK GOD YOU'RE SAFE HOPING FOR BETTER NEWS OF
OTHER LOVE FROM MUM AND ALL + 30 L/SC +

Thetis in Traeth Bychan, Moelfre, Anglesey where local men and Navy personnel are working on her. The homes on the island are still there. Today the beach has a sailing club and is a popular spot for summer visitors to the island.

Walter Arnold, his wife May, and Cammell Laird Fitter Frank Shaw on their way to the Court of Inquiry in London.

MOVING REQUIEM ON THE DEEP

At the close of the service over the spot where 99 men lie entombed in the Thetis this deeply moving picture was taken. Officers are at the salute. Others, under stress of emotion, gaze down at the silent sea. Sorrow-stricken relatives bravely brush back their tears.

WREATHS floated over the grave of the heroes of the Thetis as sailors stood with bowed heads and arms reversed while the Last Post was sounded.

Some of the floral tributes cast upon the waters.

reflection on the system of accompanying a new submarine on her first dive with a vessel lacking the sort of signalling and navigational equipment that might be required in an emergency, rather than on any decisions taken by a young officer placed in an unreasonably and unexpectedly difficult situation. Moreover, any delay on Coltart's part had been mirrored by an identical unwillingness to presuppose disaster on the part of his senior officers at Fort Blockhouse.

In its assessment of the conduct of operations from the surface, after *Thetis* had been found, the Report also omitted to comment on two important factors. During the vital period in Liverpool Bay no physically fit senior submarine officer was present; and the *Tedworth* divers, the one body of men who might have had a chance, however remote, of succouring *Thetis*, were left to kick their heels, marooned in the Clyde, while numerous facilities for transporting them were ignored. Both these omissions, had they been included, would have further shifted the emphasis of such censure as the Report contained towards 'the establishment' and away from 'the individual.' And any such re-orientation could surely only have constituted a marked improvement.

The final factor examined by the Report was the failure of more people to escape from *Thetis* by D.S.E.A. In the ultimate analysis this boiled down to the failure to begin D.S.E.A. escapes from *Thetis* considerably earlier, which in itself was a product of the general uncertainty that seemed to surround the subject of submarine escape.

It would seem that this uncertainty had pervaded a very large majority of the people concerned in the *Thetis* disaster, people both up top and down below. It is admittedly easy to point a moral and to be wise after an event. But this does not diminish the importance of any analysis of what went wrong over *Thetis*.

In the first place there seems to have been an absolute failure on the part of the Submarine Branch as a whole to realize the deadly menace, both physical and mental, of carbon dioxide build-up in a shut-down submarine. (In June 1939 submarines were not supplied with the 'candles' of oxygen and the "Protosorb" carbon-dioxide absorbent that were to become standard equipment in later years.) In spite of the initial over-crowding of *Thetis* there was tacit accept-ance aboard the submarine of the long all-night wait before taking even the first step in their own rescue plan. And up top there was the long delay in initiating search and rescue operations, and the half-hearted attempts at salvage.

Secondly, the uncertain attitude seemed to have led to insufficient training—in that none of the submarine personnel on board had

had any experience of high pressures, and none of the civilians had even done a shallow-water training escape—and to bad teaching. In the years between the wars submariners had been taught that they must wait until rescue was known to be at hand before escaping —but in *Thetis* they were waiting for almost certain death while it was flat calm and summer on the surface.

Thirdly, the uncertainty seemed to have fathered the useless, lukewarm attempts to do something from outside. If salvage is to save life in a submarine disaster it must be a flat-out and immediate operation, with every possible facility being rendered regardless of cost and under the orders of an experienced senior officer with nation-wide authority.

These were the real lessons of *Thetis*. They were far more important than any analysis of trims and bow-caps and test cocks and so on. Had it not been for the War, *Thetis* would undoubtedly have marked a vital turning-point in the history of submarine escape. Her tragedy would have seen a turning-away from a period of complacency, a period in which the provision of D.S.E.A. sets and escape hatches was considered an adequate safeguard, a time when the difficult choice between oxygen poisoning and carbon dioxide poisoning was recognized, but ignored when it became too awkward. Generally speaking, she did begin to bring about the realization that the actual getting out of a submarine was not the only problem—the defining of the waiting period, and the finding and rescue of survivors on the surface, and their survival until rescued, were also important factors.

But all this awakening knowledge was swallowed up in the exigencies of the War that the Submarine Service was so actively fighting, and it was not until the Ruck-Keene Committee on Submarine Escape in 1946 that the lessons of *Thetis* began to be seriously applied. It is not within the scope of this book to explore their application over the last 12 years.

Thetis had died. Her complement had been buried. Her body had been returned to Birkenhead. Her Report had been published.

The protagonists in her drama went their several ways. Lieutenant Frederick Woods returned to active service—but not to submarines as he had wished, for Their Lords felt that there would be an outcry from the Press if this were allowed. Leading Stoker Walter Arnold, on the other hand, was drafted to H.M.S/M. *Spearfish*, where the threads of Fate were to begin another dramatic pattern in his life. Captain Oram did not return to Fort Blockhouse after his experience. Instead, the later months of the year were to see him in successful command of a " C "-class cruiser. Frank Shaw was soon back at work at Birkenhead, although never again would he let himself be concerned with submarines.

A further man-made web of discord was soon to weave itself around *Thetis*.   After the publication of the Report of the Tribunal of Inquiry civil proceedings for damages were instituted on behalf of the next-of-kin of some of the men who died.

But on a much, much larger stage was being presented the opening act of the greatest drama of all—War.   And *Thetis*—reborn, renamed, revivified after her own tragedy—was to have a part to play that would have warmed the hearts and stirred the blood of all the ninety-and-nine who died so grievously in her service.

17

February 1940, to
December 1940

" Thunderbolt "

TELL me, Northwood, are you superstitious ? "

The Flotilla Engineer Officer of the Fifth Submarine Flotilla at
Fort Blockhouse, Portsmouth, twirled a pencil between his index
fingers. He looked at the spare, quiet, 37-year-old Warrant Officer
sitting across the desk from him. Outside the office it was a cold,
bleak February day. The year was 1940, and if the Army and the
R.A.F. were still complaining of the " phoney War," the Navy—
and especially the Submarine Service—was finding plenty of opportunity of engaging the enemy.

" Jackie " Northwood was surprised by the question. In his
seventh year as a Warrant Officer he had only a few weeks previously
returned ' home ' after his third two-year spell on the China Station.
Once his Foreign Service Leave had finished he had settled down
patiently to the routine of ' black-outs ' and ' emergency musters.'
He knew he was entitled to a coveted ' new construction ' and that
it was only a matter of waiting, but he had reached the stage of
hoping that Their Lords Commissioners would hurry up with things
before all the killings were over. But he failed to see where the
question of superstition came in.

" No, sir, I'm not."

" Well, look, Northwood. It's like this. Plans have been altered
a little. I want you to take on the *Thetis.*"

The senior officer watched the involuntary start that Northwood
gave at the news, but without waiting for a reply he continued.
" She is to be renamed *Thunderbolt*. You can pick your key men,
but they are all to be volunteers for her. That's all. Good luck."

" Thank you, sir." As Northwood closed the door behind him
his mind was already racing ahead to the problems that the forth-
coming months would bring. His disappointment and dismay had
lasted only a matter of seconds.

The atmosphere of the Birkenhead yard made a deep impression
on him. Cammell Laird had suffered a severe loss when very nearly

170

the whole of their skilled submarine staff had died in *Thetis*. Opinions were rife, and often the men with whom Northwood was working expressed themselves forcefully about the fate of their predecessors. The general opinion seemed to be that the Navy had been responsible for the mishandling of the boat, and that the salvage operations had been too tardily put in hand. But, with the odd exception, this kind of opinion appeared to be held genuinely and without acrimony. Certainly Northwood felt that he could not complain about his personal relations with, and the technical co-operation he received from, all sections of the yard.

The submarine was a hull. Cammell Laird had stripped her immediately her salvors had brought her back from Anglesey. For a few weeks they had waited for an Admiralty decision. Should she be scrapped, as a symbol of failure and misfortune, or should she be brought back to life again, as a gesture of defiance ? In the end it was the interests of the war-time economy that prevailed. Submarines were needed as fast as the Royal Navy could get them. *Thetis*, or *Thunderbolt*, could with luck be operational by the turn of the year.

As the weeks progressed Northwood was joined by his Chief and one other E.R.A., his Chief Stoker, and his Torpedo Gunner's Mate. The empty hull was cleaned and prepared. All traces of the boat's previous existence were erased. Piece by piece, the items of mechanical equipment were fitted. Gradually the characterless mass of steel began developing a new personality. She was growing away from being ' the salvaged *Thetis*,' and day by day more and more people spontaneously began thinking of her as *Thunderbolt*. No attempt had been made to enforce her new identity by means of a formal relaunching or renaming ceremony. Time, it was felt, worked best unaided.

In June she was joined by Lieutenant J. S. Stevens (now Captain J. S. Stevens, D.S.O., D.S.C., R.N.) as First Lieutenant. Stevens had had a varied nine months of war. Known as " Tubby," or alternatively as " Ginger," to his friends, he was a large young man with a red beard that was later to reach gigantic proportions. At the time of the accident to *Thetis* he had been the ' third hand ' of *Triumph*, the only " T "-class submarine at Fort Blockhouse. Later, she was to become something of a showpiece, as all the members of the Tribunal came down to inspect her, followed by a number of interested M.P.s.

With the advent of war *Triumph* had gone to sea under the command of Lieutenant-Commander " John Willy " McCoy. The closing weeks of the old year found *Triumph* on patrol in the Skagerrak. One night she was on the surface. Suddenly the Officer of the Watch caught sight of a mine; but it was too late to take avoiding action. Her bows were shattered, but by a miracle the torpedoes in the tubes did not detonate. One was blown completely out of its tube, a second had nothing but its tail remaining, a third had its explosive head crushed in. Eighteen feet of the boat's bows were missing and her pressure hull was split amidships. She was taking in a lot of water and could not dive. All that could be done was to plug the worst of the leaks and keep the pumps running at full speed, in the hope that they could keep pace with the incoming water.

Triumph was 300 miles from the nearest British port, and between her and home lay the enemy minefields in the North Sea. She wirelessed for assistance, turned for home, and proceeded slowly into the sea, hoping that the foremost remaining bulkhead would survive. Soon Beauforts of Fighter Command arrived, just in time to drive off attacks by enemy bombers. Eventually, after two nights and a day of slow, painful, dangerous, exposed progress she reached the safety of the Firth of Forth.

When *Triumph* went for repairs Stevens joined the submarine *H 50* as First Lieutenant. One day he received a chit to report to a job number at Birkenhead. Until he arrived at Cammell Laird he did not realize that he was destined for the boat he still thought of as *Thetis*. The day after he first saw her—he was, of course, in acting command—he had the sudden and unexpected honour of showing the late King George VI and Queen Elizabeth over her. The Royal Visit to the Mersey produced the War's first bombing raid on that part of the country, and that night *Thunderbolt* heard her first sound of war.

One more man joined *Thunderbolt* before her commanding officer was appointed. Petty Officer Telegraphist Yeates arrived a month after Stevens, straight from service in the submarine *Salmon*. There, under one of the earliest of the Second World War's submarine 'aces,' Commander E. O. Bickford, D.S.O., he had taken part in a patrol in which *Salmon* had sunk a U-boat, refrained from torpedoing the German liner *Bremen* on account of international law, and then, a day later, hit and severely damaged the cruiser *Leipzig*. As he unpacked his gear in his digs in Birkenhead he hoped he would find his new boat no less exciting.

Some two months later, in September 1940, as the Battle of Britain was reaching its climax, Lieutenant Cecil Bernard Crouch, Royal Navy, was appointed to *Thunderbolt* in command, from the submarine *Swordfish*. Unlike Bickford, his war patrols had not brought him any significant success. He might even have been thought—but how very wrong this would have been—an unwise choice for *Thunderbolt*.

Northwood knew him well, for they had been together in the submarine *Seahorse*, based on Malta at the time of the Abyssinian War. Crouch was renowned as a man of few words, reticent in the extreme, and a master of the art of playing everything down. It came as a little bit of a shock to Northwood, therefore, when on his first day at Birkenhead, Crouch made a short speech to the handful of officers and senior petty officers present.

" There is going to be no fuss about this boat just because she was once called *Thetis*," he said. " Each man who joins will be allowed the opportunity of declining to stay. After that he will be expected to get on with it. And there will be no backward glances."

The tenor of Crouch's approach reflected the background thinking behind his appointment. During the earlier part of the summer it had been suggested in Fort Blockhouse that some sort of special effort should be made with *Thunderbolt*, that some reasonably senior commanding officer should be nominated, and that a suitably high-ranking engineer officer should be sent up as well, to replace Northwood. But then the proposals reached Max Horton, the Flag Officer Submarines.

Horton had very strong views on the subject of submarine accidents and morale. He set his face very firmly against any flamboyant showmanship in respect of *Thunderbolt* and decreed that she should be recommissioned in the usual way, just as if she were an established boat getting a new ship's company after a lengthy refit. So Northwood stayed where he was, and a deliberately young, junior, and unforceful commanding officer was appointed. The business of having special volunteering for *Thunderbolt* was stopped and the normal drafting routine was substituted, modified only to give the officers of *Thunderbolt* preferential treatment in getting the remaining key men they wanted—Crouch reaped the benefit of the original ' special treatment ' for *Thunderbolt* by getting as his coxswain Chief Petty Officer " Charlie " Jones, a most sought-after submariner, whose transfer had been specially arranged—and also to give anyone drafted to the submarine one chance of withdrawing. On no occasion was this latter privilege invoked.

Cammell Laird had made good progress with *Thunderbolt*. Before October's mellow fruitfulness had completely given way to the drear, dank mists of November the newly fitted submarine was ready for her acceptance trials. As steering, engine, and diving tests were to be undertaken all on the same occasion, in the orthodox manner, there was no question of heightening any tension that might exist aboard by diving in Liverpool Bay. For the second time in her career as a submarine *Thunderbolt* moved off down the Mersey to try her builders' skill in Scottish waters. This time she was escorted by a Naval vessel—a change of pattern produced, not by any recollection of her earlier relationship with *Grebecock*, but instead by the demands of war.

She sailed north with only her crew on board. In the Clyde she was joined for each day's trials by a group of Admiralty and Cammell Laird representatives; but the numbers aboard never exceeded 75 to 80. Perhaps in conversation some minor prophet even proclaimed that " she'll never have over a hundred on board again." He would have been wrong.

The diving trial came last of all. Stevens and Chief Stoker Chipperfield had put the trim on before *Thunderbolt* left Birkenhead, and it was certainly a submariner's trim that Crouch and Jones found themselves with when it came to diving.

" Open main vents," ordered Crouch. No snags, no hitches, just an honest-to-God submarine, nice and heavy in the way that every submariner aboard hoped she always would be.

No time was wasted in bringing *Thunderbolt* face to face with the enemy. Early in November she reported alongside H.M.S. *Forth*, the depot-ship of the 3rd Submarine Flotilla at Dunoon, on the Clyde Estuary. Captain (Submarines) in *Forth* was the same G. C. P. Menzies who had been an Assessor at Mr Justice Bucknill's Tribunal of Inquiry.

For less than a month *Thunderbolt* was occupied with working-up exercises. Every complexity of her equipment was explored, every possible manœuvre perfected. The split-second efficiency of the crash dive, the mad stampede of ' Gun Action Stations,' the mental and physical torture of keeping at periscope depth for a protracted period at dead slow speed in a choppy sea: all were repeated, repeated, repeated—day and night, night and day—with criticism and encouragement alike coming quietly from Crouch, and an ever-mounting sense of satisfaction and pride developing throughout the boat.

The torpedo department received its fair share of the emphasis of the hectic weeks of working-up. Firing, draining, reloading, in calm conditions and in heavy seas, first at leisure, then at speed: until efficiency became automatic and the impossible shrunk into something that Torpedo Gunner's Mate Webster felt they could lay on to order. And if the bow-cap operating-levers were pushed hard against the ' Shut ' position with an extra feeling of satisfaction, and if the rear door of No. 5 tube was swung home on its seating with a little more ' shoulder ' behind it than was strictly necessary, who can say but that the exorcizing of old ghosts did in fact need to be a continuing process.

One modification in *Thunderbolt's* torpedo equipment regularly called to mind her previous identity. On the rear doors of each of the tubes there was fitted a ' *Thetis* clip,' as it was already universally known in the Submarine Service. This was a single dog-clip, which prevented the door from opening more than a fractional amount when the originally fitted ' all-round ' lever moved from ' Shut ' to ' Open.' This safeguard—while the torpedo department often cursed it as a delaying factor in their constant race against the clock— would, they knew, reduce the inflow of water in any subsequent mishap to manageable proportions.

Thunderbolt's navigator had by this stage already made his personality felt. Sub-Lieutenant R. L. " Dicky " Bird, R.N.R., had been with Stevens in *H 50*. One night, at Harwich, they had been celebrating some sort of Guest Night and, in the course of the proceedings, Bird lost his trousers. While still in this unprotected condition he sat on and broke a glass. His cut backside demanded surgical attention and, as there was no doctor on board, the job traditionally fell to the coxswain, no less a person than the well-known " Jack " Passey, who was later to train the human torpedo ' charioteers ' and midget submarine divers of the 12th Submarine Flotilla.

Crouch and his wardroom roared with laughter when Stevens described how they had a marked man among them. Soon they were to find that they had a magnificent pilot, too, for Bird seemed to have the knack of making miraculously accurate rendezvous. What was more immediately apparent about him, however, was that he seemed to consider his status as a reservist as excusing him from all the more tedious aspects of naval discipline. And his extreme untidiness—very noticeable in the narrow confines of a submarine—seemed only to make the precision of his chartwork all the more remarkable.

So it was that with a few brief weeks of working-up the submarine that had once been called *Thetis* had not only changed her name to *Thunderbolt* but had also welded into a composite personality the strengths and weaknesses of the 60 men who now formed her War crew, the noise and the reticence, the smiles and the stubborn-ness, the experience of nigh-on a year's patrolling in other sub-marines, and the keenness of inexperienced courage. The most nagging reminder of *Thetis* came from the dirty, rust-brown high-water-mark, which persisted in showing through in certain com-partments no matter how many coats of paint were superimposed.

At two o'clock in the afternoon, on December 3, 1940, His Majesty's Submarine *Thunderbolt* slipped from alongside H.M.S. *Forth.* She proceeded in company with her fellow-submarines *Tribune* and *Cachalot*, escorted by the armed yacht *Cutty Sark*.

Her instructions were to patrol off the entrance to the Gironde river on the west coast of France, not to close inside 20 miles, and to relieve the submarine already on patrol there, which turned out to be none other than her former yardmate at Birkenhead, the *Taku*.

Forty hours after acknowledging *Forth's* final " Good luck " signal the four craft parted company. *Thunderbolt* headed south for her patrol area. Nerves on board were just the slightest bit taut. Tension is always greatest at the beginning of any patrol. Speculation is always rife as to how good or bad the area is going to be. But on the first patrol of a new commission there is so much else for the ship's company to wonder about. How good is the new Skipper ? Has he a good eye ? Will he be able to shake off enemy surface-vessels without too much trouble ? And how will they all react to depth-charging ? With a bit of luck it would not be too long before they had all the answers.

One man looked completely unconcerned. Chief Stoker Chipperfield, unmoved by any gyrations that sea and *Thunderbolt* could think up between them, and untouched by any of the curiosity that abounded, spent all his non-sleeping off-watch hours sitting cramped up cross-legged in his minute storeroom right aft, where the rolling and pitching was worst. The cupboard—for it was no more—lacked even the slightest ventilation, but this did not deter Chipperfield from pulling at a large and foul-smelling pipe all the time *Thunderbolt* was on the surface. When one's eyes could penetrate the haze of thick black smoke one was obsessed by a most peculiar vision. Chipperfield had a huge black beard and, more likely than not, he was wearing only a knitted bathing-costume. During his continuing sojourn in his store—this habit never varied throughout the whole of his time in *Thunderbolt*—he kept himself assiduously employed. No idle moments were ever allowed to destroy his devotion to his one hobby—knitting. The occasional greenhorn would be foolish enough to ask him what he was producing on his large-diameter needles. " A new bathing-costume, of course," would come the answer. He never seemed to make anything else. They were quite professionally turned out, although the size of mesh which the large needles produced was sometimes almost too big for decency.

By the morning of December 15 they had been on patrol for nearly a week. Some stomachs were getting better; others had been written off by their owners as being likely never to get better. At 8.30 A.M. they were a little way south of the entrance to the river and some little distance inside their 20-mile limit. Crouch was tired of the complete inaction that had rewarded their watchfulness to date. He was looking to see if he could find any trouble closer inshore.

"Up periscope." The very moment that Crouch's eyes caught the daylight streaming in through the lower lens he saw a familiar-looking object in the middle distance.

"Looks like a submarine conning-tower, Number One," he murmured as he took a quick sweep through the remainder of the 360 degrees. Within minutes the drama developed. The alarm had been sounded and the whole boat was at diving stations. Unnecessary machinery—fans, and the like—was stopped.

Up top the object that looked like a conning-tower was joined by two trawlers. It then seemed as if smoke was coming out of the object, so Crouch reluctantly assumed that he was looking at three trawlers and that one of them was farther away than the other two. Quietly he gave orders to alter course back to the patrol area, returned to the wardroom, and commenced his breakfast.

Every few minutes the periscope hissed up again. The three craft were approaching *Thunderbolt*. It was still only 0909 when Stevens, whose watch it was, saw that the objects had suddenly altered course. The resultant shifting of the angle allowed him to see quite clearly that Crouch had been right first time. The one in the middle was a submarine. The smoke must have been an optical illusion. Crouch was called back from his breakfast.

"Port twenty. Steer 130. Keep her at Half Ahead, Group Down. Target is enemy submarine bearing . . . *that*. Distance approximately 5000 yards. Bring all tubes to the ready."

Thunderbolt, preparing for her first encounter, was a new girl to the business of war. The Italian submarine *Tarantini* (Commander Alfredo Iaschi) was not. The German Navy had been finding the blockading of Britain an undertaking that called for more submarines than they had available. The entry of Italy into the War seemed providential. She had quite a number of large submarines, and it was not long before some of these found themselves—not entirely to their crews' complete pleasure—in unfamiliar surroundings and required to carry out operations for which it could be claimed they were not designed; for Atlantic patrols, for instance, of up to five weeks.

Tarantini had just completed such a mission. She had been stationed off the west coast of Ireland, the weather had been atrocious, and they had made an abortive attack on a British convoy which had produced some rather unpleasant depth-charging. After several days without a reliable 'fix' of their position they were pleased and relieved to pick up their rendezvous with the German M-boats. It would only be a matter of hours,

T.A.R.—12

they were reckoning, before the long-awaited mail would be opened and the leave arrangements for travel to Italy announced.

Crouch was watching the decreasing gap between them, and observing the periodic alterations of course. He had to make a guess at the enemy's speed. " The disposition of the trawlers at the time was somewhat reminiscent of the start of an A/S (anti-submarine) exercise," he wrote in his patrol report, " and in consequence I gave her a low nominal speed of 6 knots." Quietly he altered course by a few degrees to come on to the firing line, and—such was his misfortune—just as he did so his target also altered course, with the result that she was plumb stern-on to him, offering the smallest possible target.

Within a few minutes he was ready to attack. He had ordered all six tubes to be fired—at 12-second intervals. Apart from the hum of the main motors, there was dead silence throughout the boat. " Fire one," called Crouch. A slight shudder shook the boat as *Thunderbolt's* first shot in anger sped away at 40 miles an hour. The silence was even more silent. Then another shudder . . . and another pause. The moment the third torpedo left its tube Crouch had a sudden fear that the target was in fact going a little slower than the 6 knots he had estimated. Quickly he called an alteration of course without interrupting the firing, so that if his fear were well founded there was less risk of all the torpedoes missing ahead.

After the sixth ' fish ' had gone the whole boat settled down to what seemed an eternity of waiting. They've all missed, thought Crouch to himself. " Up periscope," he called, and was only just in time—four minutes and nine seconds after firing the first torpedo —to see a tall column of water rise into the air. Then came an explosion which all could hear. Up went the periscope again, and this time Crouch saw what looked like the bows or stern of a submarine sticking out of the water.

Then the trawlers started depth-charging, but at such a tremendous distance from *Thunderbolt* that it was obvious that they had no idea from which direction the torpedoes came. While this was going on Crouch took another look. There was no sign of the enemy submarine. As she would not willingly have dived while her escorts were depth-charging he felt he could consider her as sunk.

A stern-on hit on a submarine was a spectacular shot at any stage of a boat's commission, but in a first-ever attack it was without precedent. *Tarantini* had, of course, no warning of the attack until she was hit. Immediately she started sinking aft. As her stern touched the sea-bed her bows came up and she turned over.

Those on the conning-tower managed to jump for it. All told, her captain, a Lieutenant Frattura, two midshipmen, a radio operator, and three or four seamen scrambled into the sea. But only Frattura and three of the junior ranks survived.

Thunderbolt continued her patrol. Two days later she was at 60 feet when an enemy sloop passed directly over the control-room. While the propeller noise was still deafening them another sound stirred their blood. It was a wire being trailed by the sloop scraping along the hull. Sure enough, *Thunderbolt* had been located. Two loud explosions came quite soon. They were unpleasant but seemed to do no internal damage. Half an hour later there were another two about the same distance away on the starboard bow. After that no more—even though the attacking vessel remained within hearing-distance for the best part of another hour. When *Thunderbolt* surfaced after dark it was found that her main aerial had been carried away, that her jumping wire had been severed right aft, and that there was various other miscellaneous upper-deck damage.

Four days later, in time for Christmas, she was manœuvring to come on the outside of the 'trot' of boats lying alongside *Forth*. Captain Menzies had ordered that all present should " Cheer ship," in recognition of *Thunderbolt's* successful first patrol. He himself decided to welcome Crouch in person. The latter remained on his bridge until he saw the berthing wires across to the next submarine. Then, spotting Menzies coming down the accommodation ladder prior to crossing the trot, he went down below to travel for'ard inside the boat. So he was not a spectator of what happened.

Between each of the submarines in the trot there were narrow planks acting as gangways. Menzies, or " The Colonel "—as he was widely known, in acknowledgment of his red and brisk appearance and aggressive manner—was on the final gangplank when it happened. One of the seamen for'ard in *Thunderbolt* allowed the rope that was holding her bows to slip. Her head swung off, and the plank, unsupported at its outboard end, descended into the water. With it went the Colonel. He was totally immersed, and when he surfaced he had lost his cap, but he climbed aboard *Thunderbolt* undaunted, and carried on with congratulating Crouch and his crew in the manner that he had planned. The cheers from *Forth* and the other submarines split the heavens and, if not all of them were for *Thunderbolt*, then every one, including the Colonel, understood.

" What a wonderful homecoming," said Jackie Northwood afterwards. " We'll never have a better."

18 *December 1940, to July 1941*

Forty-three Men and a Dog

THE group of men on the bridge were wrapped in khaki-grey, wind- and water-proof 'Ursula' suits, and black oilskins. Each of them was huddled round-shouldered against the cold and wet. It was not raining particularly hard—just the usual drizzle and penetratingly damp haze of the Iceland coast—but the white tops of the grey waves that sluiced over the bows seemed to set off the muddy pallor of the low-clouded sky and introduce a coldness that one saw with one's eyes more than felt with one's body.

Thunderbolt was on the surface, heading westward. It was morning, and her captain was sharing the discomfort 'up top' with the Officer of the Watch and the lookouts. It was their seventh day out from Dunoon bound for Halifax, Nova Scotia. The atmosphere on board was one of moderate depression.

After the undreamt-of luck of the first patrol it was almost inevitable that they should have drawn a complete blank on the second. They had been away from *Forth* for three weeks and their patrol area had once again been in the Bay of Biscay. They had had plenty of foul weather—snow, rain, gales, and bad visibility—but apart- from some distant explosions, which they took to be depth-charging aimed at some one else, they neither heard nor saw anything of the enemy.

This patrol had turned out to be their last from Scotland. Without warning they were ordered to sail for Halifax. An interval of two and a half weeks for leave and maintenance saw them away. There was much disappointment about the assignment. Not only had regular leaves at home been put out of the question, but the job itself sounded dull in the extreme. They were to escort east-bound convoys across the Atlantic until they could be met by home-based surface vessels. The idea of using submarines for this purpose was dictated partly by the lack of destroyers but also by the chance that if one of the large German surface raiders tackled a convoy there would be good opportunity for torpedo attack.

Alternatively, the presence of a submarine could be expected to frighten off any large surface warship which, quite probably, would carry little or nothing in the way of anti-submarine equipment.

It was Crouch who first spotted the indistinct shape emerging out of the mist. It was a large merchantman—a passenger liner, by the look of it.

" Challenge her, signalman," he called.

The dots and dashes of the code group flickered across the intervening distance.

For a second there was no reply. Then it came—in the form of a salvo of 6-inch shells. They fell either side of the submarine and uncomfortably close. A straddle on the first salvo would probably mean a direct hit on the second. Although in the same moment Crouch thought he recognized his adversary as the *Canton*, one of the Royal Navy's Armed Merchant Cruisers, his hand was already on the button of the klaxon.

" Dive, dive, dive," he ordered. " Off the bridge quickly. Let's hurry."

From *Thunderbolt* a wireless signal was flashed to Admiralty. " Challenged suspicious vessel. Accuracy of fire forced to dive." Crouch had decided not to speculate immediately on the identity of his assailant. A minute or two later a shout of glee came from the submarine's W/T office. They had intercepted a signal from *Canton*—for it was definitely she—also to Admiralty, which read, " Attacked and believe sunk hostile submarine." Later, twin signals were sent from Admiralty, straightening the matter out, and the more philosophical members of *Thunderbolt's* complement comforted themselves with the thought that to be attacked by one's own side was something that had to happen to every submarine, and that here was another stage of initiation safely over.

Years later, by which time he had completely forgotten about *Canton*, Northwood had reached the day of his retirement from the Navy. His pensioner servant, who was helping him pack his belongings, turned to him. " You're lucky to be retiring, sir," he said.

" Why so ? " asked Northwood. " I've done my whack."

" I know, sir. But remember the *Canton* ? " Northwood nodded. " Well, I was in one of her gun's crews and we were certain we had got you."

But it appeared that the *Thetis* luck had well and truly turned.

The next day a domestic incident broke the routine. Webster, the Torpedo Gunner's Mate, who had been attached to *Trident* at the time *Thetis* was lost and who was later appointed to

Thunderbolt, had a poisoned thumb which was obstinately refusing to react to treatment. His temperature had risen and his arm had begun to change colour. Surgical measures appeared to be called for. A submarine carries neither doctor nor sick-berth attendant. It relies instead on the handiness of the Coxswain with pill or scalpel. But surgery was one department of the Coxswain's duties in which Jones had not previously had opportunity to excel.

He consulted with Crouch and together they scoured the various medical books on board. There appeared to be nothing for it: either Jones operated or there was a risk of Webster losing his arm. By this time Webster was in such pain that he was past caring.

So the scene was set. Crouch offered his cabin as operating theatre. Jones—rather in the tradition, he recalled later, of the butchers of Nelson's navy—offered his patient a generous tot of rum in lieu of anæsthetic. Webster accepted but prevailed upon Jones to take a similar dose himself. " Because," he said, sitting bolt upright in Crouch's bunk, " you're a bloody sight whiter than I am, and the way you're waving that knife about I shall be lucky to escape with nothing more serious than a lost hand."

Jones complied—and then set to. To his intense surprise the problem was not to prevent oneself doing too much damage with the scalpel but rather to do any damage with it at all. Either it was very blunt or else the skin on Webster's thumb was particularly tough, but he had to exercise quite considerable force before succeeding. Webster recovered—and so did Jones.

The days and weeks and months at Halifax were uneventful, except for what seemed to be the certainty of bad weather whenever they went to sea. It was June 11 when Crouch sent for Jones and told him to get all the men down into the boat out of their messes in the depot-ship *Forth*—she, too, had been transferred from Dunoon—as they were proceeding to sea at the earliest opportunity. They were away within hours, almost within minutes, as long only as it took to get the last-minute supplies of food aboard.

There was much speculation in the mess-decks. The reason for the sudden departure, which at the outset only Crouch himself knew, was that Admiralty had deciphered an enemy signal asking for a U-boat to rendezvous just over 1000 miles east by south of Halifax, in a position just off the main New York/Gibraltar trade route. The appointment had been fixed for the forenoon of June 15 and *Thunderbolt* planned to be there as an uninvited guest. Crouch knew that she would have to be driven hard to make it in time. For what remained of the 11th and for the whole of the 12th and the 13th the submarine pushed eastward at maximum revolutions, although the state of the sea did not make this a very comfortable undertaking. On the 14th she proceeded dived by day and on the surface at night. And at 0150 (1.50 A.M.) on the morning of the 15th Bird announced that they had arrived.

Long before this stage of the commission Bird had demonstrated an uncanny ability with charts and sextant and tide tables and all the other paraphernalia of his trade. But it was appreciated in *Thunderbolt* that this particular task was a tall order. The weather had been bad. He had been able to get only intermittent star sights. And the spot on the ocean that he had to locate after a traverse of over 1000 miles was a very small one. Nevertheless, it was with a very confident grin on his boyish face that he stood in the control-room running a grubby hand through a head of untidy hair.

Daylight came and an almost continuous periscope watch was kept. There was no sign of any U-boat. The minutes ticked away into hours and the forenoon progressed. Still no sign. Bird's confidence seemed as high as ever, though some of the faith in him began to diminish. As midday approached he did, however, hazard the consideration that perhaps the German navigator had missed his correct position.

For the umpteenth time the periscope hoist hissed and the steel tube slid upward. Crouch bent to the eye-piece. " There she is." His quiet words stilled the boat. " Bearing Red 70 . . . a conning-tower . . . about 3½ miles . . . she's one of the 750-ton class." The time was five minutes before noon.

There was jubilation in *Thunderbolt* as the periscope slid down. Bird received an assortment of salaams. The next sight through the periscope showed no sign of anything, but, as visibility had been coming down and then lifting again almost minute by minute, this did not seem to mean that she had dived. Then the Petty Officer on the hydrophone equipment reported that he could hear her. The range was narrowing. The ' hydrophone effect ' put her revolutions at 250, which meant that she was doing about 7 knots. All six tubes were brought to the ready.

Thirty-five minutes after the first sighting the range had come down to two and a half miles. Crouch ordered a ' stop-watch ' salvo of all six tubes at 11-second intervals. " Stand by," he cautioned, as he checked the ship's head reading on the gyro compass repeater. " Stand by. . . . Now ! " The last word hissed out between almost closed lips.

Six times the firing-drill was carried out. But only four times did the group of men standing round the two periscopes in the centre of the control-room feel the characteristic shudder of a torpedo leaving the tube. Sure enough, Nos. 1 and 5—fateful No. 5 !—had misfired. For five minutes they waited to hear that one of the four remaining 'fish' had won their second U-boat. But no sound came. They had missed. Crouch looked dejected.

Several minutes later he had manœuvred *Thunderbolt* into position to bring her two upper-deck tubes to bear on the enemy. Away in due course went two more torpedoes. Again the men in *Thunderbolt* waited for the explosion. Again it did not come.

This time Crouch looked more bad-tempered than dejected. It was really not surprising that none of the six 'fish' had hit, for the huge waves of the mid-Atlantic had a tremendous rise and fall, and the draught of the target submarine was small enough in these circumstances for a torpedo to pass underneath her quite easily. But Crouch felt that Bird's masterly navigation entitled them to a kill.

"Stand by Gun Action Stations," he called. Within seconds *Thunderbolt* was prepared for surfacing and the gun's crew were closed up and ready to dash out.

"Up periscope." Crouch was taking a final look before surfacing. The gun's crew tensed themselves for their first chance of action in six months' commission. Crouch grasped the periscope handles.

"Down periscope. Flood Q. One hundred feet."

As the quick-diving tank sped them down to deeper water he explained. The U-boat had obviously seen the last two torpedoes, for when he had looked through the 'stick' he had seen her a bare 600 yards away, steaming down the tracks that the 'fish' had left, in order to destroy any chance *Thunderbolt* might have had of getting a further shot at her. *Thunderbolt* was cheated. Moreover, in going deep she got temporarily out of control, and went down below 480 feet before she was 'caught.' They had lost on every move—there always had to be a first time.

They cleared the two tubes that had misfired, fired water-shots to test them, and then re-loaded, having decided that the two failures had probably been due to insufficient firing pressure. For 10 more days they patrolled up and down the area in which the U-boat had been ordered to report, but he had clearly been scared away. For the whole of the period they neither saw nor heard any other vessel of any kind. Finally, they returned to Halifax.

It was not a port that the ship's company of *Thunderbolt* viewed with any great favour. Their pay was ridiculously small by comparison with Canadian prices and Canadian earnings; they could not get to like or understand the Canadian liquor laws; they were a long way from their families; and their share of the War was a very boring one. The Mediterranean was the theatre of operations that most of them had their eyes on.

And the Mediterranean was very much the topic of conversation aboard *Forth* when they returned. The glorious tragedy of Crete had been at its most dramatic—and, from the point of view of the Royal Navy, its most catastrophic—while they had been away on their unsuccessful patrol. The news that greeted them was that six ships had so far been lost, the cruisers *Fiji* and *Gloucester* and four destroyers. Names of shipmates probably lost were recalled, humorous incidents involving the now non-existent ships themselves were recounted. The atmosphere was one of nostalgia rather than of grief. But none of them realized that one of the ships—*Fiji*— had an acute personal connexion with *Thunderbolt*.

Leading Stoker Arnold had joined the submarine *Spearfish* in February 1940. But his nerve broke the first time she dived, and he knew that he would never be able to work in a submarine's engine-room again. In the April he was transferred to the *Fiji*. She was another new construction, and sailed for the West Indies to do her working-up exercises soon after he joined. Returning home later the same year, she was torpedoed but managed to make the Clyde under her own steam. Arnold's experience of dealing with dead bodies in awkward positions was widened when this happened, for the task of getting some of the corpses out of the stricken boiler-room fell partly to him.

After completing repairs *Fiji* eventually made her way to the Mediterranean. She took a battalion of the Leicestershire Regiment to Crete, and from then onward remained right in the thick of things. On June 21 she received multiple hits from incessant Stuka dive-bombing attacks.

Arnold was in the for'ard engine-room when a bomb fractured the fuel tanks and had them all swimming in oil. Minutes later they were hit again, and the ship took on an immediate heavy list to starboard. She was obviously sinking, and the order came round to " Abandon Ship." Getting to the upper deck from the engine-room called for Arnold's reserves of strength—inside him he could feel the same hollowness that he had known in *Thetis*. Water was entering, there was oil everywhere, most of the lighting had gone, and the angle was increasing. Moreover, he knew that she was short of boats, having already dropped a number of hers for some other ship that she had seen sunk.

By the time he reached the open she had rolled over so far that he was walking on her side, looking for somewhere to jump. The only people he could see still aboard were the Captain, the Commander, the Royal Marine Captain, and a Canteen Assistant. He had not managed to swim very far before she turned over completely. He could hear all the machinery crashing loose, and remembered thinking that the gun-turrets would have fallen out. For several hours he floated, hanging to a small piece of wood, gradually drifting among a crowd of other survivors who had got clear before he had. It was well into the night before an escorting destroyer found them. He was so exhausted that he found it almost impossible to reach the top of the scrambling net that was slung over her side. Then he was safe. First *Thetis*, then *Fiji*. What would it be next, he thought.

" What will it be next ? " was very much the cry aboard *Thunderbolt* too. To their delight they found that their period of purgatory in Halifax had been rewarded with a posting to Gibraltar. They sailed on July 8. Nine days later, on the evening of the 17th, they were signalled to try to pick up the survivors of a British merchantman, the s.s. *Guelma*, in a position midway between Madeira and the Canary Islands.

The *Guelma* (Frank C. Strick and Company) had opened her articles on Boxing Day, 1941, when her crew signed on for her 101st voyage. She was a hoary old coal-burner, unable to squeeze more than a cantankerous 7 knots out of her engines. So when she sailed for Cape Town from the Clyde, as part of a 9-knot convoy, it was not surprising that she should soon be left to her own devices. Her master, Captain W. G. Taylor, could not really arouse any dismay.

She reached the Azores, where she had cargo to unload, without incident. Unfortunately one of the items was too heavy for her derrick to lift, and the only firm on the island with a suitable set of sheer-legs was German-owned. They had no alternative. The next morning they sailed for Funchal to discharge some coal.

It was in a ship-chandlers ashore that the bombshell was dropped. " We knew you would arrive safely with the coal," a stranger remarked apropos of nothing to the *Guelma's* Chief Steward, Mr E. Jones. " You were escorted by a German submarine all the way from the Azores, to make sure that nothing happened to you," he continued. " The Germans need your coal to get some of their own merchantmen out of here." He was greeted with a laugh, which seemed to annoy him. " I should be careful when you leave," he fired as a parting shot, " because they'll have no need to safeguard you any longer." Five days later they sailed with a cargo of onions, wines, and basketwork chairs for Freetown.

They had been at sea 14 hours and it was four o'clock in the afternoon when there was a loud explosion aft. The ship reeled. Quickly she started settling by the stern. The enemy submarine surfaced and circled round her as her crew prepared to abandon ship. There were onions everywhere. Some freak of the explosion had bombarded them into cabins, offices, and machinery spaces.

Rapidly the wireless operators tapped out a last position and SOS. Speedily one or two essentials were saved—for more than one member of the crew it seemed that a bottle of whisky figured high on the list—and one man managed to do a quick change from a solitary towel around his waist to a full No. 1 uniform complete with spotless white buckskin shoes. They made sure that Nigger, the ship's dog, scrambled into one of the boats with them. In addition to him, and including two stowaways, they numbered forty-three.

As they pulled clear, the submarine—by this time they had gathered that she was an Italian—fired another torpedo which hit the *Guelma* amidships. In no time she went down—" God bless the old tub," some one murmured—echoing her relief with the explosions of her boilers. The submarine followed her, and the men in the *Guelma's* boats were alone on a desert of water with only the millions of bobbing onions for company. The sea even got up, and they were all sick. The spray made them cold and miserable, and they had to bail continuously because the boats leaked. So they entered upon an unhappy night.

Back in *Thunderbolt* " Dicky " Bird announced that they were in the position which *Guelma* had radioed at the time of her sinking. The deck-watch in the control-room showed 2.40 A.M. There was no sign of boats or survivors, so the submarine patrolled to leeward and up and down the path of the moon. At 5.28 A.M. she dived. Crouch wanted to bring in the daylight dived, in the accepted fashion, for this was one of the times a submarine was traditionally the most vulnerable. Moreover, he wanted to be able to listen for hydrophone effect, in case the enemy submarine that had sunk the *Guelma* should still be in the vicinity. By 6.20 A.M. it was fully light and there had been no " H.E."; so *Thunderbolt* surfaced.

It was Chief Mate Trattles's boat who first spotted her. All they could make out was the sinister line of the swept upper-deck broken only by the gun and conning-tower structure. She was low down on the horizon and making towards them. They wondered what nationality she was; it was impossible to tell. Captain Taylor saw her from his boat, and took off his uniform jacket and hid it under one of the thwarts. If she were a German he would be the first they would want—they made a practice of taking sunken merchant-men's captains with them—and it might be possible to say that the captain was lost in another boat. So they all waited, each with his own thoughts. Soon she had closed right in. With a defiant gesture she suddenly swung off course, and the waiting men could see a flag tugging at its halyards—it was the White Ensign.

Crouch kept her moving slow ahead all the time they were

manœuvring among the boats—they could not risk being a stationary target—and this made the embarking a tricky business. First aboard was Nigger, to a subdued cheer from the seamen on the casing. A few minutes later Crouch was able to sink the lifeboats and set course for Gibraltar.

For two more days he kept on the surface the whole time. Then, one day out from their destination, he decided to dive to check the trim. " For, after all," he told Taylor, " the last time this submarine had over a hundred people aboard she was lost in the most fearsome circumstances ! " Happily nothing untoward occurred.

So it was that the very submarine that had brought forth the complaint that underwater sailors were the complete antithesis of chivalry had itself demonstrated the injustice of that remark. The men of the *Guelma* are to this day vociferous witnesses to this effect. Everything *Thunderbolt* had was theirs, they will still tell you. They slept in the bunks—the submariners on the deck; they ate first— the submariners afterwards; they had the seats—the submariners stood. They were treated as guests throughout.

And their reception did not end with *Thunderbolt*. When the submarine tied up alongside the depot-ship *Maidstone* they found that a tremendous welcome had been organized. After plentiful hot baths they were given clean clothes and lashings of food and drink. It worried them that they could do so little in return. But they did arrange an interim payment from the local consul so that they could pass the hat round for *Thunderbolt's* mess fund. And they presented the boat with Nigger. *Thunderbolt* thought him a delightful present, even though they had to leave him in *Maidstone* when they sailed for Malta.

Crouch and his crew had enjoyed their humanitarian trip. The joviality of it—in fact, the almost Boy Scout-like, play-the-game flavour of all the scant excitement they had had since leaving Dunoon—had overshadowed their awareness of the grim and dangerous theatre of war that they were now entering. But such grimness and such danger as might lie ahead of them would be, they knew, a sort of happy grimness and a kind of pleasant danger.

For the perils that their predecessors in *Thetis* had tasted to the full had been unnatural as well as incontestable. *Thunderbolt*, by contrast, was in her element. She and her crew were doing what they had been built and trained to do. Together they would face what came with a glow in their hearts rather than with a shiver at their backs. And whatever should come would only ever be disaster, never tragedy.

19

September 1941, to
February 1943

Patrolling

For the umpteenth time since they had left Alexandria, Crouch laughed quietly to himself. They were on the twelfth day of their First Mediterranean War Patrol. It was September 1941. They were on the surface, close inshore, near Benghazi.

Never before on the commission had he come so near to riling the men who worked so willingly with and for him. Normally he had a very withdrawn sense of humour. But on this occasion, even though he laughed quietly, it was the laugh of an extrovert. He had heard the story in the depot-ship just before they sailed. " It's the funniest I've ever heard," he told them time and time again, " and it's clever and appropriate. It ends with ' and I said Blow Main Ballast,' but I can't remember the rest."

And on the twelfth day he was still repeating the punch line, still laughing, and still saying that he wished he could remember the remainder. The previous night they had closed the coast somewhere off Sirte and done a night bombardment on a likely-looking coastal village, hoping they had not injured any locals. The object had been to give the gun's crew its first real live workout. During the day they had quietly navigated round towards El Agheila, and had found a naturally protected anchorage containing some small craft and a large three-masted schooner, all nestling very cosily under a shallow cliff. After dark they crept in as close as they could to the surface, keeping nice and low in the water, and speaking in whispers—the latter more from nervousness than anything else.

" Open fire," called Crouch—and away they went. The third round hit. At that moment the shore batteries opened up, using attractively coloured tracer. After a total of 11 rounds fired at the schooner, including four hits and two possibles, target was switched to the batteries. Then *Thunderbolt* ran aground !

" Blow main ballast," shouted Crouch in an unaccustomedly loud voice. Knees went weak as the keel of the submarine grated along the bottom. But her excess buoyancy brought her clear in time, before she could ground and become a sitting target. Ten minutes later they were in deeper water, had dived, and were safely away. The schooner continued merrily on fire and was obviously a total loss.

Crouch had had his punch line brought full circle and the remedy worked. He seemed to forget his funniest-ever story forthwith. This in itself was a subject for rejoicing inside the boat, but of more serious value was the way in which the gun's crew had proved itself on its first blooding. As gun-actions continued Crouch was to speak and write very highly of his Gunnery Officer, Lieutenant Martin Hutley, R.N.R., and his Gunlayer, Able Seaman Eric Webb.

On the same patrol Crouch got an early opportunity of a complicated Mediterranean torpedo attack. They were off Benghazi in the early evening when they spotted a small convoy consisting of a steamer and two sailing vessels, with an attendant destroyer and some escorting aircraft.

At first it looked as though it would be a short attack, but then the convoy seemed to lose any idea of where it was going and wandered aimlessly to and fro, with the result that *Thunderbolt* anticipated a lot of incorrect positions. Eventually, after well over an hour's manoeuvring, Crouch was ready to fire. A matter of seconds before he called his firing order the destroyer and the steamer turned suddenly through 180 degrees. They were patently going to retrace their steps and round up one of the laggard sailing ships.

Crouch muttered bad-temperedly to himself. He now had only a stern-on view of his target. And the dusk was coming in fast. To increase his visibility through the periscope he had an old coat thrown over his head and shoulders, which made him look, as he swung the periscope round from one bearing to another, like an extremely animated photographer.

" We'll take a chance, Number One," he said, having suddenly made up his mind. " But she's not worth more than one."

So one torpedo only was fired. Sharply *Thunderbolt* turned, increased speed, and went deep. At the right interval there came two dull explosions reverberating through her steel sides. The hydrophone operator could hear distinctly the sounds of the steamer breaking up. Crouch had secured a most remarkable hit. The crew grinned. Torpedo hits were what most of them—with the obvious exception of the gun's crew—lived for.

For a few more minutes they kept up their high underwater speed. But as soon as the propeller noises of the destroyer began to close they shut down and went quiet. Minutes later their first depth-charging started. Fourteen were dropped within two hours —some unpleasantly near, but none dangerously so—until with the onset of complete darkness they were left in peace.

Bird's navigation on this patrol seemed to indicate that he was just as infallible in the Mediterranean as he had been elsewhere. His vices as well as his virtues seemed unchanging too. He was a terribly heavy sleeper, and much to the disgust—not always fabricated—of the other watch-keeping officers, it was often almost impossible to wake him.

One night Crouch decided to take a hand. Bird had had several ' shakes,' all to no avail. Quietly the men standing around the companionway watched as their captain took a grenade rifle and fitted an orange into the cup of it. Slowly he aimed just above Bird's head. The orange disintegrated against the boat's steel side and covered the sleeping navigator in a squashy pulp. Immediately Bird shot bolt upright, cracked his head hard against a valve handle that in normal circumstances he always remembered to avoid, and sank slowly back on to his pillow, dazed.

" Cor, 'e's gone back to sleep again," came an astonished rating's voice. Nor did his waking habits alter significantly. Bird was a ' character.'

As *Thunderbolt* re-entered Alexandria Harbour at the end of this first patrol in the Mediterranean she was met by a motor-boat carrying her brand-new ' Pirate ' flag. The skull-and-crossbones emblem was awarded to a boat as soon as she ' blooded ' herself on a new station. Proudly wearing her decoration, she manœuvred alongside the depot-ship *Medway*.

The Submarine Service believed that *Medway* was the biggest mistake the Admiralty had ever made. Even to-day, a decade and a half after she was sunk by the enemy, she is still acclaimed as the most comfortable, easy to work, and accommodating parent-ship ever entered in the Navy List. She was, of course, built as a parent-ship and not converted. She knew what submariners wanted and how they liked to live—well !—and she had the right sort of welcome for them when they returned to her.

She was genuinely thought of as ' Home.' There was a warmth about her sides that welcomed you as your boat nudged under her protection. The easy manner of her mess-decks (seamen and stokers were separated), the palatial space allotted to each submarine, the generous locker accommodation, the almost opulent washing and toilet facilities, and above all the tradition of ' submarines first ' that was so often lacking in other depot-ships : all went to make up perfection. When the sad news of the demise of " Mother

Medway" reached Blockhouse there was great sorrow. The lower deck knew that Admiralty would never make such a mistake twice; and, as one may still be told, they have been proved right.

For two full weeks *Thunderbolt* tasted *Medway's* luxuries. Then she was off to operate around Crete on the second of a series of five Mediterranean War Patrols that were to keep her occupied all told from the August of 1941 to the February of 1942. Her experiences were many and varied. A few were outstanding either in the form in which they figured in Crouch's extremely laconic Patrol Reports or in the reminiscences which they still awake. Together they all compose a picture of a submarine which, if less dramatic than the portrait forged by *Thetis* in Liverpool Bay, was nevertheless infinitely more true to life.

There was the time—it was, in fact, the second patrol—when they embarked the special agents to be landed in Crete. The party numbered a British Army Intelligence Officer (a Captain Jack Smith-Hughes, who was later to run the Cretan Office of Special Operations Executive in Cairo), two Commandos (the Sergeant of whom is now Major Ralph Stockbridge, O.B.E., M.C.), two Cretans, three Greeks, and one Pole. The Cretans, who had to be landed in some secluded bay on the southern shore of the island, were in appearance the oddest of the bunch.

One of them was an old chieftain, white-haired and bearded, and dressed in the loose black robes of his native land. The Germans had quite a large sum of money placed on his head, and he was returning home again—so the wardroom understood—to see if he could increase his market value. On the second day out he discovered *Thunderbolt's* store of ·45-inch revolver ammunition, which still contained the peace-time issue of lead bullets. Volubly the old man wheedled a supply out of Crouch. Contentedly he settled down at the wardroom table, nicking the heads of all the bullets with a large knife. No one quite plucked up·the courage to try to explain to him about International Law.

His colleague spoke no English at all, but apparently had a well-developed sense of humour. He worked on the principle that whenever he heard anyone else laughing he would laugh too. His jovial reputation was dimmed a little, however, when the old man proudly revealed that he was a twice-convicted murderer, who had escaped the death penalty the first time on account of a change of Government and the second time in order to fight the Germans when they attacked Greece.

The final surprise came when *Thunderbolt* located the bay where the two desperadoes had to be landed. Obviously they had been extremely indiscreet in Alexandria, for the whole village was out in small boats waiting to welcome them. Fortunately the ' buzz ' had not reached the Germans.

The other agents were scarcely less colourful, being hung around with revolvers, knives, and the like, from which—as far as the submariners could see—they were not parted even when they turned in to sleep. Just before they were due to be landed somebody remembered the food tins. In haste the off-duty E.R.A.'s. had to turn to, carefully open the bottom ends of jam and biscuit tins, secrete literally thousands of pounds' worth of local currency (not negotiable in ' Alex,' they were firmly warned) among the contents, and then solder up the tins again as neatly as they could. It was all in the day's work.

The second landing was as far from the textbook as the first, but in a different sort of a way. The gun's crew was closed up just in case of any emergency. They watched the folboat canoes come up the fore-end ladder, over the casing, and then off noiselessly inshore to cover the remaining few hundred yards in to the beach. About half an hour later the two Commandos finally returned, having ferried all the remaining agents over to the land. Just as the folboats were being restowed down into the fore ends a dim shadow came out of the darkness. It was a native caique.

Thunderbolt's First Lieutenant (Lieutenant B. J. Andrew, R.N., a relief for Stevens, who had gone off for a commanding officer's course) was still on the for'ard casing. In his best Franco-Scottish voice he hailed the shadow. " Parlez-vous français ? " The gun had swung round to bear on the target, and moving shadows of men within the boat's outline had become apparent. " Grecon soldats," came the answer. " You want feesh—we give you feesh."

Then Crouch interrupted, distrusting the naïveté of the situation. " Full astern both," he ordered. " Stand by to open fire." Without hesitation the crew of the caique jumped over the side to a man. This was what Crouch had intended, and he was free to sink her with a clear conscience. " Open fire ! " he commanded.

Gunlayer Webb pulled the firing lever. Misfire ! In his best Gunnery School manner he bawled " Misfire: change lock." But the breech worker had not brought up the spare. And when it did come up and was fitted everything else seemed to go wrong. It took them at least 12 shots to sink the caique at point-blank range. Webb felt dejected. " Gunlayer's nightmare," he murmured self-consciously when he eventually came below. " Gunlayer's nothing," a mess-deck wit answered him. " The Chef could have hit it with a handful of spuds."

On the same patrol *Thunderbolt* fired three torpedoes at a 6000-ton tanker and missed. For the next nine hours she was savagely hunted by destroyers and aircraft. It was one of the worst days she was to experience. The explosions had cracked the sump of No. 3 battery, with the result that compensating water entered the battery compartment. The first indication they got was a faint hint of chlorine gas coming into the control room. A quick glance through a battery inspection door showed the water just lapping the tops of the battery cells. Fortunately there was a lull in the attack from the surface, and they were able to run the pumps in comparative safety, and expel the water without attracting attention back to themselves.

The same attack had damaged the Asdic dome. Without this the submarine was largely deaf as well as blind underwater. And their hope of ultimately escaping from an area of the Aegean strongly infested with enemy war vessels would be greatly diminished. But it did not seem to be a soluble problem. Or such, at least, was the opinion until Jackie Northwood propounded to Crouch a daring plan. At first Crouch rejected it as too dangerous for the men involved, but finally he was persuaded—" in the interests of the rest of the ship's company," as Northwood put it.

So it was that when night fell they surfaced quietly. Nothing was in sight, although they knew that the destroyers who had kept them company during the daylight hours could not be far away. Undramatically Northwood and his Chief E.R.A. George Curtis entered the tube space. The door was shut tight behind them— the aperture that Petty Officer Mitchell in *Thetis* had tried so hard to close was, with frightening certainty for the two men for'ard, well and truly secured. They set to work.

On the stowage compartment side of the for'ard bulkhead Engine Room Artificer Glass was operating the low pressure blower. Northwood had established with him a code of signals to control the inflow of pressurized air into the tube space. In went the air and up went the pressure for'ard. Soon an excess of some seven pounds per square inch had been created, and Northwood and Curtis turned to the cover plate of the Asdic dome. What they were going to do was to open to the sea the fateful compartment which had already once been so tragically flooded, and trust to the excess pressure of air to keep the water out. In theory it was straight-forward—reminiscent of bell-jars and bowls of water in a school chemistry laboratory—but in practice a lot could go wrong.

Before they started Northwood had had to take Crouch on one side and firmly tell him " Now look. We're very close to the enemy. If an alarm's sounded you dive right away. No nonsense. I guarantee to get the false cover over the orifice and the nuts in position before she can get down."

" All right, Jackie," Crouch had replied very doubtfully. " And one more thing," continued Northwood, invoking all his years of friendship with the man who was now his captain, " don't look so bloody worried. It won't happen."

Northwood and Curtis worked fast. Off came the cover plate. The oscillator flange nuts were spun loose amid the rising water, which stopped where they had calculated it would, and the oscillator itself, the functional heart of the Asdic apparatus, was removed. They found that the stainless steel dome had been crushed and was leaking badly. Northwood reached for the copper hammer he had with him just for the purpose. Without much success he tried to reach down and beat out the dome until it was roughly cylindrical again. Then one of them had the bright idea of increasing the pressure further. This they did through a series of signals knocked through the bulkhead, until an excess pressure of some twelve pounds had been reached. Miraculously the dome behaved perfectly. Self-satisfied, they closed up the opening, had the pressure taken off, and returned to the control-room—where they found that the Asdic still refused to work !

The earlier jamming of the oscillator in the crushed dome had caused the teeth to strip off a steel driving-worm, for which they carried no spare. So for the rest of the night Northwood sat quietly filing some teeth into the worm with a half-round file. Hours later he was able to fit the new worm into its wormwheel, with a host of adjustments to take up the gap between the old size and the new. The final result—it worked, of course !—was so perfect that the Flotilla Asdic Officer in Malta, whither *Thunderbolt* had been posted for a short three weeks' refit, refused to change it, as he had only one spare in his store. Not unreasonably Northwood was eventually decorated for his devotion to duty on this patrol.

The E.R.A. who had worked the L.P. blower for Northwood— William Glass—was another of *Thunderbolt's* strong characters. He was, and still is, a devout Christian. He had volunteered for submarines before the War, believing that their job was necessary and that in war they would be defending the people at home. This he still felt deep down, but he could not stop himself also thinking that his boat's ' successes ' were really dreadful acts of violence, speeding them all on the road to Hell. He found it difficult to feel the larger issues at stake. The War, for him, was between *Thunderbolt* and her immediate opponents. Whenever they had attacked first, which was almost always, he could not stop himself feeling that in the subsequent counter-attack the justice was all on the side of the enemy, and that they in *Thunderbolt* richly deserved all that was coming to them.

During his time in *Thunderbolt* Glass was studying for the examination for Warrant Officer. The refit in Malta seemed to be an ideal opportunity, so he decided to take a room ashore, where he could get peace and quiet. After three days' fruitless search he came to the conclusion that Malta was pretty full, and decided to content himself with a cubicle in what appeared to be little more than a doss house, above a café. He thought that the Maltese proprietor looked a little askance at him when he explained what he wanted, but he was most helpful, and provided a table and an oil lamp to go in the cubicle. The lamp appeared to be the only permanent lighting in the passage. As far as he could gather sufficient light filtered through into the other cubicles to allow one to see to undress and go to bed, but there was hardly enough to read by, he mused.

So he duly spent the remainder of *Thunderbolt*'s stay in Malta studying in his cubicle during the evening and turning in early as he had to make an early start. The establishment was pleasantly quiet, he felt, although he did hear some rather odd sounds from some of the other cubicles occasionally during the night. It was not until some little while later that he discovered that his academic institution was in fact a brothel. In spite of his patent innocence his colleagues purported to disbelieve his explanation; nevertheless, he half jokingly, half seriously, decided to write and tell his wife before anyone else did.

On the night before *Thunderbolt* sailed for her third patrol one of the junior members of the engine-room department had dined ashore in Malta well, but not too wisely. The next morning he felt too ill to join the boat and was absent at 'Harbour Stations.' Chief E.R.A. George Curtis had by this time heard a rumour that the youngster was hiding in the 'heads' (the lavatories) in the dockyard. Catching Crouch's eye, he strode ashore, found the locked door in question, climbed over it, hit the offender one stout thump on the chin, slung him over his shoulder, and strode back. In full view of Crouch on the bridge and of the assembled 'brass-hatted' senior officers on the quayside, he stumped back over the gangway, dumped his burden down the fore-end hatch, turned smartly to face and salute the bridge, and reported " All engine-room hands on board, sir."

Crouch never even referred to the subject again.

It was, in fact, the very lightness of hand with which Crouch exercised his firmness of purpose that kept the crew of *Thunderbolt* happy and razor-sharp during the next two boring patrols. Explore as they might, in concealed entrances to narrow harbours, and close to the land in shallow bays, where deep diving would be out of the question, it seemed almost impossible to run into trouble. All that the west coast of Greece seemed to hold for them was interminable bad weather.

Occasionally the monotony was broken by gun actions against vessels too small to be worth a torpedo. They demanded an energetic performance by all concerned. At 30 feet the gun's crew would close up in the gun tower and remove the pins from the hatch clips. The tower contained two hatches and the Gunlayer and Trainer would emerge first, one through each hatch. At 20 feet they slipped one clip. At 10 feet the First Lieutenant's whistle shrilled out from the control-room, and they slipped the remaining clip and pushed the hatch. Needless to say, they were always soaked well before they reached the gun as the last few feet of protesting sea poured down on them before the submarine broke surface. Within seconds the first round would be away, and the Captain and Gunnery Officer would be correcting and encouraging the attack.

But action or no action, the small incidents that formed the whole web of submarine life continued. One night the Officer of the Watch was so engrossed in studying the horizon that he failed to notice that, through mistaken instructions, the complete for'ard casing had disappeared and the base of the conning-tower itself was awash. On another occasion, when they were entering Alexandria Harbour, the W/T mast, which had been hoisted to carry the ensign, fell with a tremendous crash—one of the hoisting wires had snapped—making all the occupants of the bridge save one jump out of their skins. The exception was the signalman, who, with great aplomb, sprang to attention, saluted Crouch, and reported " Sunset, sir." (' Sunset ' was the ceremony of lowering the ensign in the evening.)

Inevitably, living at such close quarters as was demanded by the scant accommodation of an operational submarine, tensions developed—sometimes over the smallest points. All sorts of small things annoyed, irritated, and rubbed on the raw. E.R.A. Glass can still remember George Curtis's invariable habit of attempting to fill his ' tot ' measure exactly to the brim, and just as invariably failing to do so, and slopping a minuscule amount of rum over the side. As patrol followed patrol this began to annoy Glass intensely; not that he thought Curtis was greedy for the last drop nor that he personally resented the waste. It was just the inevitable regularity of it he felt was almost driving him insane for that brief moment every day. Every evening when they surfaced he watched, fascinated, until the rum spilt. At times he could have screamed when it ran over the side of the measure. And yet, within a minute the two of them would resume a completely equable relationship.

The end of the fourth patrol had seen a certain alleviation of the boredom in the shape of a successful gun action against an Italian minesweeper. The early days of the fifth patrol proved that their luck had turned once again. During a bare three weeks at sea—it was the end of January and the beginning of February 1942—some of which was spent on passage to and from Alexandria, back for a third time to the west coast of Greece, they made a successful torpedo attack on an escorted merchantman, sunk a U-boat and an armed trawler by gun action, were attacked at various times by five destroyers and one Italian seaplane, and were bombarded by 60 or more depth-charges. And the bulk of the patrol had to be conducted with only the low-power periscope functioning—the high-power had been put out of action by the first counter-attack.

Behaviour during depth-charging followed a set pattern, largely devoted to keeping as quiet as possible. One day the Asdic operator was taking out a dud valve from his apparatus, at the height of an attack, only to find that it was really too hot to hold. He had no place to put it and was frightened to drop it in case it exploded; so he had to have recourse to juggling it from hand to hand, giggling the whole time.

A particular hazard in these circumstances was always the magazine hatch. The odds were ten to one that if one trod on it it would resound with a fearful clang. Inevitably as anybody approached it there would be a tense look on all the near-by faces to see whether he would tread on it; and then there would be visible relief all round when he remembered not to.

If the attack lasted any length of time it was a foregone conclusion that tea would be brewed. Whichever messman was concerned went through agony on each and every occasion to complete this simplest of domestic tasks in absolute silence.

Thunderbolt's fifth patrol had ended in February. On March 27, 1942, she secured alongside the depot-ship *Forth*, back at Dunoon. She was home for a long refit.

For a period after her refit her activities, and also those of the submarines *Trooper* and *P 311*, were identified with those of the Twelfth Submarine Flotilla. This unit was operating the Navy's midget submarine and human torpedo forces; and the human torpedo side wanted to develop a technique whereby two or three ' chariots ' (as the machines were known) could be taken to their target area by an operational submarine.

The three participating submarines had large external cylinders fitted on the casing for'ard and aft of the gun and bridge-structure. Into and out of these the chariots slid easily along polished runners. For a few months working-up exercises in various remote lochs along the west coast of Scotland served to marry the experienced submariners and the highly-trained ' charioteers.' Then the submarines sailed for Malta and the charioteers took passage via Gibraltar.

To operate with chariots, or, subsequently, with midget submarines, can scarcely have been a ' big ' submarine commander's dream of heaven. The Submarine Service normally expects, for the pains and risks it must endure, frequent opportunities of engaging the enemy. To become a ferry-boat for some one else, who is probably going to be presented by you with the chance of a lifetime, and to be told into the bargain that no potential targets below the rating of capital ships may be engaged until after the operation, can only be the sort of assignment that one wishes for one's colleague. Furthermore, it entailed incurring the greatest of all submarine risks, that of proceeding close inshore into water too shallow for a successful evasive dive. It was to the great credit of all in *Thunderbolt* therefore—as well as to the complements of the other submarines—that in no instance was their undoubted dislike of the work ever made manifest in the presence of any of the chariot party. Co-operation was always of the highest standard, the charioteers affirmed. It was bettered only by the hospitality.

So it was that as 1942 turned into 1943 the two-men crews of eight human torpedoes were housed in three submarines sailing from Malta into a hostile sea. Unfortunately, the hostility of the sea was physical as well as political. Dressing-up in awkward diving-suits was obviously not going to be anybody's idea of fun, especially as seasickness was taking its toll. *Thunderbolt* had been practical enough to provide an open-topped five-gallon oil-drum. This would save fishing for buckets, some one explained to the charioteers, and it would also allow more people to ' play ' at once.

By 9 P.M. on January 3 *Thunderbolt* was in position a few miles to seaward of the North Sicilian port of Palermo. Conditions were bad, so bad indeed that they had been rolling noticeably at 30 feet. The wind was about Force 4, coming directly offshore; as inimical a set of circumstances as could be imagined for a human torpedo operation. As *Thunderbolt* lay stopped on the surface, water was breaking hard over the casing with each wave that pounded against the pressure-hull. Hand over hand the first pair of charioteers—Lieutenant Richard Greenland, R.N.V.R., and Leading Signalman

Alec Ferrier—pulled themselves along to where their machine was
housed. To the submariners on *Thunderbolt's* bridge they looked
grotesque in their clumsy diving-suits and self-contained breathing-
sets.

Observing the well-worn tradition of "one hand for yourself
and one for the King," they had to struggle hard to keep a grip on
the container while they released the door. The drill to which
they had become accustomed in training continued. *Thunderbolt*
flooded down in the water and, as casing and containers came
awash, the machine rose off the chocks and was hauled clear. The
two riders scrambled or were flung astride. Immediately the
casing plunged down further, forced under by a particularly heavy
wave. As it did so the jumping-wire whistled past the charioteers'
shoulders, descending at such a speed that it would surely have
wrecked their chances right from the start, had it been inches
nearer.

Without further ado the tiny machine disappeared into the
blackness of the night. Quickly the procedure was repeated to
allow the second machine to leave, and *Thunderbolt* then settled
down to a night of waiting. As the rendezvous time approached
and passed there were sad faces inside the submarine. Crouch
waited long past the limit he had been given, but eventually he felt,
regretfully, that he had to abide by his instructions, and he set about
withdrawing alone.

They had not gone far to seaward when they heard two heavy
explosions from the direction of Palermo. Sure enough, the
attack had been successful. Greenland and Ferrier had sunk the
brand-new cruiser *Ulpio Traiano* and a team from *Trooper* had
badly damaged a merchantman. The adventures that were subsequently to befall the various chariot crews who made their way
inshore are, of course, another story.

A fortnight later *Thunderbolt* was engaged on a different kind of
human torpedo operation. In North Africa the Eighth Army was
fast approaching Tripoli, and the Navy was asked to immobilize
the blockships which the Germans were known to be preparing for
the harbour entrance. The task was entrusted to two chariot crews.

Launching that night had been planned for 10.30 P.M. Unfortunately on account of lack of star-sights, *Thunderbolt* was a
little farther from the shore than had been intended when she
surfaced. Crouch decided to remain 'up top' and run in at full
speed. They had not been so engaged long when an enemy E-boat
was sighted at close range. The E-boat's crew must have been
asleep, for they failed to see *Thunderbolt's* silhouette during the
whole of the 30 minutes that the submarine continued to be visible

to her. It was not, indeed, until the precise launching-position was reached that *Thunderbolt* eventually discharged the two chariots and withdrew to seaward.

Once again her waiting was unrewarded. Neither of the teams returned. Nor had the operation on this occasion been successful, although it failed purely because the undertaking of it had been delayed fractionally too long. One of the machines was, in fact, within 150 yards of the harbour entrance when two violent explosions tore open the bottom of a blockship which had already been manœuvred into its vital position.

Seventeen days later, on February 5, *Thunderbolt* started her Sixth Mediterranean War Patrol. On the 24th of the month she returned to H.M.S. *Talbot*, the submarine base in Sliema Creek, Malta. Her patrol report showed four successful and two ' possible ' gun actions, one ' possible ' torpedo attack, and the successful evasion of an attack from Italian aircraft. After her ferry-boat duties she was back on the offensive in earnest.

The new members of her crew had been blooded. There were many new faces. Andrew, Northwood, Bird, and Hutley (of the officers) had gone to other appointments; and Coxswain Charlie Jones, Chief Stoker Chipperfield, E.R.A. Glass, and Webb the Gunlayer were among the numerous lower-deck representatives who had been relieved. Crouch still remained in command. The newcomers had a tried and proven captain, and they were sailing beneath a well-endowed Jolly Roger. Their prospects looked good.

20 *March 1943*

" The Admiralty regrets . . ."

HIS Majesty's Submarine *Thunderbolt* pulled slowly away from the cat-walk.

" Half ahead both," ordered Crouch.

Imperceptibly the gap between her and the pock-marked sandstone buildings of the Malta base widened.

" Thank you," he called to two khaki-uniformed base staff officers. " And au revoir."

Their hands went up in a friendly gesture, half salute, half wave. Suddenly the gesture was formalized as the pipe of a bo's'n's call shrilled thinly across the stone paving and the wooden pontoons. Stiffly the group of men for'ard and aft on *Thunderbolt's* casing froze to attention. Another naval courtesy had been observed.

So the submarine moved on down the creek, past the background of battlements and terraced buildings, of religious ornamentation and secular colour, of cratered colonnades and multitudinous houses tightly packed elbow-to-elbow along needle-thin streets and alleys that made up Malta. She was proceeding to war yet again, on her seventh full Mediterranean patrol. Nineteen days later, before the end of March, she was due to report to the newly opened base at Algiers. But for the moment her attentions had to be concentrated on the stretches of water around the Cape San Vito area of western Sicily.

On the night of March 12–13, 1943, *Thunderbolt* was some little way to the north of the Cape. While it was still dark she sighted a convoy. It was escorted, as far as she could see, by an Italian sloop. Quietly she manœuvred for a torpedo attack on one of the larger steamers. Away went the ' fish.' Silently the tracks rippled beneath the water. There was the usual period of waiting during which *Thunderbolt* took the usual rapid evading action. Then came a loud explosion. The steamer—she was the *Esterel*—had been hit and mortally damaged.

Aboard the escorting sloop *Cicogna* the commanding officer, Capitano di Corvetta Augusto Migliorini, registered a momentary feeling of admiration at a difficult submarine operation well executed. He himself was a former submariner and, at times like this, could not resist identifying himself for a fraction of a second with the enemy captain. As this also enabled him to calculate the experienced submariner's most likely next move he became thereby an especially dangerous opponent.

For the remainder of the night and into the early daylight hours the *Cicogna* harried the never very clear traces her detection gear could give her. She dropped a number of depth-charges without very much confidence. Later in the morning she temporarily gave up the chase and hurried back into the near-by base of Trapani.

Early the same afternoon she was out again. More indistinct echoes were received, and Migliorini was worried lest, with nightfall not far off, the submarine might manage to remain undetected until she could surface and get away from the area under the shield of darkness. But as if to encourage him, the onset of the first of the night watches seemed to produce more frequent detection contacts, stronger echoes, and less fading. And yet somehow the trace always seemed to disappear just before he could make an attack.

As the hours moved round towards daylight and he continued half in and half out of touch with the submarine, Migliorini decided on a new tactic. Time and again he carried out a complete attack along the line of an echo, no matter how indistinct, pursuing the whole sequence of pointing, run, and turn away. But, never having the right sort of contact, he would never drop any charges. He was not solely being cautious. It seemed to him that the submarine, having been subjected to such a long hunt, would by this time have very low batteries and would not be able to stay down for another complete day. At least, he felt, the submarine commander would want to come up to periscope depth to see just what all these unfulfilled attacks really meant.

It was just after 7.30 A.M. on the morning of March 14 when three almost simultaneous shouts reached Migliorini's ears. The Gunnery Officer and one of the for'ard lookouts had sighted a periscope, and the rating on the detector apparatus had got a definite contact on the same bearing. By the time Migliorini had his binoculars to his eyes the tell-tale sliver of metal had disappeared. The sea was as smooth as a sheet of oil. They would be bound to see the periscope again the next time it broke the surface—and once again the good echo had suddenly faded. So, very much to the impatience of some members of his crew, Migliorini continued with his plan.

An hour later the situation had not appreciably altered. Migliorini had had ample opportunity to imagine himself in the place of his enemy. Their nautical chess match was fast approaching the end-game stage, he thought. They were worthy opponents for each other. He had set a most expert trap, and the British submarine captain had been extraordinarily adept at secreting his craft from the full beam of the echo equipment. But time was on his side.

Suddenly his perseverance was shattered. A signal arrived from the Naval Command at Trapani urging him to complete the attack or call it off in order to rendezvous with a priority convoy for North Africa. Disappointed and almost annoyed that he would not be able to complete his masterpiece in the way that his mind had imagined it, he clipped out a number of commands.

" Stand by for a depth-charge attack. Full pattern of twenty-four. Speed ten knots."

It was 8.54 A.M. As they closed the target the detector rating kept calling out the decreasing range. The bearing remained steady. On the bridge and by the depth-charge racks the men were taking shorter breaths. Their hands were tensing. They were very close now.

" Periscopio. Dritta—circa 2 metri."

The cry from the group of men in the bows tore Migliorini's attention away from the attack routine. Sure enough, it was a periscope. It was just going down as he saw it. And as he leaned over the wing of the bridge the feather of its wake passed a bare two yards away, along the starboard side of the sloop.

For a brief second he half expected to hear his keel grating across the submarine's periscope standards. Then his mind switched back to the mechanism that was still functioning. " Fire," came the order; and the 24 canisters shot up through their momentary airborne parabolas to tumble in quick series into the blue-grey water.

The sloop swung round through 180 degrees.

" Stand by to repeat the attack," called Migliorini. " Another full pattern. The last batch may well have been set to explode too deep."

But as the bows of the surface vessel steadied on a new attack course the water dead ahead erupted. The stern of the submarine staggered drunkenly up into the air, hung quivering uncertainly at an angle of almost 90 degrees from the horizontal, tipped up a little further still to show a length of bent, grey keel, and then, vibrating harshly as if in protest, plunged downward to disappear in a maelstrom of air and oil.

For the second time in her short life the submarine that had first been called *Thetis* had symbolized the ultimate in disaster with a sharp-pointed stern stuck eloquently out of a muted sea.

Calmly, almost sadly, Migliorini took the *Cicogna* over the still effervescing patch of water.

"Fire two," he called. And, as the new charges exploded, he turned and watched fresh quantities of air and oil come up to the surface.

Four minutes later, all round the place where the writhing steel cylinder had gone down, a cloud of thickish white smoke began to rise.

"Chlorine," muttered Migliorini.

He swung his command once more over the circle of sea.

"Fire one more," he ordered.

Slowly a final depth-charge curved into the pattern of wavelets left by the sloop's wake. More in salute than in anger, a final plume of water stood up from the surface. The *Cicogna* jockeyed round at half helm on to her new course and, picking up speed, was soon a blur on the horizon.

And 3000 feet down in the pitiless waters of the Mediterranean the submarine that had been first *Thetis* and then *Thunderbolt* had ended its odyssey.

It was June 2, 1943—four years and a day since she had first dived in Liverpool Bay. The *London Gazette* of that day's issue carried a further list of awards for her crew. But the Admiralty communiqué made starker reading.

"The Admiralty regrets to announce that His Majesty's Submarine *Thunderbolt* must now be considered lost," it ran.

The curtain had officially fallen.

21 *1943–1956*

Epilogue

WE don't want another *Thetis*."

It was Thursday, January 12, 1950. The time was 7.35 P.M. The submarine *Truculent*, on passage through the Thames Estuary to Sheerness after having undertaken propeller trials in a submarine exercise area, had been hit by the Swedish tanker, s.s. *Divina*, some 30 minutes previously, and had sunk in 54 feet of water. Her captain and four others had been swept off the bridge, and 11 men had been drowned at the moment of impact. The 64 remaining members of her complement of 80 officers, men, and dockyard staff were distributed between the after ends and the engine-room.

The two compartments had been shut off from each other. In the after ends *Truculent's* First Lieutenant, Lieutenant F. J. Hindes, was in command. In the engine-room it was the senior rating, Chief Engine Room Artificer F. W. Hine, D.S.M., who was in control. The parallel with *Thetis* was in many ways acute. And as Hine discussed with the other senior petty officers present whether to escape through the twill trunk apparatus—a collapsible tunnel of water-resistant twill fitted under the hatch, which had superseded *Thetis's* ' two-man-band ' escape chambers in the later " T "-class submarines—it was only natural that Liverpool Bay should be in the forefront of all their minds.

Not that they knew very clearly what had happened in Liverpool Bay. For the Navy issued no manual of submarine escape, no textbook on the problems of whether to get out and when, no case-law of previous successes and failures. Submarine commanding officers were allowed to see minutes of the relevant inquiries if they so wished; but—presumably for fear of discouraging recruiting—this facility went no further down the hierarchy. And yet *Truculent* was by no means the first submarine in which a group of chief and petty officers had held the responsibility for a large number of lives.

The persistent thought was of the dangers of remaining. " The longer escape was delayed the more polluted the air would become, and there seemed to be nothing to be gained by waiting," wrote one E.R.A. afterwards. " We could hear the sound of propellers passing overhead and were sure that rescue craft were in position," he continued. But the sound was a false hope, being only the noise of an innocent surface vessel passing unawares down the river.

So, preoccupied with the risks of remaining, they ignored the risks of not waiting—at least for a few hours, for the daylight had already gone—until they heard some sort of sign that assistance was waiting for them up top. From one extreme they swung to the other.

Truculent had sunk at 7.05 P.M. At 7.40 P.M. the twill trunks were unrolled and the flooding of the two after compartments—a necessary preliminary to this type of escape—had started. By 8.10 P.M. the first man got out. The others all followed in a matter of minutes. There were examples of great bravery—the First Lieutenant, the Chief E.R.A., Petty Officer Cook R. C. Fry, and E.R.A. L. F. Strickland were decorated for extreme gallantry (the first two posthumously)—but these were largely in vain. The cold and the current carried away 54 brave men. Only 10 survived long enough to be rescued from the water.

It was still only 9.40 P.M. when the *Hunt*-class destroyer, H.M.S. *Cowdray*, arrived on the scene. Had the 64 men who had crowded into the after ends of *Truculent* still been inside the submarine, it is inconceivable that they would not all have been saved. But they had not known how long they might safely wait. They had thought too much on *Thetis*.

In one way this marked the end of the *Thetis* story. For *Thetis* had not finally died with *Thunderbolt's* last despairing gyrations off Cape San Vito. The evil genius that had beset her had pursued its course through a threefold legal action that did not end until nearly seven years after the tragedy itself.

An initial test action in the King's Bench Division in 1943 had been brought by the widows of two of the civilian staff lost in the submarine against Cammell Laird, Wailes Dove Bitumastic, Lieutenant Woods, Mrs Bolus, and the widowed mother of Leading Seaman Hambrook. Mr Justice Wrottesley delivered a reserved judgment against Cammell Laird and held that the claims against the other defendants failed.

Then, in the Court of Appeal in 1944, before the Master of the Rolls (Lord Greene) and Lords Justices Goddard and du Parcq, an appeal was allowed on behalf of Cammell Laird and also a cross-appeal by the two plaintiffs against Lieutenant Woods.

On October 15, 1945, the House of Lords heard Woods appealing against the decision of the Court of Appeal and the two plaintiffs cross-appealing against Cammell Laird and Leading Seaman Hambrook. This final episode dragged on for a further three and a half weeks. Then, 14 weeks later, on February 27, 1946, the judgment of Viscount Simon, Lord Russell of Killowen, Lord Macmillan, Lord Porter, and Lord Simonds was made known. They had unanimously arrived at the conclusion that negligence had not been established in respect of either Woods, Hambrook, or Cammell Laird. In terms of Law the loss of *Thetis* had been a " non-negligent accident."

It is perhaps relevant to observe that the negligence or otherwise of the only other potential defendant in the matter, the Admiralty, could not legally be established, as until 1953 it was not possible to sue the Crown.

The legal ordeal had been greatest for Woods. He had given a considerable amount of evidence in front of a number of different bodies. And the steadfastness of his behaviour throughout had been remarkable.

It was on September 29, 1943, that the Attorney-General, Sir Donald Somervell, K.C., who had appeared on behalf of His Majesty's Government at the Tribunal of Inquiry and subsequently for Woods, Mrs Bolus, and Mrs Hambrook, wrote to Woods after he had given evidence on the second major occasion. The letter ran:

> MY DEAR WOODS,
> I got a kind message from you when you left the other day—I finished this morning what I had to say. I've never been more anxious to see that everything I could do for anyone in a case was done. It's no good counting chickens, but I'm not at all unhopeful. In any case—and I wanted to say this—don't you worry any more. I'm myself completely satisfied that you took all the precautions a reasonable person would have done. Apart from your gallantry after the disaster, you gained the respect of every one who heard you last time and this for the way in which you gave your evidence and answered the questions that were put to you.
> You might have looked surprised if you had heard me tell the Judge that you had had the advantage of being cross-examined by eight different Counsel. The advantage, as I said, was that the more a truthful and accurate witness is cross-examined the stronger his evidence becomes . . .
>
> (Signed) DONALD SOMERVELL

But the final judgment of the House of Lords did not rejoice Woods for long. By the spring of 1946 he was a Lieutenant-Commander on the staff of the Commander-in-Chief, Mediterranean, and the holder of the Distinguished Service Cross for services in destroyers. Not many weeks after Viscount Simon's final pronouncement Woods was on a farewell visit from Malta to the South of France, where he was killed in a road accident. He left a widow and a young son.

The Memorial set up by Admiralty over the graves of those who were lost in *Thetis* was unveiled and dedicated on November 7, 1947. Whether this, or the final verdict of the House of Lords, or the sad story of *Truculent*, was the real end of the strange saga of *Thetis*, it is difficult to say.

But whenever the history of *Thetis* was finally closed there can be little doubt but that her ultimate epitaph will contain an allusion to the ignorance that has long surrounded the manner of her ending.

It is hoped that this book will have dispelled a little of this ignorance. If, too, it has pointed to the gallantry, humour, and efficiency of those members of the Submarine Service and their associates who died while serving in His Majesty's Submarine *Thetis* and *Thunderbolt*, it will have portrayed what is in effect the nub, heart, and centre of this sad yet proud submarine story.

For what is a submarine but the men who live—and, often, die—in her?

Appendix

I. IN MEMORIAM: H.M.S/M. " THETIS "

(i) *Officers and Men of H.M.S/M. " Thetis "*

Lieutenant-Commander G. H. Bolús, R.N.
Lieutenant H. Chapman, R.N.
Lieutenant W. A. W. Poland, R.N.
Mr R. D. Glenn, Commissioned Engineer, R.N.

Chief Petty Officer G. P. Cornish
Petty Officer E. Mitchell
Petty Officer T. T. Goad
Petty Officer C. E. Smithers
Petty Officer Telegraphist J. A. Hope
Petty Officer Cook J. C. Hughes
Electrical Artificer A. W. Byrne
Chief Engine Room Artificer W. C. Ormes
Chief Engine Room Artificer P. F. Jackson
Engine Room Artificer J. C. Creasy
Engine Room Artificer H. W. E. French
Engine Room Artificer H. G. Howells
Chief Stoker H. J. Dillon-Shallard
Stoker Petty Officer J. W. Wells

Leading Seaman W. L. Hambrook
Leading Seaman W. A. Luck
Leading Seaman J. A. Read
Leading Seaman A. H. Smith
Leading Seaman S. W. G. Stevens
Leading Signalman F. B. Batten
Leading Telegraphist W. E. Allen
Leading Telegraphist G. A. Harwood
Leading Steward F. N. Stock
Able Seaman J. Costley
Able Seaman S. Crombleholme
Able Seaman E. A. Kendrick
Able Seaman N. Longstaff
Able Seaman J. A. Morgans
Able Seaman F. Rogers
Able Seaman J. H. Turner
Able Seaman T. Wilson

Telegraphist C. T. W. Graham
Telegraphist T. W. Mortimer

Leading Stoker R. S. Brooke
Leading Stoker D. Cunningham
Leading Stoker J. S. Feeney
Leading Stoker T. W. Kenney
Leading Stoker E. J. Youles
Stoker T. Bambrick
Stoker J. Craig
Stoker A. H. Dunn
Stoker L. E. Green
Stoker A. G. Hills
Stoker W. T. Hole
Stoker W. A. Matthews
Stoker W. Orrock
Stoker A. E. Yates

(ii) *Officers of Submarines building at Cammell Laird*

Lieutenant-Commander R. N. Garnett, R.N.
Lieutenant-Commander T. C. C. Lloyd, R.N.
Lieutenant P. E. J. Ryan, R.N.
Lieutenant (E) A. G. J. Jamison, R.N.

(iii) *Other Naval Officers*

Commander R. G. B. Hayter, R.N.
Commander L. G. Pennington, R.N.
Engineer Captain S. Jackson, R.N.
Lieutenant (E) C. M. H. Henderson, R.N.

(iv) *Admiralty and Overseeing Officers*

Mr W. H. Aslett
Mr F. Bailey
Mr E. Gisborne
Mr A. A. F. Hill
Mr C. W. Horne
Mr H. Horsman
Mr L. W. Hunn

(v) *Employees of Cammell Laird and Co., Ltd*

Managers and Foremen
Mr J. I. Armstrong
Mr R. W. Crout
Mr R. Kipling
Mr W. Owen

Mr A. B. Robinson
Mr R. Rogerson
Mr A. S. Watkinson

Caulker
Mr W. B. Beatty

Electricians
Mr S. Broad
Mr A. G. Chinn
Mr C. J. S. Hamilton
Mr E. H. Lewis
Mr W. H. Smith
Mr G. A. Summers

Engine Fitters
Mr F. R. Bresner
Mr W. Brown
Mr H. Eccleston
Mr J. Griffiths
Mr R. Homer
Mr J. A. Page
Mr P. L. Quinn
Mr C. Smith

Ship Fitters
Mr A. Craven
Mr G. L. Scarth
Mr W. Watterson

(vi) *Employees of Vickers-Armstrong, Ltd*
Mr T. Ankers
Mr H. T. Cragg
Mr D. V. Tyler
Mr J. Young

(vii) *Employee of Brown Bros. and Co., Ltd*
Mr D. N. Duncan

(viii) *Mersey Pilot*
Mr N. D. Willcox

(ix) *Employees of City Caterers (Liverpool), Ltd*
Mr W. G. Bath
Mr G. H. Dobells

II. IN MEMORIAM: H.M.S/M. " THUNDERBOLT "

Lieutenant-Commander C. B. Crouch, D.S.O.**, R.N.
Lieutenant G. P. Horlick, R.N.
Lieutenant R. P. Webb, R.N.
Lieutenant J. Edgar, R.N.
Lieutenant E. P. Maw, R.N.V.R.
Lieutenant (E) D. A. M. Woodcock, R.N.

Chief Petty Officer F. Ringham
Chief Petty Officer H. P. Walters, D.S.M.
Petty Officer J. A. Cale, D.S.M.
Petty Officer T. Curry
Petty Officer C. S. Elliott
Petty Officer J. A. Lee
Petty Officer H. J. Whitbread, D.S.M.
Petty Officer Telegraphist S. R. Freeman
Petty Officer Cook E. W. Bird
Petty Officer Steward T. York
Electrical Artificer S. Cook
Chief Engine Room Artificer G. W. Curtis, D.S.M.
Chief Engine Room Artificer R. Lynch, D.S.M.
Engine Room Artificer A. Downham
Engine Room Artificer J. E. Newcomb
Engine Room Artificer R. W. Spice
Stoker Petty Officer T. A. Boulton, D.S.M.
Stoker Petty Officer F. Lowe

Leading Seaman H. Crane
Leading Seaman E. Heathcote
Leading Signalman R. S. King
Leading Telegraphist T. T. Blane
Leading Telegraphist G. N. Murray
Able Seaman W. M. Bradley
Able Seaman W. T. Galloway
Able Seaman S. Gilroy
Able Seaman V. Harris
Able Seaman J. K. Hughs
Able Seaman L. D. Hussey-Yeo, D.S.M.
Able Seaman S. L. Johnson
Able Seaman R. Keenan
Able Seaman R. Kelsey
Able Seaman R. E. Mitchell
Able Seaman L. J. Moore, D.S.M.
Able Seaman D. J. Preece
Able Seaman S. Rice
Able Seaman F. Saunders
Able Seaman D. H. White

Able Seaman H. D. Wilson
Telegraphist A. W. Japp
Ordinary Seaman W. J. Trayler

Leading Stoker D. Brister
Leading Stoker S. Cooper
Leading Stoker M. Daly
Leading Stoker V. W. Hines
Leading Stoker R. Newton
Stoker M. Cannon
Stoker W. G. Doughty
Stoker W. H. Golding
Stoker E. McGow
Stoker D. McLeod
Stoker D. McNally
Stoker F. C. Newman
Stoker R. J. Norwood
Stoker F. W. Prince
Stoker C. Stanley

III. H.M.S/M. " THUNDERBOLT ": AWARDS FOR GALLANTRY

February 5, 1941

D.S.O.	Lieutenant C. B. Crouch, R.N.
D.S.C.	Lieutenant J. S. Stevens, R.N.
D.S.M.	Chief Petty Officer C. S. Jones
	Chief Engine Room Artificer G. W. Curtis
	Petty Officer T. Webster
	Petty Officer Telegraphist T. Yeates
	Stoker Petty Officer J. Chipperfield

May 15, 1942

Bar to

D.S.O.	Lieutenant-Commander C. B. Crouch, D.S.O., R.N.
D.S.C.	Lieutenant B. J. Andrew, R.N.
	Mr J. W. Northwood, Commissioned Engineer, R.N.
D.S.M.	Chief Petty Officer H. P. Walters
	Petty Officer T. Maughan
	Engine Room Artificer W. R. Glass
	Stoker Petty Officer T. A. Boulton
	Able Seaman E. Webb

June 30, 1943

Bar to

D.S.O.	Lieutenant-Commander C. B. Crouch, D.S.O.*, R.N.
D.S.M.	Chief Engine Room Artificer R. Lynch
	Petty Officer J. A. Cale
	Petty Officer H. J. Whitbread
	Able Seaman L. D. Hussey-Yeo
	Able Seaman L. J. Moore

IV. LIST OF THE EIGHT VESSELS BEARING THE NAME H.M.S. " THETIS "

1. A ship of the 5th rate; 720 tons; 44 guns; 250 men.
   Built at Liverpool; launched April 15, 1747.
   On July 14, 1761, captured the French man-of-war *Bouffonne* (32 guns).
   Sold June 9, 1767.

2. A ship of the 5th rate; 685 tons; 32 guns; 220 men.
   Built at Buckler's Hard; launched November 2, 1773.
   Wrecked at St Lucia May 12, 1781.

3. A ship of the 5th rate; 700 tons (approx.); 38 guns; 238 men.
   Built on the River Thames; launched September 23, 1782.
   In 1795 captured the French storeships *Prevoyante* and *Raison*; in 1801 took part in Keith's expedition to Egypt; in 1809 assisted in cutting out the French man-of-war *Nisus* (16 guns) at Guadaloupe, and took part in the storming of the batteries at Anse-le-Barque; in 1810 took part in the capture of Guadaloupe.
   Sold June 9, 1814.

4. A ship of the 5th rate; 1081 tons; 46 guns; 300 men.
   Built at Pembroke; launched February 1, 1817.
   In 1824 took part in the defence of Cape Coast Castle.
   Wrecked off Cape Frio December 5, 1830, with £160,000 of treasure, which was subsequently salvaged.

5. A ship of the 5th rate; 1553 tons; 36 guns; 360 men.
   Built at Devonport; launched August 21, 1846.
   Handed over to the Prussian Government in exchange for two gun-vessels, in 1855.

6. Screw corvette; 1854 tons; 14 guns.
   Built at Devonport; launched October 26, 1871.
   Between 1873 and 1877 took part in the repression of the slave trade on the east coast of Africa and in the Red Sea.
   Sold November 1887.

7. Second-class Protected Cruiser; 3400 tons.
   Built at Clydebank; launched December 13, 1890.
   Took part in South African War, 1899-1900.
   Sunk as a blockship at Zeebrugge April 23, 1918.

8. Submarine.

Index

Postscript
by   David Roberts

In Greek mythology, Thetis was the most famous of the Neriad gods. She was wooed both by Zeus, the supreme deity, and by Poseidon, god of the sea, until they learned of the prophecy that she would bear a son who would be mightier than his father, when they withdrew their suits. She eventually married Peleus and was the mother of Achilles.

When Achilles was a child his mother dipped him into the River Styx to make him immortal. The waters made him invulnerable except for the heel by which his mother held him. At the battle for the city of Troy, Achilles was killed by sustaining an injury to his heel, his one unprotected part. Thus we come today to what we know as an Achilles heel, a fatal flaw in an otherwise invulnerable armour.

So it was with the tragic submarine Thetis. Built at Cammell Lairds' shipyard in Birkenhead, she was lost in Liverpool Bay in 1939 taking 99 souls with her, still today the worst ever submarine disaster in British history. Her Achilles heel was a small blob of bitumastic enamel paint, just enough to block a half- inch tell tale hole on one of her torpedo tubes and delude those aboard into thinking that the tube was dry when in fact the sea was bursting to get in. This was the Achilles heel amongst many many other things that went wrong for Thetis. Detailed in the story are the many difficulties she had experienced even before she sailed that fateful day in June.

The sea did come into Thetis and pulled her down into a position that she found it impossible to free herself from. Only four men out of 103 escaped from the stricken submarine, Lt. Frederick Woods, Captain H.Oram, an overseeing Captain- not the Captain of the Thetis, Walter Arnold, and Frank Shaw. Woods and Oram were Naval officers, Walter Arnold a Navy Stoker and Frank Shaw a Cammell Lairds' Fitter.

The British Navy has long followed its own traditions, not least among these the divisions between the lower decks and the wardroom, between officers and men, what those ashore might refer to as class divisions. Derek Arnold, the son of the only rating or non-officer to survive Thetis, in his excellent foreword to this book has alluded to his fathers treatment at the hands of the Admiralty after the loss of the submarine.

Stoker Walter Arnold was obviously a fit and well built man. His son Derek shares the same physique. Certainly it was Arnold's strength of mind and body that got him and Frank Shaw out of the escape chamber and to the surface, yet the rating was the only man to be given an injection and told to rest on the rescue vessel Brazen. The result was that he was sedated for many hours and upon waking was very annoyed to find that the others survivors, two officers and a Cammell Laird man, had effectively been spirited away.

Leading Stoker Arnold is on record as saying at the time "it's not just the hint of snobbery, but I'm just as anxious and interested as the officers are about the safety of the rest of the blokes in Thetis".

The Admiralty could probably rely upon its officers to 'tell no tales' - they would have no control over the civilian, Frank Shaw, but could probably rely on the submarine builders, Cammell Laird, to protect their interest in the Admiralty building programme and thus ensure their employees' compliance with 'the official line'. But a rating! Possibly a loose cannon with a looser tongue? Who could be sure?

Was Leading Stoker Arnold ' taken out of the picture' until the wardroom dwellers had, to use a nautical expression, 'got all their ducks in a row?' He was certainly debriefed by the top brass at Admiralty HQ. in London before giving his evidence when the inquiry sat, and was obviously given gagging orders until then, witness his telegram to his wife May ' Arrive Liverpool 1.5 am.... don't tell a soul'.

The Admiralty were so frightened of Stoker Arnold 'saying the wrong thing', that he was placed in an isolated private medical ward at the Naval Hospital Plymouth. His parents travelled from Portsmouth to visit him but were not allowed in until the Stoker had identified them through his ward window!

Leading Stoker Arnold was to be of great value to the Admiralty over the coming weeks in identifying his former shipmates and attending the various ceremonies held in their memory. The onlooker could be forgiven for thinking that if the Admiralty were to keep on the right side of anyone concerned with the whole affair, it would be Leading Stoker Walter Arnold. Yet, as Derek Arnold points out and Warren and Benson confirm, Walter Arnold, having survived the submarine trauma and the loss of all his shipmates that he had come to know and trust during the working up period of the new submarine, was off -pay and had to fight tooth and nail to get some sort of subsidence to send home to Merseyside to support his wife and family. This went on for nearly six months!!

Did the officers who escaped from the stricken submarine suffer the same ignominy? This is highly unlikely and assuming this is so, only serves to confirm the class divisions within the British Navy even in the aftermath of a catastrophe that shook the whole country.

Stoker Walter Arnold, whilst shuttling between Holyhead and Birkenhead, was,'*left alone, almost ignored*'. Was this again a symptom of the class distinction of the late 1930's, perhaps still with us today? A man has a 'country accent' and is thus presumed to be 'not the sharpest knife in the draw?' In Arnold's case nothing could be further from the truth. I have seen his highly detailed and neat drawings of the layout of Thetis and her multiplicity of on board systems. These precision documents are not the product of a country yokel.

A final indicator to the deep rooted divisions of class in the Navy came when the authors of this book interviewed the Leading Stoker amongst others, wrote the book and presented a signed copy to the surviving rating.

Warren and Benson were officers, Leading Stoker

Arnold was not. Walter Arnold had served in and survived the Thetis, the authors had not.

The signed copy was inscribed, many years after the end of the Second World War 'To Arnold, with Thanks.' Not Walter, Wally, or even 'a fellow submariner', not even his well known nickname of 'Mac'.... just 'Arnold'... surnames only for ratings. Such was the Navy way, the Navy system, and perhaps more than anything else, it was 'the system' itself that failed those aboard Thetis.

Decisions were made that proved fatal to the men aboard Thetis in Liverpool Bay. Her position was lost, found, lost again and found again. Help from the surface was slow in coming because of old technology and the need for ships to 'get up steam'.

Of all the decisions made in those terrible hours was the decision to wait. To wait, wait and wait, to see if the handful of men that had escaped from the submarine would be added to. They never were.

Being born and bred in Birkenhead, from a shipbuilding family, and serving my own apprenticeship in Lairds, I had always remembered my Dad telling me his version of the story, the detail wasn't there but I'd always had the notion that it was a bad business. In my Dad's words he'd always said "they could've got those poor buggers out you know". Now I too know that this was effectively true.

If the wrong things had not happened at the wrong times, if those above had acted instead of waited, if, if, if..

Perhaps though the largest part of the blame, if we can blame any one thing without pointing to the next mistake and the next, lies with the pressure of war itself. The 1st of June 1939 was just weeks before the official start of the Second World War. Everyone knew it was coming and so the pressure was on to equip the armed forces for the impending conflict.

Did the Navy want the submarine more than it did the men? If access to the pressure hull had been gained (and at one stage it clearly could have been) the men could have escaped, but there would be a grave risk to the submarine itself. Thetis was a piece of hardware worth some £300,000, no mean sum in 1939, but more than the cost, submarines take time to build, and the Navy, and the country, were going to war. The fact that Thetis was salved, refitted at Cammell Laird, renamed Thunderbolt and saw action in the self-same war indicates that the Navy indeed did *need* the submarine.

It is hard to know how much the *need* for Thetis influenced the decisions of those above the surface, all that can be said with any certainty is that some highly unfortunate decisions were made, decisions which ultimately contributed to the loss of those trapped in Thetis.

Whenever I think of this disaster I imagine the women and loved ones shut outside Cammell Lairds gate at the bottom of Green Lane in Birkenhead, waiting for news that nobody was giving them, some of them there all night long. All they knew was that 'Thetis had failed to surface'. They must have suffered almost as much as the men aboard the submarine.

According to the authors of this book there was *'an apparent lack of sufficient concern at top level in the Navy'*, suitably couched phraseology that I translate today as 'nobody seemed to have any sense of urgency or care'.

During the terrible hours when messages were being radioed from one end of the country to the other, ships and equipment were being organised and then reorganised (and arguably *disorganised*), decisions were being *thought* about but not taken, all that was actually happening was that the men on Thetis were dying or dead.

At the same time, down at the submarine HQ at Fort Blockhouse on the South coast of England, a bunch of navy ratings, who probably knew as much as anyone else from actually serving on submarines, felt strongly enough to complain about some aspect of the disaster, by daubing a painted message across the parade ground in the middle of the night. It was erased the next morning.

What did it say?

In all my research into these events I have been unable to find out. I can only guess. Maybe it said, like my

Dad had said to me, 'Get them out!'

There are no longer any living survivors from the Thetis tragedy in 1939. Derek Arnold has his memories and his memorabilia, he was lucky enough to know his father, live with him and grow up in his house. Many many children of those lost on the Thetis did not.

Up until 1989, fifty years after the events off the coast of Anglesey, those that did not come home were remembered at an annual commemorative service at the Thetis memorial in Holyhead, Anglesey. Forty- four of the dead made their last short journey by land from where the Thetis was eventually beached at Bychan Beach (Traeth Bychan), Moelfre, to the sleepy little cemetery close to Holyhead railway station. The names of all those lost on the Thetis are inscribed here.

Just across the road from the train station, on the corner of Holborn Road stands the aptly named New Harbour Inn. Holborn Road leads to Maeshyfryd Road and then down the narrow lane to the Maeshyfryd cemetery. The Thetis memorial stands out from all the others.

If you are ever in the Anglesey area, try to take time to go and take a look at their memorial. Spare a thought for them and their loved ones, and how it could all have been so different.

David Roberts, Avid Publications, 1997

Lusitania - On the 7th May 1915 the Cunard vessel *Lusitania* was torpedoed by a German submarine off the Old Head of Kinsale on the south west coast of Ireland, resulting in the loss of the vessel itself and 1,201 men, women, and children. An act of brutal aggression? Or a cynical plot to bring the United States into the First World War?

More than eighty years on the story of the *Lusitania* continues to be shrouded in mystery and suspicion. What was her real cargo? Why wasn't she protected? Why did she sink so quickly?

Lord Mersey, the great grandson of the man who chaired the enquiry into the *Lusitania* disaster, (who he calls 'the Old Man'), has been extremely helpful and was kind enough to write a new foreword for this Special Edition.

Containing rare photographs from Germany and elsewhere, it is a truly intriguing and fascinating tale.

'A book that clamours to be read' - Observer.

'The truth at last' - The Sunday Times.

By Colin Simpson. ISBN 1 9521020 6 4.   £9.50.

IRON CLIPPER

'TAYLEUR' - THE WHITE STAR LINE'S 'FIRST TITANIC'

by H.F. Starkey

'Iron Clipper' is subtitled 'The First Titanic' for it tells the story of the first White Star liner to be lost on her maiden voyage. The *'Tayleur'* tragedy of 1854 and the *'Titanic'* catastrophe of 1912 are disasters which have so much in common that the many coincidences make this book appear to be a work which is stranger than fiction.

'Iron Clipper' is an intriguing story of hope, bravery, incompetence and horror. It graphically illustrates an event that foreshadowed the famous *Titanic* disaster half a century later. The discovery of both wrecks and the recovery of artefacts from the seabed have exited public interest in the two great liners.

PRICE £7.50 & £1.40 p&p in UK

Just Nuisance AB
– his full story
by Terence Sisson

The amazing but true story of the only dog that was officially enlisted into the British Royal Navy, a Great Dane whose name was Nuisance, his official name and rank was AB Just Nuisance.

Famed for his preference for the company of navy ratings (he wasn't too keen on Officers) in and around the famous World War II naval base of Simonstown, South Africa, Nuisance helped many a sailor rejoin his ship after a night on the town.

Today his own statue overlooking the bay off the Cape of Good Hope commemorates AB Just Nuisance.

£7.50 + £1.00 P&P in UK

Faster Than The Wind - the Liverpool to Holyhead Telegraph. A guide to and history of this fascinating maritime communications system from North Wales to the busiest port in the world, Liverpool, in the early 19th century. This book will take the reader on two journeys. The first is a real journey, to places with superb views along the North Wales and Wirral coasts, including full details of how to find the substantial remains of the Liverpool to Holyhead Telegraph Stations. The second is a journey into the workings of such a telegraph, and into the experiences of the people

involved in creating and using the signalling system. By Frank Large. ISBN 1 9521020 9 9. £8.95

Life At Lairds - Memories of working shipyard men at Cammell Lairds world-famous shipyard in Birkenhead. *'The time may not be far off when young people will ask, what did they do, what were they like, those who worked there? This book answers the questions.'* - Sea Breezes.
'A book full of anecdotes and rich in humanity...a piece of social history.' - Liverpool Echo.
By David Roberts. ISBN 0 9521020 1 3 £6.99

Cammell Laird - the golden years. Looks back at the yard's history with particular focus on the 1960s and 70s when Lairds were engaged in the building of the Polaris nuclear submarines.
'Captures life in the prosperous years of the historic Birkenhead shipyard' - Liverpool Echo.

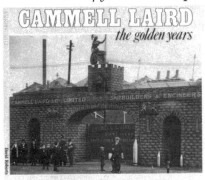

David Roberts - Foreword by Frank Field M. P.

'Puts into perspective...the strikes...the Polaris contract...and those who worked at the yard' - Sea Breezes.
By David Roberts. Foreword by Frank Field MP.
ISBN 1 9521020 2 1. £5.99

Off The Cuff - Ex-Merseyside Sergeant Swasie Turner tells the stories of real-life policing on the streets of the area. A book to raise your eyebrows - and sometimes your hair! Foreword by Alison Halford, former Asst. Chief Constable, Merseyside.
By Swasie Turner. ISBN 1 9521020 4 8. £8.99.

If The Cap Fits - The follow-up to the bestselling 'Off The Cuff' brings you more yarns from the sharp end of Merseyside police work. Foreword by Michael Chapman, Executive Producer of TVs 'The Bill'.
By Swasie Turner. ISBN 1 9521020 7 2.. £8.99.

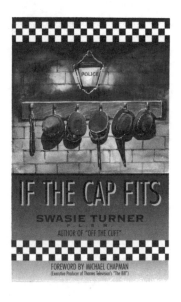

SCHOONER PORT

– Two Centuries of Upper Mersey Sail

by H.F. Starkey

If it were possible to identify one factor which above all others made possible the Industrial Revolution, it might well be the improved rivers and canal system of England. With its location as a focal point amidst the inland waterways of a major region, the Port of Runcorn played a vital part in the development of three Cities, their hinterlands and of industrial mid-Merseyside.

Before the days of good roads and railways, the mills of Manchester depended on the improved upper Mersey and the canals for their supplies of raw cotton and for the transport of their manufactured cloth to a world market. Similarly, the prosperity of the Stoke-on-Trent region was built on supplies of materials from Cornwall, Devon and France carried on the upper Mersey for transhipment to the Five Towns, the return journey being made with cargoes of pottery. Equally, Liverpool's rise to prominence in the eighteenth century was largely due to the Cheshire salt trade, which supplied the basic raw material for the town's early industries whilst salt was exported to Europe, the West Indies and North America. Every ton of salt and much of the coal to reach Liverpool came via the river Weaver and the upper Mersey in small sailing flats. Later, in the nineteenth century, the establishment of the chemical industry on mid-Merseyside and the cheap transportation of its heavy goods was only made possible by water borne carriage.

Schooner Port tells the story of the part Runcorn and navigation of the upper Mersey played in the Industrial Revolution and the contribution of merchants, the shipbuilders, and the crews in making Britain 'The Workshop of the World'. Also recounted is something of the courage and tragedy which was the lot of many flatmen and seamen who helped build British industry.

'Recognised as the only authoritative work on this particular subject' - *Sea Breezes*

'Packed with hard facts and illustrated with some rare old photographs, this rare book should command a wide readership'. - *Liverpool Echo*

£8.95 + £1.50 P&P

Videos

Cammell Laird, Old Ships and Hardships - the history and true story of this world-famous shipyard - on video. Contains rare archive footage of famous vessels and comments from the men who built them. £12.99.

All In A Day's Work Vol. 1 - the story of a living, working river - the River Mersey - and the ordinary people that work upon it. Features : Mersey Pilots; Pilot Launch Crews; Shipbuilding and Shiprepairing workers; Dredger crews, and much more. £12.99

Also available -
All In A Day's Work Vol 2 - More stories from the Mersey, on video. Features : Rock Boats; Mersey Ferries; Tugs and Tug management; the Bunker boats and crews; the Vessel Tracking System; New vessels on the river including cruise liners and car ferries, & much more. £12.99